Data Quality Management with Semantic Technologies

Christian Fürber

Data Quality Management with Semantic Technologies

Foreword by Prof. Dr. Martin Hepp

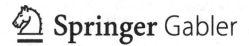

Christian Fürber
München, Germany

Dissertation Universität der Bundeswehr München, Neubiberg, 2015

OnlinePlus material to this book can be available on
http://www.springer-gabler.de/978-3-658-12224-9

ISBN 978-3-658-12224-9   ISBN 978-3-658-12225-6 (eBook)
DOI 10.1007/978-3-658-12225-6

Library of Congress Control Number: 2015959354

Springer Gabler
© Springer Fachmedien Wiesbaden 2016

Printed on acid-free paper

Springer Gabler is a brand of Springer Fachmedien Wiesbaden
Springer Fachmedien Wiesbaden is part of Springer Science+Business Media
(www.springer.com)

Für Tanja

Foreword

In contrast to physical machinery, computer-based information systems operate on the basis of *models of reality*. While traditional forms of automated systems directly handle the actual objects of a task, computers must rely on representations of the input objects of processing, and they return representations of the results when they are done. For the information to be processed, these representations are in the form of digital data, and for the details of the processing, they are computer programs, i.e. executable instructions.

By being models, both computer data and computer programs are purpose-bound abstractions of reality, and their appropriateness can only be judged in the light of the information processing task at hand.

Now, the overall reliability of an information system critically depends on how well the data represents the relevant subset of reality, and on how well the computer programs represent appropriate processing steps. This is valid for all computer-based information processing, from the most simplistic digital weather station up to the complex transaction support systems in entire value chains. This sounds like a triviality, but even if it was, it is an important one, because it helps understand the origin of many practical problems of computer information systems.

Reality shows that our ability to use computers for the automation of business processes is severely limited by our ability (1) to represent information and processing instructions properly in the form of data and computer programs, and (2) to keep these artifacts in alignment with the ever-changing reality. Our customers move from one address to another, while our customer database will typically contain at least some outdated addresses. Product designs change, but almost every Web shop will, every now and then, show outdated product images and product descriptions, and the picture of me on my university Web page does obviously not match with how I really look while writing this foreword. Data and programs are human-made artifacts, and they do not automatically align with changes in the environment they represent.

This problem at the interface between reality and the representations of reality in the components of computer information systems is one of the root causes whenever computers do not behave as we expect them to do: When they make wrong decisions, provide wrong information, or cancel business processes unexpectedly. If a customer database contains outdated address data, a shipment to that address will fail, if the weight of a product in data differs from the actual weight, incorrect shipping charges will be computed; and if a part number for consumables or spare parts is missing in a database of inventory, the automatic procurement of those items will fail. Relevant examples can be found in every major organization.

Since the 1990s, the systematic analysis of the quality of computer data has become an established field of research, known as "Data Quality Management" (DQM), and its broader notion "Information Quality Management" (IQM). One of the early works on this topic is the thesis by Mark David Hansen, entitled "Zero Defect Data"[1], published in 1991. In the following years, numerous theoretical concepts, technical solutions and practical implementations have emerged. In business practice, there is a wealth of products and services available that promise to systematically improve the quality of data or information in enterprises and value chains.

Sadly, though, data quality in many organizations is still insufficient. One reason for this is that the interface between reality and representations of reality in computer systems is itself not accessible for computer-based solutions. In essence, a computer program cannot determine whether its components properly represent reality, because it lacks a sufficient sensory apparatus. For instance, a Web application that supports declaring your income tax cannot validate whether its processing matches the latest state of the tax laws. Admittedly, computers can increasingly validate the consistency *within* those representations, e.g. spot outliers in data based on statistical approaches or compute logical contradictions within formally specified business models. Still, the interface between reality and the models of reality itself remains inaccessible to them.

Typical approaches in data quality management therefore focus either (1) on helping human actors to better collect and maintain data and process specifications, or (2) on spotting and correcting problems within the model world of a computer, as in the validation of data based on syntactic validation rules.

In computer science, the fundamental problem of the interface between reality on one hand and models of reality inside computers on the other has been studied for about 20 years under the term "ontologies". Ontologies are specifications of models of reality that aim at being consensual among many people and applicable to a broad range of

---

[1] Hansen, M. (1991): Zero Defect Data. MSc thesis, Sloan School of Management, Cambridge, Mass. (USA): MIT, http://hdl.handle.net/1721.1/13812.

scenarios. They typically include at least some formal axioms and the underlying modeling decisions are influenced by philosophical principles, e.g. regarding the identity and unity of objects. The formal axioms enable a computer to spot contradictions in the models, draw additional conclusions, and to automatically translate between multiple data models of the same subject area, at least to a certain degree. The philosophical grounding can increase the general validity of the model.

Ontologies are a promising attempt to improve the consistency and accuracy of models of reality. While they do not take away the fundamental barrier between reality and the model world of computers, because they are models themselves, they add a formally specified and philosophically grounded intermediate level, which can reduce the problem.

In 2001, Berners-Lee, Lassila and Hendler applied the idea of ontologies in computer science to the problem of information interchange on the World Wide Web and described the vision of a "Semantic Web", in which computers are increasingly able to process information at the level of meaning[2].

In this thesis, Christian Fürber analyzes the use of the ideas and technological components of the Semantic Web, in particular ontologies, for better data quality management. His approach is characterized by the following two main innovations.

(1) While traditional data quality management formulates requirements and metrics at the very low level of system-specific database schemas, he lifts these to a generic, business-level understanding of a domain of interest.
(2) He proposes the use of a Semantic-Web-powered Wiki for organizing the elicitation and management of validation rules and metrics, thus increasing the inclusion of domain experts into these processes.

In essence, this approach can increase the quality and reusability of data quality knowledge. It will be easier for domain experts to be involved, it will be less effort to validate the consistency of data quality rules and metrics, and the rules and metrics can be applied to a broad set of data sources, because they abstract from the implementation details of a particular database schema.

---

[2] Berners-Lee T., Hendler J., Lassila O. (2001): The Semantic Web. Scientific American. 284(5): 28-37.

The topic of this thesis is practically relevant to almost any organization, and the proposed solution is a very promising application of the Semantic Web technology stack to real-world problems. I sincerely recommend this work and am confident it can help improve both our understanding and the state of implementations of data quality management as a whole.

Dr. Martin Hepp

Professor of General Management and E-Business

Universität der Bundeswehr München

Preface

As this thesis is being published, we are in the middle of the digital age in which people utilize their mobile devices to permanently share and consume data, while society still struggles with data protection issues and credibility of information. Moreover, we are entering an age, in which the massive amount of data is being used to increase the degree of automation and to precisely predict future events. Data quality issues will more and more hinder these developments, unless suitable architectures will be provided that help to reduce them.

This dissertation, therefore, describes an innovative way on how to manage data quality by utilizing knowledge representation and processing technologies which have been brought up by the Semantic Web initiative of the World Wide Web Consortium (W3C) and the Semantic Web research community. Based on a literature analysis of typical data quality problems and typical activities of data quality management processes, I developed the Semantic Data Quality Management (SDQM) framework as a major contribution of this thesis. The SDQM framework consists of three major components:

(1) an ontology for the machine-readable representation of quality-relevant knowledge,

(2) a semantic wiki that is connected to the ontology to facilitate structured capturing of quality-relevant knowledge, and

(3) a Web-based reporting frontend for data quality monitoring and assessment based on the captured knowledge.

The framework has been evaluated in three different use cases based on real-world data. Moreover, we compared SDQM with conventional data quality software to identify strengths and weaknesses of the approach. Besides technical results, this thesis delivers four theoretical findings, namely

(1) a comprehensive typology of data quality problems of information systems and Semantic Web data,

(2) ten generic data requirement types,

(3) a requirement-centric data quality management process fitted to the needs of the SDQM framework, and

(4) an analysis of related work.

This dissertation would not have been possible without the support of my family, colleagues, and friends. Therefore, I would like to thank my supervisors, Prof. Dr. Martin Hepp and Prof. Dr. Michael Eßig, for the precious discussions, their guidance, and their dedication to support my thesis project.

Moreover, I would like to thank Andreas Radinger, Alex Stolz, Dr. Mouzhi Ge, Uwe Stoll, Dr. Bene Rodriguez-Castro, Leyla Jael García-Castro, Prof. Dr. Heiner Stuckenschmidt, Dr. Holger Knublauch, and everyone else from the Semantic Web community who supported me with valuable hints and discussions.

I would also like to thank my parents, Magrit and Claus-Dieter Fürber, for encouraging me to always follow my passion. But most of all, I have to thank my wife Tanja for her love and support over all these years and for giving me the freedom to spend so much time on this thesis.

Dr. Christian Fürber

Table of Content

Table of Content XIII

List of Figures XIX

List of Tables XXIII

List of Abbreviations XXV

PART I – Introduction, Economic Relevance, and Research Design 1

1   Introduction 1

1.1   Initial Problem Statement 1

1.2   Economic Relevance 3

1.3   Organization of this Thesis 6

1.4   Published Work 6

1.4.1 Book Chapters 7

1.4.2 Papers in Conference Proceedings 7

1.4.3 Other Publications 7

2   Research Design 8

2.1   Semantic Technologies and Ontologies 8

2.2   Research Goal 9

2.3   Research Questions 11

2.4   Research Methodology 12

2.4.1 Design Science Research Methodology 13

2.4.2 Ontology Development Methodology 18

PART II – Foundations: Data Quality, Semantic Technologies, and the Semantic Web 20

3 Data Quality 20

   3.1 *Data Quality Dimensions* 21

   3.2 *Quality Influencing Artifacts* 24

   3.3 *Data Quality Problem Types* 26

      3.3.1 Quality Problems of Attribute Values 28

      3.3.2 Multi-Attribute Quality Problems 30

      3.3.3 Problems of Object Instances 32

      3.3.4 Quality Problems of Data Models 34

      3.3.5 Common Linguistic Problems 38

   3.4 *Data Quality in the Data Lifecycle* 39

      3.4.1 Data Acquisition Phase 40

      3.4.2 Data Usage Phase 41

      3.4.3 Data Retirement Phase 42

      3.4.4 Data Quality Management throughout the Data Lifecycle 42

   3.5 *Data Quality Management Activities* 43

      3.5.1 Total Information Quality Management (TIQM) 43

      3.5.2 Total Data Quality Management (TDQM) 47

      3.5.3 Comparison of Methodologies 49

   3.6 *Role of Data Requirements in DQM* 49

      3.6.1 Generic Data Requirement Types 50

      3.6.2 Challenges Related to Requirements Satisfaction 54

4 Semantic Technologies 56

   4.1 *Characteristics of an Ontology* 56

   4.2 *Knowledge Representation in the Semantic Web* 58

      4.2.1 Resources and Uniform Resource Identifiers (URIs) 58

      4.2.2 Core RDF Syntax: Triples, Literal Triples, and RDF Links 59

      4.2.3 Constructing an Ontology with RDF, RDFS, and OWL 60

      4.2.4 Language Profiles of OWL and OWL 2 63

   4.3 *SPARQL Query Language for RDF* 64

4.4　　Reasoning and Inferencing 65

4.5　　Ontologies and Relational Databases 67

5　　Data Quality in the Semantic Web..69

5.1　　Data Sources of the Semantic Web 69

5.2　　Semantic Web-specific Quality Problems.. 71

5.2.1　Document Content Problems... 72

5.2.2　Data Format Problems.. 72

5.2.3　Problems of Data Definitions and Semantics...................................... 73

5.2.4　Problems of Data Classification 74

5.2.5　Problems of Hyperlinks 75

5.3　　Distinct Characteristics of Data Quality in the Semantic Web 76

PART III – Development and Evaluation of the Semantic Data Quality
Management Framework...78

6　　Specification of Initial Requirements..78

6.1　　Motivating Scenario... 78

6.2　　Initial Requirements for SDQM.. 79

6.2.1　Task Requirements.. 80

6.2.2　Functional Requirements 82

6.2.3　Conditional Requirements 83

6.2.4　Research Requirements 85

6.3　　Summary of SDQM's Requirements 86

7　　Architecture of the Semantic Data Quality Management
Framework (SDQM) 87

7.1　　Data Acquisition Layer 88

7.1.1　Reusable Artifacts for the Data Acquisition Layer................................ 89

7.1.2　Data Acquisition for SDQM... 90

7.2　　Data Storage Layer 91

7.2.1　Reusable Artifacts for Data Storage in SDQM..................................... 91

7.2.2　The Data Storage Layer of SDQM.. 92

7.3   *Data Quality Management Vocabulary* *94*

    7.3.1 Reuse of Existing Ontologies 95

    7.3.2 Technical Design of the DQM Vocabulary 96

7.4   *Data Requirements Editor* *99*

    7.4.1 Reusable Artifacts for SDQM's Data Requirements Editor 100

    7.4.2 Data Requirements Wiki 101

7.5   *Reporting Layer* *104*

    7.5.1 Reusable Artifacts for SDQM's Reporting Layer 105

    7.5.2 Semantic Data Quality Manager 105

8   Application Procedure of SDQM **110**

8.1   *Prerequisites* *110*

8.2   *The Data Quality Management Process with SDQM* *111*

9   Evaluation of the Semantic Data Quality Management Framework (SDQM) **122**

9.1   *Evaluation of Algorithms* *122*

    9.1.1 Algorithm Evaluation Methodology 122

    9.1.2 Application Procedure 123

    9.1.3 Results 124

9.2   *Use Case 1: Evaluation of Material Master Data* *124*

    9.2.1 Scenario 125

    9.2.2 Setup and Application Procedure of SDQM 125

    9.2.3 Results and Findings 127

9.3   *Use Case 2: Evaluation of Data from DBpedia* *132*

    9.3.1 Scenario 132

    9.3.2 Specialties of Semantic Web Scenarios 133

    9.3.3 Setup and Application Procedure 133

    9.3.4 Results and Findings 135

9.4   *Use Case 3: Consistency Checks Among Data Requirements* *141*

    9.4.1 Scenario 142

    9.4.2 Application Procedure 142

    9.4.3 Summary 144

9.5   Comparison with Talend OS for Data Quality....................................... 145

    9.5.1   Representation and Management of Data Requirements.................... 145

    9.5.2   Data Quality Monitoring and Assessment Reporting 148

    9.5.3   Summary 151

PART IV – Related Work...153

10   Related Work 153

10.1   High-Level Classification Schema... 153

10.2   Categorization Schema 154

    10.2.1 Supported Data Lifecycle Step... 154

    10.2.2 Supported Data Representation... 155

    10.2.3 Supported Data Quality Task.. 156

10.3   Conventional Rule-Based Approaches.. 157

10.4   Ontology-based Approaches.. 158

    10.4.1 Information System-oriented Approaches 158

    10.4.2 Web-oriented Approaches 165

10.5   Summary.. 168

PART V - Conclusion...171

11   Synopsis and Future Work 171

11.1   Research Summary.. 171

11.2   Contributions 173

11.3   Conclusion and Future Work.. 174

Appendix A – Comparison of TIQM and TDQM...................................177

Appendix B –Rules for the Evaluation of SDQM.................................182

Appendix C – Test Data for SDQM's Evaluation 187

**Appendix D – Evaluation Results of SDQM's Data Quality Monitoring
Queries 191**

Appendix E – Evaluation Results of SDQM's Data Quality Assessment Queries 193

References 195

List of Figures

Figure 1: Extended DIKW hierarchy
(cf. Bodendorf, 2006, p. 1; Rowley, 2007, p. 164) 2
Figure 2: Simplified illustration of the relationship between
business processes and data 4
Figure 3: Impact of poor data quality on organizational success 5
Figure 4: Design methodology as applied in this thesis (cf. Peffers et al., 2008) 13
Figure 5: Problem identification and motivation process as applied in this thesis 14
Figure 6: Process for the definition of solution objectives as applied in this thesis ... 15
Figure 7: Design and development process as applied in this thesis 16
Figure 8: Demonstration and evaluation process as applied in this thesis 17
Figure 9: Ontology engineering methodology as applied in this thesis 19
Figure 10: Layers in the perception of data consumers
(inspired by Redman, 2001, p. 72) 25
Figure 11: Terminology applied to tabular data 27
Figure 12: Attribute value problems 28
Figure 13: Multi-attribute quality problems 30
Figure 14: Instance-related quality problems 32
Figure 15: Quality problems of data models 35
Figure 16: Example of a data value attribute conflict 37
Figure 17: Example of an attribute entity conflict 38
Figure 18: Example of a data value entity conflict 38
Figure 19: Data lifecycle (cf. Redman, 1996, p. 217) 40
Figure 20: Total Information Quality Management (cf. English, 1999, p. 70) 44
Figure 21: Fundamental stages of the TDQM methodology by (Wang, 1998) 48
Figure 22: Challenges of requirement satisfaction 55
Figure 23: Syntax of RDF triples (cf. Klyne & Carroll, 2004) 59
Figure 24: Linking Open Data (LOD) cloud diagram
(Cyganiak & Jentzsch, 2011a) 70
Figure 25: Typology of requirements for artifact design 80
Figure 26: High-level architecture of the SDQM framework 87
Figure 27: Visualization of the DQM vocabulary (cf. Fürber & Hepp, 2011b) 98
Figure 28: Example for an inline query and its result (cf. Dauw et al., 2014) 102
Figure 29: Architecture of SDQM's data requirements wiki 104

Figure 30: Web-based user interface of the Semantic Data Quality Manager 106

Figure 31: Configuration of data quality assessment reports in SDQMgr 108

Figure 32: Data quality assessment report of SDQMgr 109

Figure 33: DQM process as supported by SDQM (based on Wang, 1998) 111

Figure 34: SDQM's form to register new tested classes 112

Figure 35: SDQM's property requirement form 113

Figure 36: Code for a wiki page to maintain lists in the data requirements wiki 113

Figure 37: Example of new wiki page for the maintenance of legal value lists 114

Figure 38: Example of SDQM's form to add legal values 114

Figure 39: Example of legal value list in SDQM's data requirements wiki 114

Figure 40: SDQM's form to define conditions 115

Figure 41: SDQM's conditional requirement form 116

Figure 42: SDQM's functional dependency reference rule form 117

Figure 43: SDQM's form for timeliness requirements 118

Figure 44: SDQM's duplicate instance rule form 119

Figure 45: Data quality monitoring report of SDQMgr 120

Figure 46: SDQM application procedure (based on Wang, 1998) 121

Figure 47: Report with legal value range violations 127

Figure 48: Report with semantic accuracy score based on
            value range requirement 128

Figure 49: Result of legal value requirement analysis in DBpedia 135

Figure 50: Infobox source code of Wikipedia page "Janet Wood"
            as of June 27, 2011 136

Figure 51: Wikipedia page "Cy (Cyclon)" as of June 10, 2012 136

Figure 52: Out of range values for property "population" in DBpedia 137

Figure 53: Wikipedia page "Downsville, Louisiana" as of June 19th 2011 138

Figure 54: Data quality assessment report displaying syntactic accuracy results ... 138

Figure 55: SPARQL query and result displaying duplicate property requirements . 143

Figure 56: SPARQL query for identification of inconsistent property requirements 144

Figure 57: SQL business rule in Talend OS for Data Quality 146

Figure 58: Selecting SQL business rules in Talend OS for Data Quality 147

Figure 59: Data quality assessment report in Talend OS for Data Quality 149

Figure 60: Data quality monitoring report of Talend OS for Data Quality 149

Figure 61: High-level classification of DQM frameworks 153
Figure 62: Categorization schema for related work 154
Figure 63: Own classification of related work 170

All figures can be accessed on www.springer.com under the author's name and the book title.

List of Tables

Table 1: Common data quality definitions.. 20

Table 2: Data quality dimensions and their definitions according to
 Wang and Strong (Wang & Strong, 1996) 23

Table 3: First example schema "employee"... 36

Table 4: Second example schema "employee" 36

Table 5: Generic data requirements as published in
 (Fürber & Hepp, 2011a, p. 3; 2011b, p. 3) 53

Table 6: Simplified mapping between RDBs and ontologies (cf. Astrova, 2009) 67

Table 7: Tasks in the SDQM framework and their equivalencies in the
 TDQM method (based on Wang, 1998) 81

Table 8: Summary of functional requirements including expected deliverables........ 83

Table 9: Initial requirements for the development of the SDQM framework 86

Table 10: Requirements for the data acquisition layer...................................... 88

Table 11: Analysis of existing data acquisition tools with RDF conversion support.. 89

Table 12: Requirements for the data storage layer... 91

Table 13: Analysis of existing triplestores regarding their use for SDQM 92

Table 14: Requirements for the data quality management vocabulary.................... 94

Table 15: Ontologies in the data quality space of Linked Open Vocabularies 96

Table 16: Requirements for the data requirements editor 100

Table 17: Forms provided by SDQM's data requirements wiki 103

Table 18: Requirements of the reporting layer... 105

Table 19: Reports of SDQMgr 106

Table 20: Data requirements that were collected and applied for use case 1 126

Table 21: Evaluation results of SDQMgr's data quality
 monitoring reports (use case 1) 129

Table 22: Evaluation results of SDQMgr's data quality
 assessment reports (use case 1)... 130

Table 23: Assumed data requirements of use case 2....................................... 134

Table 24: SDQMgr's data quality assessment results on DBpedia......................... 139

Table 25: Qualitative comparison of SDQM and Talend OS for
 Data Quality regarding data requirements management 148

Table 26: Qualitative comparison of Talend OS for Data Quality and
 SDQM regarding data quality reporting 150

Table 27: Results of performance analysis between Talend OS for
Data Quality and SDQM 151

Table 28: Comparison of TIQM and TDQM, part one 177

Table 29: Comparison of TIQM and TDQM, part two 178

Table 30: Comparison of TIQM and TDQM, part three 179

Table 31: Comparison of TIQM and TDQM, part four 180

Table 32: Comparison of TIQM and TDQM, part five 181

Table 33: Overview of rules used for the validation of the SDQM algorithms 182

Table 34: Location test data for evaluating SDQM's algorithms 187

Table 35: Product test data for evaluating SDQM's algorithms 188

Table 36: Stock quantity test data for evaluating SDQM's algorithms 188

Table 37: Test reference data for evaluating SDQM's
"FuncDepReferenceRules" with two properties 189

Table 38: Test reference data for evaluating SDQM's
"FuncDepReferenceRules" with three properties 189

Table 39: Test reference data for evaluating SDQM's
"FuncDepReferenceRules" with four properties 190

Table 40: Test reference data for evaluating SDQM's
"FuncDepReferenceRules" with five properties 190

Table 41: Evaluation results of SDQM's data quality monitoring queries 191

Table 42: Evaluation results of SDQM's data quality assessment queries 193

List of Abbreviations

BIS	=	Business Information Systems
COIN	=	Context Interchange
CPU	=	Central Processing Unit
CRM	=	Customer Relationship Management
CSV	=	Comma-separated Value
DIKW	=	Data, Information, Knowledge, Wisdom
DQ	=	Data Quality
DQM	=	Data Quality Management
DSRM	=	Design Science Research Methodology
DSV	=	Delimiter-separated Values
DTD	=	Document Type Definition
ETL	=	Extraction, Transformation, and Loading
FDR	=	Functional Dependency Rule
FN	=	False Negative
FP	=	False Positive
FuncDepReferenceRule	=	Functional Dependency Reference Rule
HTTP	=	Hyper Text Transfer Protocol
IQ	=	Information Quality
IP	=	Information Product
IS	=	Information System
ISO	=	International Organization for Standardization
JSON	=	JavaScript Object Notation
KPI	=	Key Performance Indicator

LOD	=	Linked Open Data
MDM	=	Master Data Management
MIT	=	Massachusetts Institute of Technology
OS	=	Open Studio
OWL	=	Web Ontology Language
OXC	=	Ontology-based XML Cleaning
PHP	=	Hypertext Preprocessor
RDB	=	Relational Database
RDBMS	=	Relational Database Management System
RDF	=	Resource Description Framework
RDFS	=	RDF Vocabulary Description Language
RQ	=	Research Question
SCROL	=	Semantic Conflict Resolution Ontology
SDQM	=	Semantic Data Quality Management Framework
SDQMgr	=	Semantic Data Quality Manager
SMDM	=	Semantic Master Data Management
SMW	=	Semantic MediaWiki
SPARQL	=	SPARQL Protocol and RDF Query Language
SPIN	=	SPARQL Inferencing Notation
SQL	=	Structured Query Language
SSN	=	Social Security Number
SWRL	=	Semantic Web Rule Language
Talend OS for DQ	=	Talend Open Studio for Data Quality
TDQM	=	Total Data Quality Management

TIQM	=	Total Information Quality Management
TQDM	=	Total Quality Data Management
TP	=	True Positive
TSV	=	Tab-separated Values
UDF	=	User-defined Function (SPARQL)
URI	=	Uniform Resource Identifier
URL	=	Uniform Resource Locator
W3C	=	World Wide Web Consortium
WWW	=	World Wide Web
XML	=	Extensible Markup Language

PART I – Introduction, Economic Relevance, and Research Design

1 Introduction

In this chapter, we will provide a brief introduction into the thesis topic, clarify our understanding of the term "data" and its dependency to business processes and decisions, and discuss the economic relevance of the systematic management of data quality. Moreover, we give a short overview of the thesis structure.

1.1 Initial Problem Statement

Data has become an important resource for our business and social life. We use data every day for transactional and decision making processes. For example, we use data when driving to a certain place with a navigation system (e.g. Skog & Handel, 2009), when carrying out business tasks (e.g. Otto et al., 2011), when shopping online (e.g. Barnes & Vidgen, 2002), or when traveling from one place to another (e.g. Redman, 1996, pp. xvii-xviii). Data as society's core information resource is in the focus of this thesis. At present, there is no common definition of data (cf. Rowley, 2007, pp. 163, 170-172), but many definitions of data and information utilize the Data-Information-Knowledge-Wisdom hierarchy (DIKW) as depicted in figure 1 (Fink et al., 2005, p. 66f.; Rowley, 2007, p. 163f.). The DIKW hierarchy originates from a poem by Eliot (Eliot, 1934) and an article of Ackoff (Ackoff, 1989). Bodendorf extends the DIKW hierarchy by adding the characters layer to the bottom of the hierarchy (Bodendorf, 2006, p. 1). Although there is no common understanding about the transformation process between the layers of the hierarchy in detail (Rowley, 2007, pp. 163, 170-172), it assumes that (1) information is created based on data, (2) knowledge is created based on information, and (3) wisdom is created based on knowledge (cf. Rowley, 2007, p. 164).

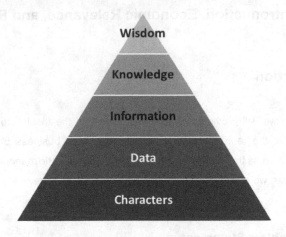

Figure 1: Extended DIKW hierarchy (cf. Bodendorf, 2006, p. 1; Rowley, 2007, p. 164)

Additionally, Bodendorf argues (1) that data are created from characters of a character set based on defined syntax rules and (2) that data become information by assigning meaning to data (Bodendorf, 2006, p. 1). Other definitions of data also regard data as "discrete, objective facts or observations" without meaning or value on its own (Rowley, 2007, p. 170f.). However, many definitions of information consider data as the major ingredient of information that is associated with meaning, context, relevance, and purpose during processing (Rowley, 2007, pp. 170-172). In other words, the definitions state that data processing makes data "meaningful, valuable, useful and relevant" (Rowley, 2007, p. 172) and, therefore, data processing generates information. Throughout this thesis, we regard data as "re-interpretable representation of information in a formalized manner suitable for communication, interpretation, or processing" (ISO/IEC, 1993, Section 01.01.02). For the remaining chapters of this thesis, we do not clearly distinguish between data and information and, therefore, use the terms "data" and "information" interchangeably. Moreover, based on the relationships within the hierarchy, we assume that "high-quality information can only come from high-quality data." (Redman, 1996, p. 11). Hence, if the consumed data is incorrect, we may derive wrong information and, therefore, make wrong decisions or processes that rely on wrong data may fail (cf. English, 1999, pp. 10-12; Redman, 1996, pp. 6-11).

Researchers and practitioners have addressed the issues of data quality for over two decades (cf. Ge & Helfert, 2007; Madnick et al., 2009, pp. 2-4), yet many people within organizations still do not fully trust their own data (Grosser & Bange, 2009, p. 10). According to studies by Madnick and Zhu, many data quality problems may be drawn back to misinterpretations of data due to heterogeneous semantics (Madnick & Zhu, 2006). Semantic technologies, such as the representation of knowledge in ontologically grounded structures (cf. Gruber, 1993, pp. 200-203), may help to improve data quality since they provide means for the concise semantic interpretation of data and its intended uses by machines (cf. Hepp, 2008b, pp. 13-15). Recently, a wide range of semantic technologies predominantly originating from artificial intelligence and knowledge management have been used in line with the Semantic Web initiative led by the World Wide Web Consortium (W3C) to publish, share, integrate, link, and consume data on web-scale (cf. Berners-Lee et al., 2001; Bizer, Heath, et al., 2009). Thereby, many technologies have evolved which may also be applied in the field of data quality management. Moreover, the availability of data on web-scale and its reuse for data quality management may significantly reduce the manual effort.

This thesis examines how we can use semantic technologies and data published on the Semantic Web for data quality management. The examination thereby focuses on data quality problems in relational databases as used by many information systems, but also addresses quality management of heterogeneous data for the Semantic Web.

1.2 Economic Relevance

Many researchers and practitioners of the data quality community agree that the level of data quality influences the economic success of an organization (e.g. Batini & Scannapieco, 2006, p. 1f.; Eckerson, 2002; English, 1999, pp. 6-13; Loshin, 2001, p. 10; Olson, 2003, pp. 12-14; Redman, 1998). However, there is only little evidence that the economic success of an organization is indeed influenced by data quality (cf. Ge & Helfert, 2013, p. 75). Today, it is widely known that the execution of business processes relies on information technology that facilitates the creation, maintenance and retrieval of data about entities and events (cf. Porter & Millar, 1985). People and machines that interact within these processes create or retrieve information to perform tasks. Information is thereby represented as data. The information system acts as an intermediary between actors of processes and data itself. Therefore, the information system provides functions and access facilities for information creation, maintenance and retrieval (cf. Redman, 2001, pp. 43-45). Figure 2 illustrates this relationship between business processes, information systems, and data.

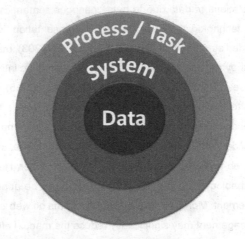

Figure 2: Simplified illustration of the relationship between business processes and data

Due to this dependency between business processes and data, we assume that incorrect data can negatively influence the execution of an organization's processes and tasks. Our assumption is supported by a study that discovered that 83 % of the participants believe that poor data quality influences the potential of creating business value (Grosser & Bange, 2009, p. 11). Redman states that data quality affects an organization on all levels, i.e. on operations, tactical and strategic level (Redman, 1998, p. 80f.). He defines the activities that are performed on the operations level as "day-to-day tasks such as order entry, customer support, and billing" (Redman, 1998, p. 80), the activities performed on the tactics level as "decisions made by (usually) mid-level managers that have consequences in the short-term to mid-term" (Redman, 1998, p. 80) and the activities performed on the strategic level as "long-term business directions" (Redman, 1998, p. 80). Based on these definitions, we categorize business processes into operational processes and decision-making processes. We thereby understand a business process as "a collection of activities that takes one or more kinds of input and creates an output [...]" (Hammer & Champy, 2002, p. 35).

In operational processes, incorrect data may lead to the incorrect execution of a task (cf. Redman, 1996, p. 4f.). For example, if the bank account details of a customer are incorrect, payments cannot be made and, therefore, revenue will not be achieved or a wrong account will be charged. Moreover, wrong address data in the customer database can lead to wrong or delayed delivery of an ordered product which may cause a decrease in customer satisfaction and, therefore, reduce the probability for future revenues from that customer (Redman, 1998, p. 80). In decision-making processes, incorrect data raises the risks to make incorrect decisions (Redman, 1996, p. 9f.). For example when performing make-or-buy decisions based on aggregated cost values, unawareness about missing cost figures within the aggregated results may lead to wrong assumptions about the real costs. Thus, the risk for an incorrect make-or-buy decision is much higher with poor data.

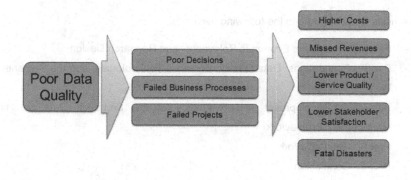

Figure 3: Impact of poor data quality on organizational success[3]

In consequence, poor data quality may impact the satisfaction of stakeholders (e.g. customers and employees), cause unnecessary costs (e.g. data correction costs or costs of failure), reduce product and service quality, reduce revenues, and even cause fatal disasters (Fisher & Kingma, 2001; Redman, 1996, pp. 6-14, 39). Figure 3 summarizes the impact of poor data quality on organizational and economic success.

However, the quantification of the economic impact of data quality is difficult (Ge & Helfert, 2013, p. 75). According to findings by Redman, we can estimate the average total costs of poor data quality in businesses as high as 8-12 % of a company's revenues (Redman, 1998, p. 80). The Data Warehousing Institute even estimates that poor customer data quality costs U.S. companies more than 600 billion US Dollar per year (Eckerson, 2002, p. 5).[4]

Without the systematic management of data quality, business processes and decisions are at risk to be affected by data quality issues, especially in systems that automatically

---

[3] Summary based on (Eckerson, 2002; English, 1999, pp. 3-13,209-212; Redman, 1998)
[4] It must be stressed that the authors do not provide many details about how these estimates have been generated.

5

perform actions based on data (cf. Loshin, 2001, p. 171). Thus, with the growing use of information systems and the reduction of human intervention and supervision, data quality management becomes critical for the economic success of businesses and organizations in general (cf. English, 1999, p. 13; Ge & Helfert, 2013, p. 75; Redman, 1996, p. 12).

1.3 Organization of this Thesis

This thesis is separated into the following five parts:

- Part I - Introduction: Economic Relevance, and Research Design
- Part II - Foundations: Data Quality, Semantic Technologies, and the Semantic Web
- Part III - Development and Evaluation of the Semantic Data Quality Management Framework
- Part IV - Related Work
- Part V - Conclusion

Part I outlines the initial problem, sketches its economic relevance and describes the research methodology for this thesis. Part II provides the theoretical foundations and defines terminology required for the understanding of the thesis. Part III describes the design process, solution architecture, application process, and evaluation results of the Semantic Data Quality Management Framework (SDQM) which has been developed as part of this thesis project. Part IV discusses related work in the area of data quality management with Semantic Web technologies. Part V summarizes the results of the research project, derives conclusions from the findings, and outlines future work.

1.4 Published Work

With permission by the PhD committee and in accordance with the regulations at the Universität der Bundeswehr München, parts of the work presented in this thesis have been published at peer-reviewed conferences or in other venues. The following is a complete list of such publications.

1.4.1 Book Chapters

Fürber, C., and Hepp, M. (2013). Using Semantic Web Technologies for Data Quality Management. In: Handbook of Data Quality: Research and Practice, (pp. 141-161), Editor: Sadiq, S., Springer, Berlin Heidelberg.

1.4.2 Papers in Conference Proceedings

Fürber, C. and Hepp, M.: SWIQA – A Semantic Web Information Quality Assessment Framework, in: Proceedings of the 19th European Conference on Information Systems (ECIS 2011), June 9th – 11th, 2011, Helsinki, Finland.

Fürber, C. and Hepp, M.: Towards a Vocabulary for Data Quality Management in Semantic Web Architectures, in: Proceedings of the 1st International Workshop on Linked Web Data Management (pp. 1-8), March 25th, 2011, Uppsala, Sweden.

Fürber, C. and Hepp, M.: Using Semantic Web Resources for Data Quality Management, in: Proceedings of the 17th International Conference on Knowledge Engineering and Knowledge Management (pp. 211-225), 2010, Lisbon, Portugal, Springer LNCS Vol. 6317.

Fürber, C. and Hepp, M.: Using SPARQL and SPIN for Data Quality Management on the Semantic Web, in: Proceedings of the 13th International Conference on Business Information Systems (pp. 35-46), 2010, Berlin, Germany, Springer LNBIP Vol. 47.

1.4.3 Other Publications

Fürber, C. and Hepp, M.: Ontology-Based Data Quality Management – Methodology, Cost, and Benefits, Poster at the 6th Annual European Semantic Web Conference, 2009, Heraklion, Greece.

2 Research Design

In this chapter, we first provide a definition for the terms "semantic technologies" and "ontologies" to provide a basic understanding for the following chapters. After that, we define the research goals and research questions. This chapter concludes with the research methodology that has been applied to generate the answers to the research questions and achieve the research goals.

2.1 Semantic Technologies and Ontologies

Originally, the use of the term "semantics" as a noun or "semantic" as an attribute was limited to the academic fields of

(1) semiotics, i.e. "the study of signs and symbols" (McComb, 2004, p. 9),
(2) linguistics i.e. "the study of language" (McComb, 2004, p. 8).

In semiotics, semantics is the name for studying the relationships between signs and meaning (cf. Hoyningen-Huene, 1998, p. 251). In linguistics, it is "the study of meaning in language" (Riemer, 2010, p. i). In computer science, the term "semantics" has been used in the context of programming languages since the 1960s, with work by Floyd (Floyd, 1967) being the most prominent initial reference. In this context, "semantics" stood for the formal analysis of the execution of programs. With the advent of artificial intelligence as a field, the notion of "semantics" in computer science got broader, including the representation of terminological and factual knowledge by data structures (cf. Sowa, 2014).

In 2001, Berners-Lee et al. described the vision of a "Semantic Web" as an evolution of the World Wide Web into an ecosystem in which information would be represented and interlinked in ways accessible to computers and not just human consumers of a visual rendering (cf. Berners-Lee et al., 2001). This contribution has triggered a broad usage of the term "semantics" as study of representation, sharing, and processing of meaning in computer systems (cf. Hitzler, 2008, p. 13). Semantic technology is then the broad range of approaches for contributing to that end. Therefore, this thesis sees "semantic technologies" as technical approaches that facilitate or make use of the interpretation of meaning by machines. A prerequisite for machine interpretation of knowledge is the collection and storage of relevant knowledge in a way that machines can understand. This can be achieved via knowledge representation languages such as the Resource Description Framework (RDF) (Manola & Miller, 2004) and the Web Ontology Language (OWL) (Bechhofer et al., 2004).

The term "ontology" is frequently used in the context of semantic technology, and there are many different options to define it (cf. Hepp, 2008b, pp. 3-6). It originates from philosophy and expresses the study of existence (cf. Gasevic et al., 2006, p. 45). In computer science, we can understand an ontology as "an explicit specification of a conceptualization" (Gruber, 1993, p. 199). "Conceptualization" can be seen as "an abstract model of some phenomenon in the world which identifies the relevant concepts of that phenomenon" (Alexiev et al., 2005, p. 16). "Explicit" means that these concepts and their restrictions are explicitly represented within an ontology (Alexiev et al., 2005, p. 16). Grimm et al. extend this definition by additional characteristics of ontologies in the context of knowledge representation and define it as "a formal explicit specification of a shared conceptualization of a domain of interest" (Grimm et al., 2007, p. 69). Based on these definitions, we understand ontologies as a formal and sharable means to explicitly model some real-world phenomenon for machine-readable knowledge representation. A detailed discussion about the characteristics of ontologies will be provided in section 4.1.

2.2 Research Goal

This thesis aims to investigate the usefulness of ontologies to support data quality management activities. Ontologies promise the concise representation of domain knowledge with its entities and relationships in a machine-readable way (cf. Grimm et al., 2007). In the context of data quality management, ontologies could provide the following benefits:

Knowledge reuse: The management of data quality requires capturing business knowledge in the form of logical rules that define the characteristics how to recognize incorrect data (cf. Loshin, 2001, p. 179). According to Loshin this knowledge "reflects the ongoing operations of a business" (Loshin, 2001, p. 185) and the same knowledge may also be relevant for other business areas (cf. Loshin, 2001, p. 286). For example, data requirements, such as the definition of credible values for a certain data element, could not only be used for data quality measurement, but also for the verification of

9

new data entries or imported data (cf. Loshin, 2001, p. 9). In many systems, such knowledge is often hidden within application logic. In order to make such knowledge reusable and transparent to business users, it is necessary to move it out of the application logic into an explicit representation (cf. Loshin, 2001, p. 279). One possible solution to preserve and publish data knowledge in a reusable way could be the structured representation of that knowledge via ontologies. E.g. data requirements could be represented with help of an ontology and linked to the accordant data element. Moreover, the data element could be linked to the data owner and the business tasks in which the data is being processed to support organizational tasks of data quality management.

Semantic reconciliation: Due to the expressivity of ontologies, it is possible to precisely define the semantics of data. When requesting information, we often ask ambiguous questions that may lead to completely different answers depending on the interpretation of an individual. With the use of ontologies, we are able to explicitly represent the concise semantics of data and annotate formal and informal definitions. This may lead to a reduction of misunderstandings and misinterpretations (cf. Madnick & Zhu, 2006).

Creation of a shared understanding: Explicit knowledge representation of a domain in form of an ontology facilitates communication about different viewpoints and thereby supports the creation of a shared understanding about a domain (cf. Fensel, 2001, p. 2; Hepp, 2008b, p. 5; Uschold & Gruninger, 1996, p. 8f.) Moreover, it is possible to enrich the elements of an ontology by textual definitions. If maintained precisely, such human-readable definitions may additionally reduce ambiguity and, therefore, support a common understanding (cf. Hepp, 2008b, p. 13).

Content integration: Several research approaches discuss the usefulness of ontologies for data and content integration within and across enterprises (cf. Alexiev et al., 2005; Fensel, 2002; Kokar et al., 2004; Niemi et al., 2007; Perez-Rey et al., 2006; Skoutas & Simitsis, 2007; Souza et al., 2008; Wache et al., 2001). The distribution of data and quality-relevant knowledge requires superior integration capabilities when managing data quality. Data quality management may, therefore, benefit from the integration capabilities of ontologies.

Deduction of implicit knowledge: Due to the explicit representation of concepts and relationships including their semantics within ontologies, it is possible to infer implicit knowledge, e.g. through reasoning engines (Hepp, 2008b, p. 15). This novel feature of ontology-based information systems may open up additional capabilities for business cases, such as data quality management.

2.3 Research Questions

In order to evaluate the potential benefits of semantic technologies, we develop a prototype that utilizes ontologies to support data quality management tasks. We address the following research questions (RQ).

RQ1: What kind of data quality problems exist?

Data quality management aims to improve data quality. In order to investigate the usefulness of ontologies in this domain, we first need to know the types and causes of data quality problems that may occur in information systems. Hence, we initially examine the characteristics of data quality problems.

RQ2: Which activities have to be performed during data quality management?

In order to identify the required capabilities which may be supported by semantic technologies, we have to analyze the data quality management process for the tasks that have to be performed to manage data quality.

RQ3: Which knowledge has to be represented to support data quality management?

Based on the identification of activities which are part of data quality management and the types of data quality problems, we need to identify the knowledge required to perform these tasks.

RQ4: How can we represent knowledge relevant for data quality management to reduce manual work?

The identified knowledge shall be represented with modeling elements of an ontology language. The ontology shall thereby be processable by both humans and machines to reduce manual efforts for data quality management.

RQ5: How can we utilize knowledge for data quality management represented within ontological structures?

Once the data quality management knowledge is captured and represented in ontological structures, we need to find ways to use this knowledge for performing data quality management tasks. Thus, artifacts are needed to process the represented knowledge to serve data quality management tasks.

In order to satisfy the reusability of the findings, this thesis aims to provide domain independent solutions to the above research questions.

2.4 Research Methodology

According to Hevner et al. the information systems discipline is dominated by two research paradigms: behavioral science and design science. "The behavioral-science paradigm seeks to develop and verify theories that explain or predict human or organizational behavior. The design-science paradigm seeks to extend the boundaries of human and organizational capabilities by creating new and innovative artifacts" (Hevner et al., 2004, p. 75). This thesis focuses on the design science paradigm to develop an innovative framework based on semantic technologies, called the Semantic Data Quality Management framework (SDQM), which aims to improve and extend the capabilities required for data quality management by providing efficient mechanisms to store and retrieve quality-relevant knowledge. Part of the framework is an ontology for sharing and utilizing quality-relevant knowledge, which we will refer to as the DQM Vocabulary in the following. The development procedure of SDQM is, therefore, based on two development methodologies: (1) the design science research methodology (DSRM) process by Peffers et al. (Peffers et al., 2008, p. 52ff.) for the development of the general framework of SDQM, and (2) the ontology engineering methodology by Uschold and Gruninger (Uschold & Gruninger, 1996) for the development of the DQM Vocabulary. Both methodologies will be explained in the following sections.

2.4.1 Design Science Research Methodology

The design science research methodology (DSRM) is based on an analysis of similarities between several different design methodologies to identify a consensual way to perform design science research (cf. Peffers et al., 2008, p. 52). In detail, DSRM has the following six processes (Peffers et al., 2008):

(1) Problem identification and motivation

(2) Define the objectives for a solution

(3) Design and development

(4) Demonstration

(5) Evaluation

(6) Communication

We chose to adjust the original DSRM by procedures and tools that have been proven to be pragmatic means during the development of the framework. For instance, we use a motivating scenario to illustrate the problem domain (cf. Uschold & Gruninger, 1996) and a requirements register to keep track of SDQM's requirements throughout its development. Figure 4 shows an adjusted version of the DSRM as chosen for this thesis including the generated outputs of the process steps.

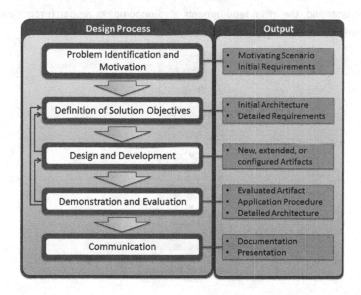

Figure 4: Design methodology as applied in this thesis (cf. Peffers et al., 2008)

13

The pure sequential execution of DSRM may not be possible in many cases due to incomplete knowledge (cf. Peffers et al., 2008, p. 56). For example, important technical requirements or defects in the developed artifacts may be initially discovered during the evaluation phase and, therefore, require to change the requirements register as part of the "Definition of solution objectives" phase and cause a change of the artifact in the development phase. Therefore, we added iteration paths that have occasionally been used during this thesis project to return to previous process steps. In the following, we will describe each process of the adjusted DSRM as applied in this thesis.

Problem identification and motivation: The design science research process typically starts with the identification of the research problem and the justification of its relevance (cf. Peffers et al., 2008, p. 52f.). In this thesis, we initially describe the general problem and its economic relevance in chapter 1. We further specify the problem by defining and motivating the research goals in section 2.2 and research questions in section 2.3. Since the research goals and research questions by themselves are not sufficient for the development of an artifact that shall be used in practical settings, we further specify the problem definition by deriving initial requirements from a motivating scenario in chapter 6. The motivating scenario is based on a practical problem setting in which the artifact shall be used (cf. Uschold & Gruninger, 1996, p. 29f.). Besides the practice-oriented requirements from the motivating scenario, the initial requirements also encompass research requirements derived from the research goals of this thesis.

Figure 5: Problem identification and motivation process as applied in this thesis

Definition of solution objectives: Solution objectives are the objectives that the developed solution shall fulfill. Based on the initial requirements, we design a high level architecture with components that shall meet the requirements that were defined in the previous process. We then describe the purpose of each component and map the initial requirements to the accordant components of the solution architecture. At this point, new requirements may arise due to increasing knowledge about the problem domain. The new requirements should, therefore, be added to the initial requirements during the "review initial requirements" process step. The execution of this process differs from the original process as described in (Peffers et al., 2008, p. 55) as we already start to sketch a solution architecture and map requirements to define the objectives of the solution components. We argue that our procedure is more pragmatic and reduces complexity, since our objectives are defined as concrete deliverables based on the initial requirements which encompass the research requirements. Finally, we already start to analyze and collect related work to identify reusable artifacts.

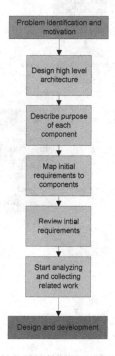

Figure 6: Process for the definition of solution objectives as applied in this thesis

Design and development: Before we start to actually develop the artifact, we first analyze whether existing artifacts can be reused for the components of our framework. The analysis is based on the description of components and its accordant requirements from the previous process. In cases of more than one reusable artifact for one component, the most appropriate artifact has to be chosen. In cases where an existing artifact only partially fulfills the requirements, the artifact may be extended before its reuse. In cases where no suitable existing artifact can be found, a new artifact has to be developed from scratch according to the component's requirements. Moreover, the components of the architecture usually have to be integrated into a single framework and initially configured as part of the development process. Figure 7 illustrates the "Design and development" process as applied in this thesis.

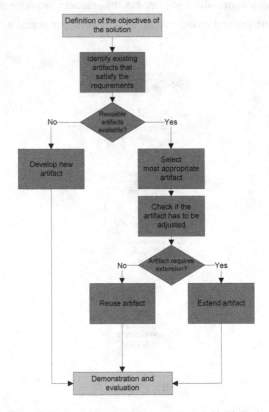

Figure 7: Design and development process as applied in this thesis

Demonstration and evaluation: We combined the activities "demonstration" and "evaluation" (which are originally separated in DSRM) to one process due to the tight interaction of demonstration and evaluation. Demonstration is the application of the developed artifact to the problem domain (cf. Peffers et al., 2008, p. 55). Evaluation identifies how well the developed artifact fulfills its intended use (cf. Peffers et al., 2008, p. 56). Therefore, it is typically performed based on information that has been collected during the demonstration (cf. Peffers et al., 2008, p. 56). In this thesis project, we perform the demonstration and evaluation process in two stages. After the development of the artifact has been finished, we initially demonstrate and evaluate the artifact as a prototype in a controlled environment. After the prototype has been evaluated successfully, we continue the demonstration and evaluation in a real-world environment as a practical use case. In cases where the evaluation identifies unacceptable limitations, we may need to return to the design and development process to enhance the artifact. For this project, we chose two major use cases: (1) data quality management of material master data (section 9.2) and (2) data quality management of Semantic Web data (section 9.3) to investigate the applicability of the artifact in both environments.

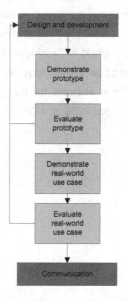

Figure 8: Demonstration and evaluation process as applied in this thesis

Communication: The DSRM ends with the communication of the research project which is performed by this thesis. Additionally, parts of this project have been published at scientific conferences. A list of conference papers that are related to this research project can be found in section 1.4.

2.4.2 Ontology Development Methodology

The development of the DQM Vocabulary is based on the ontology engineering method by Uschold and Gruninger (Uschold & Gruninger, 1996). Similar to the development of SDQM, we start with motivating scenarios for the use of the DQM Vocabulary to illustrate the problem domain and justify its relevance (cf. Uschold & Gruninger, 1996, pp. 103, 112f.). From the scenarios, we derive stratified competency questions that shall be answerable by queries that will be asked against the DQM Vocabulary (cf. Uschold & Gruninger, 1996, pp. 113-117). The competency questions serve as the requirements for the ontology. In fact, the terms used in the competency questions are extracted and informally defined as foundation for the definition of the ontology elements. Therefore, these terms are first classified into objects, properties of objects, and relationships between objects. Based on this classification and the terms derived from the competency questions, a basic ontology can be coded (cf. Uschold & Gruninger, 1996, p. 114). To reduce ambiguity, definitions are added to the elements of the ontology (cf. Uschold & Gruninger, 1996, p. 114). The evaluation is done by storing instances based on the ontology and executing queries against the ontology that attempt to retrieve answers for the previously defined competency questions (cf. Uschold & Gruninger, 1996, p. 113f.).

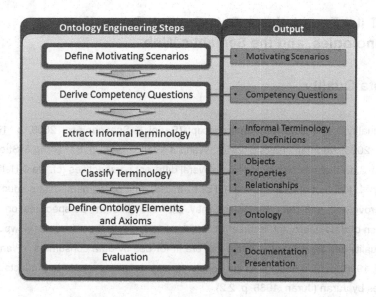

Figure 9: Ontology engineering methodology as applied in this thesis

PART II – Foundations: Data Quality, Semantic Technologies, and the Semantic Web

3 Data Quality

Data quality is a multidimensional concept (Batini & Scannapieco, 2006, p. 19ff.; Eppler, 2006; Redman, 1996, p. 245ff.; Wand & Wang, 1996, p. 87; Wang & Strong, 1996, p. 22f.) that can be defined from several different perspectives (cf. Ge & Helfert, 2007, p. 1; Kahn et al., 2002, p. 185). For example, data consumers, data producers, data providers, and data custodians may all have different perspectives on the definition of data quality (cf. Kahn et al., 2002, p. 184). From the consumer viewpoint, data quality can be defined as "data that are fit for use by data consumers" (Wang & Strong, 1996, p. 6) in analogy to the popular quality definition related to products and services by Juran (Juran, 1988, p. 2.2).

Table 1: Common data quality definitions

Authors	Year	Data Quality Definition
Wang and Strong	1996	"data that are fit for use by data consumers." (Wang & Strong, 1996, p. 6)
Redman	2001	"Data are of high quality if they are fit for their intended uses in operations, decision making, and planning. Data are fit for use if they are free of defects and possess desired features." (Redman, 2001, p. 74)
Kahn, Strong, and Wang	2002	"conformance to specifications" and "meeting or exceeding consumer expectations" (Kahn et al., 2002, p. 185)
Olson	2003	"[...] data has quality if it satisfies the requirements of its intended use." (Olson, 2003, p. 24)

From a more technical perspective, data is of high quality when it is "free of defects" and "conforms to specifications" (cf. Kahn et al., 2002; Redman, 2001, p. 71ff.). Table 1 summarizes common data quality definitions from data quality research. All of the above definitions of data quality share the assumption that data quality is relative to formally or informally defined quality expectations, such as (1) consumer expectations and intentions, (2) specifications, or (3) requirements imposed by the usage of data, e.g. to execute certain tasks. According to these definitions, the level of data quality is determined by comparison of the actual state of the data (status quo) to a desired state. The desired state is named "fitness for use", "specification", "consumer expectations", "defect-free" "desired features", or simply "requirements" in the above definitions. According to ISO 9000:2005, quality is defined as the "degree to which a set of inherent characteristics fulfils requirements" (ISO, 2005, p. 18). Therefore, we define data quality as the degree to which data fulfils requirements. The requirements can thereby be defined (1) by quality requirements of several different individuals or groups of individuals, (2) by standards, by (3) laws and other regulatory requirements, (4) by business policies, or (5) even by expectations of data processing applications, e.g. when they only process certain values or structures.

In the following, we describe relevant aspects of data quality which are important for the understanding of this thesis. In sections 3.1 and 3.2, we describe facets of the user perspective, namely data quality dimensions and quality influencing artifacts. In section 3.3, we describe the technical perspective of data quality, namely data quality problem types. In section 3.4, we briefly explain the data lifecycle with regard to data quality. In section 3.5, we provide an overview of common management methodologies for data quality management. Finally, we explain the role of data requirements for data quality management and define generic data requirement types in section 3.6.

3.1 Data Quality Dimensions

From a consumer perspective, data quality can be judged by multiple different data quality dimensions, i.e. "attributes that represent a single aspect or construct of data quality" (Wang & Strong, 1996, p. 6). Wang and Strong (1996) conducted an empirical study to identify important quality dimensions from the perspective of data consumers (Wang & Strong, 1996). Based on a set of over 100 data quality dimensions, they identified fifteen most important dimensions as perceived by data consumers when judging data quality. The dimensions can be classified into intrinsic, contextual, representational, and accessibility dimensions (Wang & Strong, 1996, p. 18f.). Intrinsic quality dimensions contain attributes of data quality "that data has on its own" (Batini & Scannapieco, 2006, p. 39). Contextual dimensions encompass quality attributes that can only be perceived when using data in task contexts (cf. Wang & Strong, 1996, p. 20f.). For example, completeness can only be judged together with completeness requirements for the task at hand. The representational category includes dimensions related to format and meaning of data such as the consistent representation of data or the ease to understand the data at hand (cf. Wang & Strong, 1996, p. 21). The accessibility category considers quality attributes regarding the access to data and data access security (cf. Wang & Strong, 1996, p. 21). Table 2 provides an overview of all fifteen dimensions including their definitions.

Table 2: Data quality dimensions and their definitions according to Wang and Strong (Wang & Strong, 1996)

Category	Dimension	Definition
Intrinsic	Believability	"The extent to which data are accepted or regarded as true, real and credible." (p. 31)
	Accuracy	"The extent to which data are correct, reliable and certified free of error." (p. 31)
	Objectivity	"The extent to which data are unbiased (unprejudiced) and impartial." (p. 32)
	Reputation	"The extent to which data are trusted or highly regarded in terms of their source or content." (p. 32)
Contextual	Value-added	"The extent to which data are beneficial and provide advantages from their use." (p. 31)
	Relevancy	"The extent to which data are applicable and helpful for the task at hand." (p. 31)
	Timeliness	"The extent to which the age of the data is appropriate for the task at hand." (p. 32)
	Completeness	"The extent to which data are of sufficient depth, breadth, and scope for the task at hand." (p. 32)
	Appropriate amount of data	"The extent to which the quantity and volume of available data is appropriate." (p. 32)
Representational	Interpretability	"The extent to which data are in appropriate language and units and the data definitions are clear." (p. 31)
	Ease of understanding	"The extent to which data are clear without ambiguity and easily comprehended." (p. 32)
	Representational consistency	"The extent to which data are always presented in the same format and are compatible with previous data." (p. 32)
	Concise representation	"The extent to which data are compactly represented without being overwhelming (i.e., brief in presentation, yet complete and to the point)." (p. 32)
Accessibility	Accessibility	"The extent to which data are available or easily and quickly retrievable." (p. 32)
	Access security	"The extent to which access to data can be restricted and hence kept secure." (p. 32)

Although it is often ultimately the data consumer who judges data quality (Wang & Strong, 1996, p. 6), a plain adaption of consumer dimensions for data quality management in practical settings is not constructive for several reasons:

- Data consumers usually do not to distinguish between data, application, and hardware when judging data quality (cf. Kahn et al., 2002, p. 186). E.g. poor hardware performance during data consumption may result in low data quality perception by data consumers although the quality of data may be perfect.
- Many data quality dimensions from table 2 are difficult to measure, since they rely on very user- and context-specific preconditions and requirements that partially depend on the individual experience, background, and intentions of data consumers (cf. Kahn et al., 2002, p. 185).
- Data consumers are not the only stakeholders who have data requirements as stated in the previous section. For example, data producers, data custodians, and data providers may also have data requirements that may be different from the consumer requirements (cf. Kahn et al., 2002, p. 184).
- The description of data quality dimensions from a consumer perspective may neglect potential quality problems in data.
- The single view on data quality from a consumer perspective may miss important quality dimensions, such as data redundancy.

Solely considering the perspective of data consumers is not enough, when aiming to develop artifacts for practical data quality management settings. However, the above dimensions may serve as a starting point for structuring data quality evaluation reports.

3.2 Quality Influencing Artifacts

Data consumers usually do not access plain data directly. They rather use query interfaces or information systems to consume data. So the data quality perception may be influenced by several other artifacts than just data values when using intermediaries to access the data. We can categorize the data quality influencing artifacts into the data layer, the data model layer, the presentation layer, and the access layer (cf. Redman, 2001, p. 72).

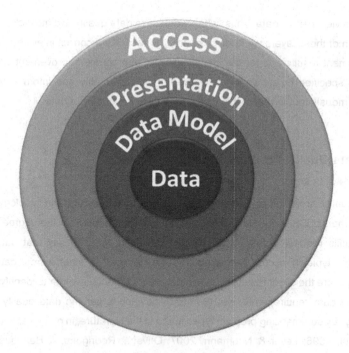

Figure 10: Layers in the perception of data consumers (inspired by Redman, 2001, p. 72)

The *data layer* consists of plain data, i.e. values composed by characters according to certain syntactical rules (Bodendorf, 2006, p. 1). The *data model layer* represents the contextual information of data. It contains a schema, i.e. a formally described data structure, integrity constraints, operators, and inferencing rules (cf. Codd, 1980, p. 112). In the understanding of this thesis, it may additionally contain classifications, restrictions, and metadata, i.e. data about data. The *presentation layer* is usually the first visible presentation of data to data consumers. The data may be represented in separately designed user interfaces. The presentation layer may itself contain transformations of data at run-time (e.g. aggregations) and separate labels of schema objects (cf. Goeken, 2006, p. 42f.). Finally, the *access layer* contains all artifacts that facilitate a user's access to data. Authorizations, i.e. user access rights to view, modify, create, or delete certain data, are the central artifact in the access layer (cf. Codd, 1990, p. 325f.). Moreover, hardware and network infrastructure may influence the ability of a user to access data at the right speed.

In general, all components of these layers may be a source of own quality problems. In fact, the quality of data may be perfectly flawless, while the perception of data quality may be poor in the eyes of a data consumer, e.g. because he or she lacks access rights to view certain data. Thus, when we assess data quality, we must clearly define to which of these layers we refer to, in order to facilitate a correct interpretation of the assessment results and for the identification of appropriate improvement objectives. Unless specified otherwise, we use the terms data quality and information quality synonymously for the rest of this thesis to refer to the quality of data.

3.3 Data Quality Problem Types

Data quality problems are an important source to understand the typology of data requirements. Earlier in this chapter, we defined data quality as "the degree to which data fulfils requirements". Based on this definition, we can say that data quality problems typically occur, if requirements are not met. In other words, data quality problems are the direct result of violated data requirements. In order to identify different types of data requirements, we, therefore, develop a generic data quality problem typology by summarizing problem types found in the literature, in particular in (Kashyap & Sheth, 1996; Leser & Naumann, 2007; Oliveira, Rodrigues, & Henriques, 2005; Oliveira, Rodrigues, Henriques, et al., 2005; Rahm & Do, 2000). The problems are thereby classified from two perspectives: (1) the problem location perspective and (2) the scenario perspective (cf. Leser & Naumann, 2007, pp. 318-322; Rahm & Do, 2000, pp. 2-5). The problem location perspective classifies the different data quality problems according to the location in which the problem occurs. Thus from the data location perspective, problems are classified into (1) attribute value problems, i.e. problems in values within a single attribute, (2) multi-attribute problems, i.e. problems where values of two or more attributes are involved, (3) problems of object instances which are represented via tuples in case of a table format, and (4) problems of the data model. The problem locations refer to the data and data model layer from the previous section. Figure 11 illustrates the terms attribute, tuple / instance, and schema as we can find them in a table representation.

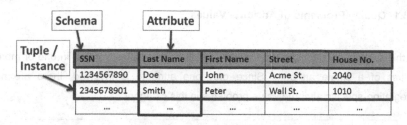

Figure 11: Terminology applied to tabular data

The scenario perspective classifies data quality problems into two different scenarios in which data quality problems typically occur. Hence from the scenario perspective, we can distinguish between (1) single-source problems, i.e. problems that occur within a single data source, and (2) integration-specific problems, i.e. problems that only occur when integrating data from two or more sources. Besides this general classification there are linguistic problems that may result in data quality problems. Based on this classification, we will describe typical data quality problems that have been identified by means of a thorough literature analysis. It must be stressed that many integration-specific problems are caused by heterogeneous ways to represent the same domain and, therefore, should not always be regarded as errors. Moreover, in the understanding of this thesis a data quality problem should only be seen as an error when it violates a previously defined requirement. The examples below assume that data requirements have been violated. Problems of artifacts related to the presentation and access layer, which have been defined in section 3.2, are not addressed by this thesis and, therefore, not covered by the typology.

3.3.1 Quality Problems of Attribute Values

In this section, we describe data quality problems that typically occur in one or more values of a single attribute. Since only one attribute is involved, there are no integration-specific attribute value problems in this category.

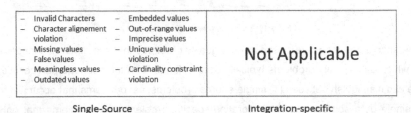

| Single-Source | Integration-specific |

Figure 12: Attribute value problems

Invalid characters: Invalid characters are characters that are not supposed to be part of the value (cf. Oliveira, Rodrigues, & Henriques, 2005, p. 5). E.g. a numeric zip code contains a letter.

Character alignment violation: Character alignment violations occur when whole substrings or characters of a value are in the wrong position according to predefined syntax rules (cf. Oliveira, Rodrigues, & Henriques, 2005, p. 4; Oliveira, Rodrigues, Henriques, et al., 2005, p. 3). E.g. the value "20.03.09" violates the syntax "MM/DD/YYYY" where M represents the index position for numerical month values, D for numerical day values, and Y for numerical year values. Misspelling errors and word transpositions can also be subsumed by this category.

Missing values: Missing values are empty values or NULL values in attributes that require a value (cf. Leser & Naumann, 2007, p. 320; Oliveira, Rodrigues, & Henriques, 2005, p. 4; Oliveira, Rodrigues, Henriques, et al., 2005, p. 3; Rahm & Do, 2000, p. 4). Furthermore, a value may be considered as missing when only a default value or a whitespace value is available (cf. Rahm & Do, 2000, p. 6).

False values: False values are possible values for the object, but do not represent the correct state of the underlying entity (cf. Leser & Naumann, 2007, p. 320; Oliveira, Rodrigues, & Henriques, 2005, p. 4; Oliveira, Rodrigues, Henriques, et al., 2005, p. 4; Rahm & Do, 2000, p. 3). E.g. the attribute "age" of customer "Peter Johnson" has the value "28", but Peter Johnson's real age is 39.

Meaningless values: Meaningless values are values that do not have a corresponding real-world entity (cf. Oliveira, Rodrigues, Henriques, et al., 2005, p. 4). E.g. the attribute name contains a value "ABC XYZ".

Outdated values: Outdated values are values of an attribute or types that represent an obsolete state of the accordant real-world entity (cf. Oliveira, Rodrigues, Henriques, et al., 2005, p. 3). E.g. Peter married on March 1st, 2009, but the employee database still shows the family status "single".

Embedded values: Embedded values are substrings in a value that represent additional information (cf. Leser & Naumann, 2007, p. 320; Oliveira, Rodrigues, & Henriques, 2005, p. 5; Oliveira, Rodrigues, Henriques, et al., 2005, p. 4; Rahm & Do, 2000, p. 4). Embedded values that do not fit to the intension of the attribute are also called invalid substrings (cf. Oliveira, Rodrigues, & Henriques, 2005, p. 5). E.g. the attribute name holds also the titles of the person, i.e. "Dr. Peter Miller" instead of "Peter Miller".

Out-of-range values: Values are out of range if they are outside of a predefined interval (cf. Leser & Naumann, 2007, p. 319; Oliveira, Rodrigues, Henriques, et al., 2005, p. 3; Rahm & Do, 2000, p. 3). E.g. the attribute salary must not contain negative values.

Imprecise values: Imprecise values are ambiguous values that cannot be precisely mapped to a corresponding real-world entity or state (cf. Oliveira, Rodrigues, & Henriques, 2005, p. 5; Oliveira, Rodrigues, Henriques, et al., 2005, p. 4). E.g. the textual attribute country has a value "D" which could indicate the countries "Denmark", "Djibouti", "Dominican Republic", or even "Germany". Imprecise values can occur in textual attributes, e.g. when using abbreviated or cryptic values (cf. Leser & Naumann, 2007, p. 320; Rahm & Do, 2000, p. 4), or in numerical attributes, e.g. one position after the decimal point may not be precise enough to indicate the currency rate. Moreover, imprecise values can be caused by homonyms, i.e. values that have more than one meaning.

Unique value violation: Some attributes must not contain the same value more than once. Hence, a unique value violation occurs if the exact same value occurs more than once with the same attribute (cf. Leser & Naumann, 2007, p. 319; Oliveira, Rodrigues, & Henriques, 2005, p. 6; Oliveira, Rodrigues, Henriques, et al., 2005, p. 4; Rahm & Do, 2000, p. 3). E.g. the attributes license_plate_no, tax_payer_no, and `social_security_no` may need to obtain unique values for each tuple. The most important types of such attributes are those that hold values that are meant to be used as identifiers for entities for cross-references.

Cardinality constraint violation: The cardinality of an attribute is violated, if the allowed amount of values per one entity is exceeded if given (cf. Rahm & Do, 2000, p. 6). E.g. the attribute `date_of_birth` must have exactly one value per person.

3.3.2 Multi-Attribute Quality Problems

In this section, we describe data quality problems that occur between two or more attributes.

− Functional depdency violations − Referential integrity violations − Incorrect / outdated reference − Conditional missing values − Misfielded values	− Heterogeneity of syntaxes − Heterogeneity of units of measuerment − Data precision conflicts − Default value conflicts
Single-Source	Integration-specific

Figure 13: Multi-attribute quality problems

Functional dependency violation: Functional dependencies can be defined as the dependency between two or more attribute values within the same tuple or among different tuples of different entities and data sources (cf. Leser & Naumann, 2007, p. 319; Oliveira, Rodrigues, & Henriques, 2005, p. 7; Oliveira, Rodrigues, Henriques, et al., 2005, p. 5f.; Olson, 2003, p. 174; Rahm & Do, 2000, p. 4). E.g. if the attribute `ZipCode` contains "85577" and the country is "Germany", then the city must be "Neubiberg".

Referential integrity violation: If an attribute of one entity comprises values that refer to tuples of another entity, the we can call the values of the first attribute "foreign keys" (cf. Codd, 1970, p. 380). In case of a referential integrity violation a foreign key value does not have a matching value in the referenced entity (cf. Leser & Naumann, 2007, p. 319; Oliveira, Rodrigues, & Henriques, 2005, p. 8; Oliveira, Rodrigues, Henriques, et al., 2005, p. 6; Rahm & Do, 2000, p. 3). Thus, referential integrity is violated when (1) a foreign key is wrong and, therefore, cannot have a corresponding tuple in the referenced entity or (2) a foreign key is correct, but the referenced entity does not contain the corresponding tuple. E.g. the attribute `ZipCode` of the table `Customer` comprises the values "4000" and "40027" that both do not exist in the referenced table LocationZipCodes and, therefore, currently violate referential integrity. In case of "4000", the postal code does not exist in reality. Thus, the foreign key is wrong. In case of the postal code "40027", the value exists in reality. Hence, the referenced table Customer misses a tuple.

Incorrect / outdated reference: Between two entities, an attribute comprises foreign keys that refer to wrong tuples in the referenced entity (cf. Leser & Naumann, 2007, p. 320; Oliveira, Rodrigues, & Henriques, 2005, p. 8; Oliveira, Rodrigues, Henriques, et al., 2005, p. 6; Rahm & Do, 2000, p. 4). E.g. the attribute ZipCode of the table Customer comprises the value "51111" that refers to the tuple for "Cologne" in the table LocationZipCodes, although the correct reference would be the zip code "40027" referring to the tuple for "Düsseldorf". An incorrect reference may also be caused when a relationship, such as an address of a customer, has changed over time and was not updated in the data source. In this case, we also talk about an outdated reference (cf. Oliveira, Rodrigues, Henriques, et al., 2005).

Conditional Missing Values: Some attributes require a value only in certain contexts, i.e. when other attributes obtain certain values (cf. Fürber & Hepp, 2011b). E.g. the attribute state may only require a value when the attribute country has the value "USA".

Misfielded values: Misfielded values are correct values that do not fit to the intension of their attribute, but to another attribute of the same tuple (cf. Leser & Naumann, 2007, p. 320; Rahm & Do, 2000, p. 4). E.g. the attribute city comprises the value "Germany" which should be located in the attribute country of the same tuple.

Heterogeneity of syntaxes: Attribute values may represent the same real-world entity or state, but use different syntactic representations (cf. Kashyap & Sheth, 1996, p. 287; Leser & Naumann, 2007, p. 321; Oliveira, Rodrigues, & Henriques, 2005, p. 9; Oliveira, Rodrigues, Henriques, et al., 2005, p. 7; Rahm & Do, 2000, p. 4). E.g. there are several different possibilities to represent the current date, for example in the format "dd.mm.yyyy" or in the format "mm/dd/yyyy". Heterogeneity of syntaxes also encompasses the representation of attribute states via cryptic values or codes. In this context, it is also called heterogeneity of representation (cf. Leser & Naumann, 2007, p. 321).

Heterogeneity of units of measurement: The same real-world concept may be represented using different scales (cf. Kashyap & Sheth, 1996, p. 287; Leser & Naumann, 2007, p. 321; Oliveira, Rodrigues, & Henriques, 2005, p. 10; Oliveira, Rodrigues, Henriques, et al., 2005, p. 7; Rahm & Do, 2000, p. 4). E.g. the weight of an object may be represented in one data source using grams, while another data source represents the weight in pounds. Heterogeneity of units of measurement is also known as a data scaling conflict (Kashyap & Sheth, 1996, p. 287).

Data granularity mismatch: Two or more attributes coming from different sources may refer to the same entity, but on different levels of granularity (cf. Leser & Naumann, 2007, p. 322; Oliveira, Rodrigues, Henriques, et al., 2005, p. 8; Rahm & Do, 2000, p. 4). Data granularity mismatches typically occur when data with different aggregation levels are integrated (cf. Leser & Naumann, 2007, p. 322; Rahm & Do, 2000, p. 4). E.g. the table `DepartmentSalaries` of data source one contains salary values aggregated to departments, while another table of data source two contains salary values detailed on the level of individual employees. Hence, the data cannot be easily compared or joined, since they contain summarized values on different levels of detail. Data granularity mismatches are also known as aggregation or generalization conflicts (Kashyap & Sheth, 1996, p. 291f.).

Default value conflicts: Different data sources may assign different default values for semantically similar attributes in absence of the real-world information (Kashyap & Sheth, 1996, p. 287). E.g. the attribute `LegalAge` of data source one may have the default value "18" to indicate adults, while data source two may assign the default value "21" for the same purpose.

3.3.3 Problems of Object Instances

In the following, we describe data quality problems that are related to object instances and tuples.

– Inconsistent duplicates	– Heterogeneity in cardinality
– Approximate duplicates	– Heterogeneity in time reference
– Contradictory relationships	– Source specific identifiers
Single-Source	Integration-Specific

Figure 14: Instance-related quality problems

Inconsistent duplicates: Two or more object instances that represent the same real-world entity are called inconsistent duplicates, when their attribute values represent contradicting states (cf. Leser & Naumann, 2007, p. 321; Oliveira, Rodrigues, & Henriques, 2005, p. 8; Oliveira, Rodrigues, Henriques, et al., 2005, p. 8; Rahm & Do, 2000, p. 4). E.g. tuple one ("135", "Johnson, Peter", "SSN123454321") and tuple two ("19", "P. Johnson", "SSN123456789") are inconsistent duplicate instances, assuming that the tuples represent the same person who can only have one social security number (SSN).

Approximate duplicates: Approximate duplicates are duplicate instances that do not have attribute values representing contradicting states (Oliveira, Rodrigues, & Henriques, 2005, p. 7f.; Oliveira, Rodrigues, Henriques, et al., 2005, p. 8). E.g. tuple one ("135", "Johnson, Peter", "Main Street 1010", "New York City") and tuple two ("19", "P. Johnson", "Main St. 1010", "NYC") are approximate duplicates, since they do not contain values for the same attribute that represent a contradicting real-world state. Approximate duplicates may also have identical values for their attributes with exception of the technical identifier, e.g. the primary key, which uniquely identifies the tuple. Note that approximate duplicates may evolve into inconsistent duplicates if the data about one instance is updated while the second one is kept unchanged.

Contradictory relationships: Contradictory relationships occur when two or more relationships between object instances are contradictory (cf. Oliveira, Rodrigues, & Henriques, 2005; Oliveira, Rodrigues, Henriques, et al., 2005). E.g. if product B is a subclass of product A, then product A cannot be a subclass of product B at the same time. Depending on the design and the data storage medium, contradictory relationships can also be located in the data model or ontology.

Heterogeneity in cardinality: Relationships between instances may have different cardinality restrictions in different sources (cf. Leser & Naumann, 2007, p. 77). E.g. in data source one the relationship between department and employee may always be one to one, i.e. every employee can work for exactly one department, while in data source two an employee may work for several departments.

Heterogeneity in time reference: Tuples of two or more sources may refer to different points in time. Hence, the tuples might contain different values representing different historical states of characteristics of an entity (Kashyap & Sheth, 1996, p. 290; Rahm

& Do, 2000, p. 4). E.g. data source one contains a tuple for "Peter Miller" with family status "single", while data source two contains family status "married" for the same person. In our example, data source one refers to a point in time before the marriage of Peter Miller. Thus, the data sources refer to a different time resulting in different values. As illustrated, heterogeneity in time references can come along with at least one outdated value.

Source-specific identifiers: Data sources typically use their own identifiers in their tuples to uniquely identify an entity. Thus, semantically identical entities represented in two or more data sources often have different identifiers in each source (cf. Kashyap & Sheth, 1996, p. 288; Rahm & Do, 2000, p. 4). E.g. the table EMPLOYEE1 from data source one contains the identifier "1234567890", while table EMPLOYEE2 from data source two contains the identifier "employee_123421" for the same employee. This increases the risk of introducing inconsistencies by future operations on the data.

3.3.4 Quality Problems of Data Models

In this section, we describe quality problems that typically occur in data models, i.e. at the schema level. An important contribution to the development of data models was made by E.F. Codd in 1970 when he initially proposed a relational model for databases (cf. Codd, 1970). According to Codd, the relational model aimed to describe "data with its natural structure only – that is without superimposing any additional structure for machine representation purposes" (Codd, 1970, p. 377). Therefore, the relational model should allow changes to the data structure without impairing application programs (cf. Codd, 1970, p. 377f.). Codd argued that a data model is a combination of (1) "a collection of data structure types [...]", (2) "a collection of operators or inferencing rules [...]" and (3) "a collection of general integrity rules [...]" (Codd, 1980, p. 112). In 1976, Chen argued that the relational model "can achieve a high degree of data independence, but it may lose some important semantic information about the real world" (Chen, 1976, p. 9). Thus, Chen proposed the entity-relationship model which sees data models as representations of entities and relationships (cf. Chen, 1976, p. 9). The entity-relationship model has been widely used for several decades as a popular diagramming technique to design data models (cf. Simsion & Witt, 2005, p. 65). Our understanding of the term "data model" is based on Chen's entity-relationship model. Therefore, we regard a data model as an independent artifact that defines the entities, their properties and relationships between the entities of a certain domain as a structure for data storage (cf. Chen, 1976, pp. 10-19; Simsion & Witt, 2005, p. 4; West, 2011, p. 5). Hence, quality problems at this level relate to the structure in which the data is being stored, not to data values. However, the proper design of data models may be relevant to achieve high quality also on object instance or on attribute value level because data models dictate the way in which data relate to each other and how they are used (cf. West, 2011, p. 5). Since data models are costly to change due to their integration with interfaces for data access and storage, workarounds, such as the misuse of conceptual elements, are sometimes used to avoid changes to the data model (cf. West, 2003, p. 1). Hence, a well-thought and approximately complete design of the data model may mitigate the necessity of such workarounds that cause poor data quality or misinterpretations on instance level.

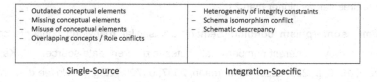

– Outdated conceptual elements	– Heterogeneity of integrity constraints
– Missing conceptual elements	– Schema isomorphism conflict
– Misuse of conceptual elements	– Schematic descrepancy
– Overlapping concepts / Role conflicts	
Single-Source	Integration-Specific

Figure 15: Quality problems of data models

Outdated conceptual elements: Conceptual elements, i.e. attributes, tables, relationships, and constraints may become obsolete over time (cf. Hogan et al., 2010, p. 6). E.g. the table `Groceries` of an information system of a retail company is outdated, since the company has a new table `Products` in which all the products of the company shall be stored. Thus, if some groceries are still only stored in the table `Groceries`, then table `Products` will not be complete.

Missing conceptual elements: Sometimes conceptual elements may be missing in the data model, e.g. when a new kind of information becomes relevant that has not been represented in the data model before. Thus, attributes, tables, or other conceptual elements may be missing (cf. Kashyap & Sheth, 1996, p. 289).

Misuse of conceptual elements: Existing schema elements may sometimes be used to store data values that do not fit to the intension of the schema element due to misinterpretation of the semantics of the schema element or due to inflexibility to extend existing schemata (cf. Hogan et al., 2010, p. 8). E.g. the attribute `lastname` may be misused to store names of organizations in the `Customer` table.

Overlapping concepts / role conflicts: A real-world entity can be part of two or more different real-world concepts at the same time. The concepts may have very different semantics, but due to the membership of the individual to both concepts, they are not disjunctive (cf. Leser & Naumann, 2007, p. 75f.). E.g. a soccer player can also be coach, but the data model design only allows the membership of each entity in one class. In many cases, this shows a lack of normalization of the database schema. For normalization in database schemata, see Simsion and Witt (Simsion & Witt, 2005, p. 391ff.).

Heterogeneity of integrity constraints: The constraints on two or more semantically similar attributes can be inconsistent with each other (cf. Kashyap & Sheth, 1996, p. 287; Leser & Naumann, 2007, p. 77; Rahm & Do, 2000, p. 4). E.g. the attribute age in data source one requires values higher than 18, while the attribute age in data source two requires values higher than 21.

Schema isomorphism conflict: Semantically similar real-world concepts can be represented by a different number of attributes in different data sources (cf. Kashyap & Sheth, 1996, p. 288; Leser & Naumann, 2007, p. 70ff.). E.g. employee data may be represented in data source one by a table Employee with attributes employee_ID, name, and gender, while in data source two the same information is represented within a table Employee with attributes employee_ID, name, male and female. Please see the following tables for an illustration of the above example.

Table 3: First example schema "employee"

Employee_ID	Name	Gender
1	Peter Smith	Male
2	Jennifer Myer	Female

Table 4: Second example schema "employee"

Employee_ID	Name	Male	Female
1	Peter Smith	X	
2	Jennifer Myer		X

Schematic discrepancy: If the schematic differences are not only related to the amount of attributes, but the same information is also represented by different schema elements, i.e. data values, attributes, or tables, then we can call this a schematic discrepancy (cf. Kashyap & Sheth, 1996, p. 291; Leser & Naumann, 2007, p. 70ff.; Rahm & Do, 2000, p. 4). According to Kashyap and Sheth (Kashyap & Sheth, 1996, p. 291f.), there are three different types of schematic discrepancies, i.e.

- data value attribute conflicts,
- attribute entity conflicts and
- data value entity conflicts.

Data value attribute conflicts occur "when the value of an attribute in one database corresponds to an attribute in another database" (Kashyap & Sheth, 1996, p. 291). Figure 16 shows an example of a data value attribute conflict between two tables of two different data sources.

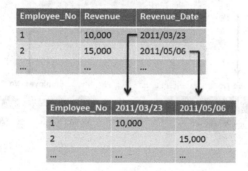

Figure 16: Example of a data value attribute conflict

Attribute entity conflicts occur "when the same entity is being modeled as an attribute in one database and a relation in another database" (Kashyap & Sheth, 1996, p. 291f.). Figure 17 shows an example of an attribute entity conflict.

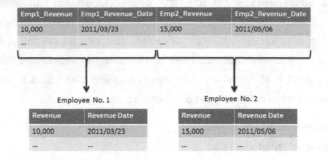

Figure 17: Example of an attribute entity conflict

A data value entity conflict occurs "when the value of an attribute in one database corresponds to a relation in another database" (Kashyap & Sheth, 1996, p. 292).

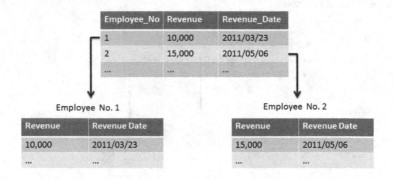

Figure 18: Example of a data value entity conflict

3.3.5 Common Linguistic Problems

In this section, we explain the most common linguistic problems that may cause data quality problems in attribute values, object instances, and data models independent of a specific scenario.

Existence of synonyms: Two or more values, instances, or names of conceptual elements can be identical in meaning, but denoted with different terms (Kashyap & Sheth, 1996, p. 286f.; Leser & Naumann, 2007, p. 74ff.; Oliveira, Rodrigues, & Henriques, 2005; Oliveira, Rodrigues, Henriques, et al., 2005; Rahm & Do, 2000, p.

4). E.g. the attribute `occupation` contains the synonymous values "coach" and "trainer" which represent the same real-world occupation. Synonymous values, instances, and conceptual elements are especially problematic during data integration and aggregation, since the synonym relationships must be known in order to produce precise results.

Existence of homonyms and polysemes: Two or more values, instances, or names of conceptual elements can be denoted with the same term, but represent a totally or partly different real-world entity (Kashyap & Sheth, 1996, p. 286f.; Leser & Naumann, 2007, p. 74ff.; Oliveira, Rodrigues, & Henriques, 2005; Oliveira, Rodrigues, Henriques, et al., 2005; Rahm & Do, 2000, p. 4). E.g. the attribute `name` could indicate a customer's name, a product's name, a vendor's name, etc. Homonyms may, therefore, easily lead to data quality problems as a consequence of misinterpretations. The term "polyseme" is sometimes used interchangeably for homonym, although it has a slightly different meaning. A polyseme is a word or a sign that has two or more different senses, but the senses are related to each other in opposite to homonyms which can have unrelated meanings (Klein & Murphy, 2002, p. 548). An example of a polyseme is the word "paper" which can (1) be the surface we use to write down words or (2) be an essay which is also written on paper (cf. Klein & Murphy, 2002, p. 548f.).

Existence of hypernyms: A word is a hypernym to another word if it represents a more general meaning than the second one (cf. Leser & Naumann, 2007, p. 75). E.g. "Instructor" is a hypernym to both "professor" and "teacher". Hypernymy can be particularly relevant for DQM among pairs of names for tables, attributes, entities, and values. It is then e.g. difficult to identify the proper semantic relationship in multi-source scenarios. Also, it may happen that a database manager maps respective conceptual elements with an equivalence relation in lieu of a proper subtype or type of relation, which can hamper the proper interpretation of the original data at a later point. Data granularity mismatches are frequently caused by the existence of hypernyms.

3.4 Data Quality in the Data Lifecycle

The data lifecycle can roughly be separated into data acquisition, data usage, and data retirement as illustrated in figure 19 (cf. Redman, 1996, p. 217). Data quality problems may occur in any of these phases. Hence, activities for data quality management are

39

required throughout the entire data lifecycle. In the following, we describe each phase according to the understanding underlying this thesis and emphasize the role of data quality management for each phase.

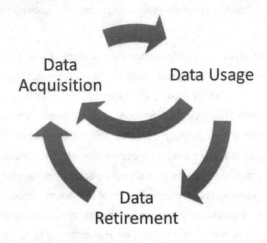

3.4.1 Data Acquisition Phase

Data acquisition relates to the problem of (1) generating new or (2) retrieving existing data and storing it onto some kind of medium, e.g. in a spreadsheet, relational database, or triplestore of the Semantic Web (cf. Olson, 2003, p. 44f.; Redman, 1996, pp. 219-222). Data can thereby be generated manually, e.g. via forms, or automatically, e.g. via sensors or algorithms that derive new data from existing data. Also, existing data may be retrieved via data migration and extraction tools. During its retrieval, data may be filtered or transformed. Hence, during data acquisition data may be filtered according to their quality or transformed to cleanse incorrect data before passing it to data usage (cf. English, 1999, p. 241). This latter improvement possibility can be used in cases where existing data is transferred to another system and the source data cannot directly be manipulated, e.g. when data manipulation in the source is not possible or not desired. But since data quality problems are not removed in the data source, data cleansing during data acquisition may cause the recurrence of the same problems. Hence, data should better be corrected in the data source if possible.

Moreover, users of the target system will not know about quality problems in the source data, if data cleansing transformations during data retrieval are not explicitly communicated. During data generation, data may be validated prior to its storage, e.g. through algorithms and constraints in forms that check the entered data for conformance with specified criteria. However, simple constraints, such as mandatory field constraints in a form, may easily be bypassed, e.g. by entering imaginary values. Thus, constraints can also cause new data quality problems. Besides constraints and cleansing capabilities, it is also important to provide transparency about quality problems and the overall quality state of the retrieved data sources as a foundation for data cleansing activities and for the selection of appropriate data sources.

3.4.2 Data Usage Phase

In the usage phase, data is used as an information source for humans and machines in operational or decision-making processes (cf. Redman, 1998, p. 80f.). Data may be altered, filtered, enriched or aggregated to derive additional information in this phase (cf. Redman, 1996, p. 222f.). Moreover, the used data may again be retrieved for distribution to other systems in cases where centralized storage for data usage is not possible or not desired (cf. Redman, 1996, p. 223). In other words, the same data may sometimes be stored redundantly in different systems for data usage or used by other systems to derive new data, which causes additional data quality problems (cf. English, 1999, p. 149f.). As illustrated in section 1.2, a lack of awareness about quality problems in the used data may result in incorrect or incomplete information for operations or decision-making processes. In the case of data usage by multiple different agents, a single data quality problem may cause multiple different consequent problems (cf. Loshin, 2009, p. 205f.). Therefore, the quality state of data should be frequently analyzed during the data usage phase. Moreover, the multiple uses of data may come along with (1) dependencies that need to be considered before cleansing data and (2) different quality expectations. E.g. interfaces that use data to derive new data may expect a data value among the used data that is considered to be deficient from another perspective. Hence, corrections of the deficient value may cause new problems without previous communication to all data users.

3.4.3 Data Retirement Phase

Finally, data retirement encompasses deleting, deactivating and archiving data (cf. Loshin, 2009, p. 223). This phase is often entered when data is not used anymore or system performance slows down due to huge amounts of data to be processed (cf. Loshin, 2009, p. 223). Data that shall be archived is moved to another repository and may be retrieved again for data usage when required. In this case, the characteristics of the data retrieval and data usage phase apply in principle. However, it must be stressed that it may not be appropriate to alter archived data, since it may damage legal evidence. Therefore, data cleansing activities may not always be feasible for retired data.

3.4.4 Data Quality Management throughout the Data Lifecycle

All phases of the data lifecycle, but especially the acquisition and usage phase, require core data quality management capabilities in order to minimize the negative impact of poor data quality on operations and decision making processes, namely

- **data quality monitoring reports** to identify instances with data quality problems
- **data quality assessment reports** to provide transparency about the quality state of a data source
- **data cleansing functionalities** to remove data quality problems
- **data constraints**, i.e. data quality rules that can be automatically applied by an information system to avoid the generation of data quality problems
- **requirements management** to manage the quality criteria used for data quality assessment, monitoring, and data cleansing

A special focus of data quality management lies in the acquisition phase where data quality problems can be identified and corrected before deficient data impacts operations and decisions. However, a narrow focus of data quality management on the data acquisition phase disregards the facts that (1) not all data quality problems may be discovered during the data acquisition phase, (2) quality requirements may change during data usage, (3) data may be altered during its usage, and (4) data may become outdated. In cases (2) to (4), previously correct data may change to an incorrect state while remaining in a system for data usage. Hence, data quality management activities should not only be focused on data acquisition, but cover the whole data lifecycle, and in particular cater for the fact that there may exist multiple contexts of usage for the same data, which may require diverse and even conflicting data management activities.

This thesis is mainly concerned with the management of data quality during data usage, i.e. when data is already stored on a medium. This is motivated by the heterogeneity of data quality requirements in this stage, and the context dependence of those requirements. Also, from the perspective of value chains, the point and time of data entry will frequently be outside the sphere of influence of the entity actually using the data.

3.5 Data Quality Management Activities

Several methodologies have been developed which attempt to describe a procedure of how data quality can be continuously improved. In the following, we will describe the data quality management activities of the two most popular methodologies in data quality management, namely Total Information Quality Management (TIQM) and Total Data Quality Management (TDQM) (English, 1999; Wang, 1998). After describing the operational activities of these two methodologies in sections 3.5.1 and 3.5.2, we compare both methodologies and identify common activities (section 3.5.3) which provides the basis for the design to meet the requirements and opportunities of the novel, ontology-based data quality management approach developed by this thesis.

3.5.1 Total Information Quality Management (TIQM)

The Total Information Quality Management (TIQM) methodology (formally known as Total Quality Data Management / TQDM) is a comprehensive data quality management methodology that aims to integrate data quality management and beneficial behavioral patterns into the culture of an organization (cf. English, 1999, p. 69f.). It was originally designed for data warehouses, i.e. reporting systems, but it is also applicable to other information systems (Batini & Scannapieco, 2006, p. 174). Besides operational processes it also contains guidelines to create an information

43

quality management culture within an organization, i.e. to raise awareness about the importance of high quality information for the organizational success (cf. English, 1999, p. 71f.). This thesis is aiming to provide artifacts that support operational data quality managing activities. Therefore, we focus on the operational processes of TIQM rather than the tools and methodologies to establish an information quality culture in an enterprise.

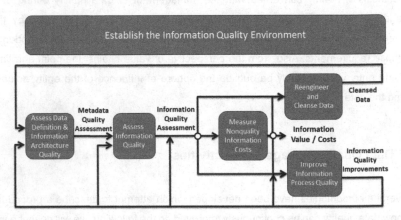

Figure 20: Total Information Quality Management (cf. English, 1999, p. 70)

The operational processes of the TIQM methodology start with an analysis of the quality of information architecture and data definitions, i.e. data about data's "names, definitions, valid value sets, and pertinent business rules"[5] (English, 1999, p. 72). TIQM sees data definitions as "product specifications" of data which are a prerequisite before information quality can be assessed (cf. English, 1999, p. 72). Thus, TIQM's first process group aims to "assess data definition and information architecture quality" with the following process steps (English, 1999, pp. 72-74):

- Identification of the organization's minimal quality requirements regarding their data definitions as the basis for the generation of technical metrics,
- selection of important information groups for the assessment,
- identification of stakeholder categories of the selected information groups , and
- assessment of the quality of (1) data definitions, (2) information architecture / database design, and (3) customer satisfaction with data definitions.

---

[5] Business rules in this context are policies that govern business actions that result in constraints on data relationships and values.

The identified quality problems of data definitions and information architecture serve as input for the "improve information process quality" process group which is described later on in this section. After the quality of data definitions was checked and their quality is regarded as sufficient, the quality of information itself is assessed with the following processes of the "assess information quality" process group, which includes the following steps (English, 1999, pp. 74-76):

- Reconfirmation or identification of information groups that shall be analyzed,
- establish information quality objectives and measures,
- identification of the "information value and cost chain" of the relevant information groups,
- identification of the objects for the assessment, i.e. files, databases, or processes,
- identification of appropriate reference sources for data validation,
- extraction of a random sample of the data to be assessed,
- measurement of information quality based on the sampled data via automated or physical assessment[6], and
- presentation and interpretation of assessment results.

The third process group "measure nonquality information costs" provides guidelines for measuring the costs of poor quality data and contains the following subtasks (English, 1999, p. 76f.):

- Identify business performance measures / business drivers that may be effected by information quality problems, such as profits, customer satisfaction, or costs,
- analyze cost of information, e.g. cost for infrastructure, value delivery, and cost-adding developments,
- determination of costs resulting from data quality problems including cost of caused process failures,
- identification of customer segments for customer lifetime value calculation,
- calculation of customer lifetime value as basis of lost opportunity costs, and
- calculation of missed and lost opportunity cost resulting from information quality problems (Nonquality).

---

[6] Automated assessment is assessment through data analysis; physical assessment is assessment through comparison with real-world objects.

The improvement processes of TIQM are organized into two process groups, namely "reengineer and cleanse data" and "improve information process quality". The "reengineer and cleanse data" process group contains the following subtasks (English, 1999, pp. 77-80):

- Identification of data sources that require data cleansing or reengineering,
- extraction and analysis of the relevant source data for anomalies and patterns,
- data standardization, i.e. the reduction of synonymously used data values and patterns,
- manual or automated correction or completion of data,
- consolidation of duplicate data,
- analysis of data defect types,
- data transformation to target state (data warehouse-specific),
- (re-)calculation of aggregates and derivations (data warehouse-specific), and
- audit and control of Extract-Transform-Load (ETL-)processes (data warehouse-specific).

The "improve information process quality" process addresses the analysis and correction of deficient information processes in order to resolve root causes for poor data quality and, therefore, covers the following activities (English, 1999, p. 80f.):

- Initiation of process improvement activities including problem definition, identification of relevant processes, and establishment of a process improvement team,
- creation of an improvement plan including the identification of the root causes,
- implementation of changes for process and information quality improvement,
- effectiveness assessment of implemented changes, and
- standardization and enterprise-wide implementation of effective changes.

Due to the completeness and the level of detail, it may not make sense to implement all processes of TIQM (cf. Batini & Scannapieco, 2006, p. 200). Instead, many of the described activities may be optional in certain settings, e.g. when the costs of poor information are unnecessary to assess because data quality problems could cause so severe damage that avoiding them is not based on a cost / benefit rationale. While the "reengineer and cleanse data" process group of TIQM may perfectly fit the needs of data warehousing systems, it cannot serve as a guideline for data cleansing in transactional systems, since transactional data must remain audit-proof and cannot always be easily updated when already used in transactions.

3.5.2 Total Data Quality Management (TDQM)

Total Data Quality Management (TDQM) is a data quality management methodology invented by Richard Wang in 1998 (Huang et al., 1999, pp. 16, 33-83; Lee, 2006; Wang, 1998). One core idea of TDQM is that it applies the notion of a Deming cycle (see Deming, 1986) and the approaches from Total Quality Management (TQM, see Juran, 1988) to the task of data quality management. Same as the Deming cycle, the TDQM cycle is also structured into four phases, namely (1) the definition phase, (2) the measurement phase, (3) the analysis phase, and (4) the improvement phase (Wang, 1998, p. 60).

During the definition phase the characteristics of so called information products (IP)[7] are captured, such as its information requirements[8], its core information objects[9] and components, and its relationships (cf. Wang, 1998, p. 61). Moreover, the importance of data quality dimensions in the perception of IP suppliers, manufacturers, consumers, and managers are identified via surveys that capture a first judgment of the quality of the underlying IP (cf.Wang, 1998, p. 61f.). Furthermore, the information manufacturing system is documented via a so called "information manufacturing analysis matrix" (Ballou et al., 1998, p. 472) as a foundation for further analysis and improvement (cf. Wang, 1998, pp. 61-63).

In the measurement phase, data quality metrics are initially developed. The metrics need not necessarily directly deal with data, but also with the production or access process, e.g. who updated how much data or how many unauthorized accesses occurred (cf. Wang, 1998, p. 64). The developed metrics are implemented in a system and applied to the data in order to periodically measure an IP's data quality. Based on the measurement results, the root causes of the identified data quality problems are analyzed during the analysis phase (Wang, 1998, p. 64).

---

[7] An information product is the output of an information manufacturing system. From a more technical perspective, an information product is "a collection of data element instances" (Lee, 2006, p. 126) where a data element is "the smallest unit of named data" Lee (2006, p. 137), e.g. the date of birth of a customer in a customer database.

[8] Information requirements are called "functionalities" in the referenced literature.

[9] Core information objects are called "basic units" in the referenced literature.

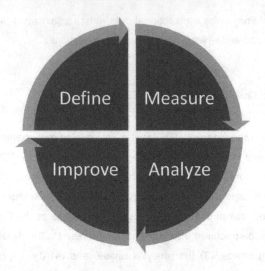

Figure 21: Fundamental stages of the TDQM methodology by (Wang, 1998)

Also the metrics are subject for further analysis, since they may occasionally need to be adjusted, extended, or improved (cf. Wang, 1998, p. 64f.). Finally, the identified causes of quality problems need to be removed during the improvement phase. Therefore, it is necessary to identify the required improvements, e.g. the adjustment of information and workflows with its infrastructure or the modification of IP characteristics according to business needs (cf. Wang et al., 2001, p. 14). The activities of the improvement phase are again supported by the "information manufacturing analysis matrix", which has been initially created during the definition phase (Wang, 1998, p. 65). Moreover, a framework developed by Ballou and Tayi (see Ballou & Tayi, 1989) can be used to support decisions related to the allocation of resources for data quality improvement (Wang, 1998, p. 65).

Although often cited, the TDQM methodology as described in (Wang, 1998) is not directly applicable to practical settings as discovered by Wijnhoven, et al. (Wijnhoven et al., 2007). In detail, TDQM in its original version has the following weaknesses (cf. Wijnhoven et al., 2007, p. 936):

- Several data quality management activities are missing pointers or details to appropriate toolsets or examples how to apply the methodology in practical settings,
- important (but mostly obvious) activities are missing,

- certain activities, such as the definition of information manufacturing systems, are described as mandatory, although they may already exist in other forms or they may not be necessary since the root cause is not located within the respective system.

3.5.3 Comparison of Methodologies

Both, TIQM and TDQM, share the same objective, i.e. to provide a methodology to continuously improve the quality of data. While TIQM was strongly influenced by practical experience, TDQM is a result of several years of research. However, both share in principle the following core activities (cf. Batini & Scannapieco, 2006, p. 171f.):

- identification and definition of quality-relevant metadata and requirements,
- information quality measurement and assessment,
- analysis of the root causes of identified data quality problems, and
- resolution of the identified root causes.

Moreover, both methodologies assume a continuous execution of data quality management activities. Besides these commonalities, TDQM also proposes to identify and document the information production process and the characteristics of information products. The more detailed TIQM also considers quality assessment of metadata and information architecture, as well as the calculation of costs resulting from poor data quality. Furthermore, TIQM clearly differentiates between the improvement of data, i.e. data cleansing, and the improvement of processes. A comparison of the process steps of both methodologies can be found in Appendix A.

3.6 Role of Data Requirements in DQM

The International Organization for Standardization (ISO) defines a requirement as a "need or expectation that is stated, generally implied or obligatory" (ISO, 2009). We adapt this definition for the data domain and define the term "data requirement" accordingly as needs and expectations on data that are stated, generally implied or obligatory. During the data quality management process, data requirements play a crucial role. They are first captured and formulated during the definition phase (cf.

English, 1999, pp. 119-121; Wang, 1998, p. 61). Subsequently in the measurement phase, they are converted into metrics to generate reports about the deficient data, i.e. data instances that violate requirements, and reports with dimensional quality scores (cf. Wang, 1998, p. 64). In other words, the measurement phase uses the requirements to identify and count requirement violations. The identified requirement violations are then analyzed to find the root causes of the requirement violations during the analysis phase (cf. Wang, 1998, p. 64f.). Finally, in the improvement phase the requirement violations are resolved to rebuild the state according to the requirement (cf. Wang, 1998, p. 65).

Consequently, the management of data requirements is the central and most critical part of data quality management, since they are used to formally express the desired state of data throughout the whole management cycle. In other words, data requirements represent the knowledge about the characteristics that constitute high quality data. Consequently, if data requirements are in an unnoticed incomplete or incorrect state, then they will most likely lead to the generation of poor data. In data quality literature, data requirements are also known as data quality rules (cf. Chiang & Miller, 2008; Fürber & Hepp, 2011a; Loshin, 2001).

3.6.1 Generic Data Requirement Types

Data quality problems can be seen as non-fulfillment of data requirements (cf. ISO, 2005, p. 27). Therefore, we can use the typology of generic data quality problem types from section 3.3 to derive generic data requirement types. Table 5 contains a list of the derived generic data requirements and its corresponding data quality problem types that represent a violation of the requirement. In the following, we define each generic data requirement type and provide an illustrating example. A first version of the generic data requirements typology was already published in (Fürber & Hepp, 2011a) and (Fürber & Hepp, 2011b).

Property completeness requirements: Property completeness requirements are data requirements that specify the need for data values in a specific attribute for all instances or for a specific subset of instances of a table (cf. Leser & Naumann, 2007, p. 320; Loshin, 2001, pp. 172-174; Oliveira, Rodrigues, & Henriques, 2005, p. 4; Oliveira, Rodrigues, Henriques, et al., 2005, p. 3; Rahm & Do, 2000, p. 4). Example:

50

The attributes indicating the latitude and longitude must exist and have values for all instances of table `Location` to facilitate navigation to each location.

Syntactic requirements: Syntactic requirements are data requirements that define the type of characters and/or the pattern of attribute values (cf. Loshin, 2001, p. 177; Oliveira, Rodrigues, & Henriques, 2005, p. 4f.; Oliveira, Rodrigues, Henriques, et al., 2005, p. 3). Example: Values for the attribute `country-name` must only contain letters.

Legal value requirements: Legal value requirements are data requirements that explicitly define the allowed values for a certain attribute (cf. Loshin, 2001, p. 174; Oliveira, Rodrigues, Henriques, et al., 2005, p. 4). Example: The property `gender` must only contain the values "`male`", "`female`", "`m`", or "`f`".

Legal value range requirements: Legal value range requirements are data requirements that explicitly define the allowed value range for a specific numeric attribute (cf. Loshin, 2001, p. 176). A value range contains an upper and / or lower limit. Example: The attribute `population` must only contain non-negative values.

Illegal value requirements: Illegal value requirements are data requirements that explicitly define values that must not be assigned for a certain attribute (cf. Loshin, 2001, p. 176). Example: The attribute `EAN13` may not contain the value "`1234567890123`".

Functional dependency requirements: Functional dependency requirements are data requirements that represent the dependencies between the values of two or more different attributes within a table or across different tables (cf. Loshin, 2001, p. 183f. and 189f.). Example: The values for the attribute `zip-code` is dependent to the values for the attribute `city,` `county,` and `country,` since certain cities of certain counties in certain countries have specific zip-codes.

Unique value requirements: Unique value requirements are data requirements which define that the values of a specific attribute must not exist more than once in a specific table (cf. Leser & Naumann, 2007, p. 319; Oliveira, Rodrigues, & Henriques, 2005, p. 6; Oliveira, Rodrigues, Henriques, et al., 2005, p. 4; Rahm & Do, 2000, p. 3). Example: The attribute `supplierID` may only contain unique numbers.

Duplicate instance identification requirements: Duplicate instance identification requirements are data requirements that specify the attributes which (in combination) uniquely identify an object (cf. Leser & Naumann, 2007, p. 321; Oliveira, Rodrigues, & Henriques, 2005, p. 8; Oliveira, Rodrigues, Henriques, et al., 2005, p. 8; Rahm & Do, 2000, p. 4). Example: The values of the attributes `zip-code`, `city-name`, `county`, `state`, and `country` uniquely identify a city. Instances with identical values for these attributes can be considered as duplicates.

Update requirements: Update requirements are data requirements that specify the maximum duration tolerated without any updates of an instance (cf. Oliveira, Rodrigues, Henriques, et al., 2005, p. 3). Example: Instances of the table `currency_rates` have to be updated every 24 hours to stay timely.

Expiration requirements: Expiration requirements are data requirements which define that an instance may not exceed its expiration date (cf. Oliveira, Rodrigues, Henriques, et al., 2005, p. 3). Example: Instances of the table `Offer` are outdated, if its value for the attribute `validThrough` is elder than the current date and time

It is important to note that the above data requirement types focus on instance data. Generic requirement types for the quality of schemata may also exist, but are not subject of this thesis.

Table 5: Generic data requirements as published in (Fürber & Hepp, 2011a, p. 3; 2011b, p. 3)

Data Requirement	Data Quality Problem Type	Example
Property completeness requirements	Missing values, conditionally missing values	Attributes `latitude` and `longitude` must have values in table `Location` to be able to navigate to each location.
Syntactic requirements	Syntax violations, misspelling / mistyping errors, Embedded values, imprecise values	The attribute `country-name` must only contain letters and no numbers.
Legal value requirements	Syntax violations, misspelling / mistyping errors, embedded values, imprecise values, false values, meaningless values, misfielded values	The attribute `gender` must only contain the values "male", "female", "m", or "f".
Legal value range Requirements	Out of range values, meaningless values, false values	The attribute `population` must only contain non-negative values.
Illegal value requirements	False values, meaningless values, misspelling / mistyping errors	The attribute `gender` may never contain the value "mail".
Functional dependency requirements	False values, referential integrity violations, incorrect references, contradictory relationships	The attribute `city` is always dependent to the value for the attribute `country`, since certain city names only exist in certain countries.
Unique value requirements	Unique value violations	Each value for the attribute `ISBN` in instances of table `Book` may not occur more than once.
Duplicate instance identification requirements	Inconsistent duplicates, approximate duplicates	Instances with the same value for the attribute `ISBN` and instances with texts that have a similarity greater than 90 % can be considered as duplicates.
Update requirements	Outdated values	Instances of the table `Quote` are outdated, if their last modification is more than two years ago.
Expiration requirements	Outdated values	Instances of the table `Quote` are outdated, if their value for the attribute `validUntil` is prior to the current date and time.

3.6.2 Challenges Related to Requirements Satisfaction

From a practical perspective, the management and satisfaction of data requirements involves at least three major challenges. The first challenge relates to the problem of how to collect and express data requirements in an objective and unambiguous form (cf. Loshin, 2001, p. 8f.). Knowledge about data requirements is usually distributed across several sources (cf. Loshin, 2001, p. 8f.). For example sources for requirement knowledge are individuals, e.g. data consumers, stakeholder groups, documents, legal regulations, operations procedures, business policies, contracts, standards, or tasks. Moreover, basic requirements may not be explicitly stated, but are indispensable for satisfying user requirements (cf. Kano et al., 1984; Pohl et al., 2005, p. 181f.). In order to be able to produce and deliver high quality data, it is necessary to gain a nearly complete picture about the data requirements stemming from several of these sources. To avoid ambiguous or imprecise statements, such as "the data must be timely" or "the data must be accurate", it is also necessary to guide knowledge workers during the process of expressing data requirements. Pohl et al. (Pohl et al., 2005, p. 198) propose to use a requirements modeling language for the proper representation of requirements.

The second challenge relates to the problem of conflicting requirements. Due to heterogeneous needs and desires, requirements may contradict each other, so that it is impossible to fulfill all of them at the same time (cf. Boehm & In, 1996; Nuseibeh, 1996). The severity of the problem increases with the degree of integration of an information system, since integrated systems usually attempt to avoid data redundancy and heterogeneity. Hence, in highly integrated systems, such for Enterprise Resource Planning (ERP), it is necessary to harmonize the conflicting requirements (cf. Batini & Scannapieco, 2006, p. 9). Otherwise one data element would have to satisfy multiple different desired states which may sometimes not be possible (see figure 22 for an illustration of the problem). It must be stressed that in some cases, it will be possible to combine the quality perspectives to generate a harmonized picture that satisfies all perspectives.

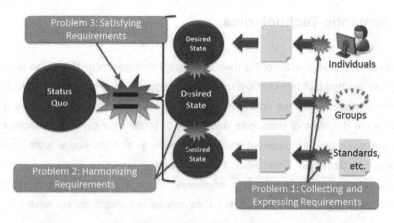

Figure 22: Challenges of requirement satisfaction

The third problem refers to the satisfaction of data requirements in which the current state of data (status quo) shall match with the desired state of data, once the desired state is known and harmonized (cf. Loshin, 2001, p. 282f.). This latter challenge is closely related to the process of data quality improvement.

Figure 22 illustrates three major challenges of requirement satisfaction. Thus, from a requirements perspective these three challenges should at least be addressed by solution approaches that aim to improve data quality.

4 Semantic Technologies

As discussed in section 2.1 of this thesis we regard semantic technologies "as technical approaches that facilitate or make use of the interpretation of meaning by machines". Ontologies are one of the core elements of semantic solutions. In the following, we review the definition of ontologies and briefly describe their general characteristics. Moreover, we discuss important concepts for ontology and knowledge representation within the Semantic Web. After that, we explain ways to process knowledge representations, such as reasoning, inferencing, and querying. Due to the focus of this thesis, we finally describe how relational databases and ontologies are related.

4.1 Characteristics of an Ontology

In section 2.1, we derived the following definition for ontologies: Ontologies are "a formal and sharable means to explicitly model some real-world phenomenon for machine-readable knowledge representation". According to this definition, ontologies have at least five important characteristics, namely "formality, explicitness, being shared, conceptuality and domain-specificity" (Grimm et al., 2007, p. 69f.). In the following, we will explain the term "ontology" along these five characteristics.

Formality: With ontologies, real-world phenomena and their relationships among each other can be described in a machine-readable way by using formal elements, i.e. concepts, relationships, instances, and axioms (cf. Grimm et al., 2007, p. 88). Ontologies are therefore used to structure and store knowledge about a domain of interest. The degree of formality of ontologies and their expressiveness to represent real-world elements varies from natural language descriptions to highly formal axioms (cf. Smith & Welty, 2001, p. 6f.; Uschold & Gruninger, 1996, p. 98). In fact, there are several different knowledge representation languages that offer modeling constructs to represent different levels of formality. The degree of formality thereby influences the ability of machine-interpretation of the represented knowledge. With increasing formality, the machine interpretation capabilities rise, but also the complexity of ontology development and maintenance increases.

Explicitness: While much knowledge usually relies in people's minds, the development of a materialized ontology documents expert knowledge in an explicit way. Moreover, the design of formal ontologies for machine interpretation promotes the rigorous explicit representation of knowledge within the ontology and the automated identification of misconceptions, i.e. inconsistencies within the ontology / understanding of a domain (cf. Grimm et al., 2007, p. 70; Hepp, 2008b, p. 16).

Being shared: Ontologies are usually developed for a certain community, e.g. to capture the knowledge of domain experts. For its successful adaptation it is, therefore, necessary to achieve agreement about the ontology among large parts of the community (cf. Grimm et al., 2007, p. 70). Once an agreement can be established, the chance for widespread adoption of the ontology as a standardized means to represent knowledge rises. Thereby ontologies may help to improve communication, enable reuse of shared knowledge, and facilitate interoperability while keeping schematic heterogeneity at a minimal level (cf. Gasevic et al., 2006, p. 48).

Domain specificity: Due to the complexity of representing concise knowledge and achieving agreement, ontologies are usually limited to a certain domain (cf. Grimm et al., 2007, p. 70). Despite domain specificity, ontologies can be combined with other ontologies to represent knowledge of multiple domains.

Conceptuality: The represented knowledge within ontologies is organized into concepts and relationships. The concepts and relationships can also be represented in hierarchies so that different levels of abstraction may be represented while being connected to each other. Instead of explaining individual phenomena, ontologies provide a framework for as many tasks as necessary within the domain of interest (Grimm et al., 2007, p. 70).

In summary, the use of ontologies for the representation of domain knowledge promises the following benefits (cf. Hepp, 2008b):

- Reduction of ambiguity through the formal and explicit representation of knowledge,
- conservation of implicit knowledge through explicit representation,
- knowledge sharing and reuse through the provision of a common vocabulary / ontology,
- reduction of manual work through the reuse of shared knowledge,
- reduction of manual work through a formal, machine-interpretable knowledge representation,

- automated inference of implicit facts through the formal representation of knowledge,
- automated identification of misconceptions through the formal, explicit representation of knowledge, and
- improved interoperability through the use of a common vocabulary / ontology.

Collections of actual instances that use the elements of ontologies to represent knowledge are known as knowledge bases and should not be confused with ontologies that provide the vocabulary to express knowledge (cf. Hepp, 2008b, p. 6). In the following, we use the term "ontology" to name the schema of knowledge and the term "knowledge base" to refer to an ontology-based representation of knowledge instances.

4.2 Knowledge Representation in the Semantic Web

Ontologies and knowledge bases in Semantic Web architectures are typically represented by using and combining elements of the "Resource Description Framework" (RDF)[10], "RDF Vocabulary Description Language" (which is also known as "RDF Schema" (RDFS)[11]), and the "Web Ontology Language" (OWL)[12]. The following subsections will give a brief overview about the most important language constructs of the Semantic Web, namely resources and Uniform Resource Identifiers (URI), the core RDF Syntax, and important vocabulary elements of RDF, RDFS, and OWL related to the topics of this thesis.

4.2.1 Resources and Uniform Resource Identifiers (URIs)

Semantic Web languages describe resources and relationships among resources. The term "resource" has thereby a very generic meaning which is not constrained to any subset of concepts. A resource can be a Web site, a product, a document, a service, a plan, a person, or anything else (cf. Berners-Lee et al., 2005). Resources are

---

[10] Resource Description Framework (RDF), http://www.w3.org/TR/2004/REC-rdf-syntax-grammar-20040210/
[11] RDF Schema (RDFS), http://www.w3.org/TR/2004/REC-rdf-schema-20040210/
[12] Web Ontology Language, http://www.w3.org/TR/2004/REC-owl-guide-20040210/, recently updated to OWL 2, http://www.w3.org/TR/2009/REC-owl2-overview-20091027/

identified by Uniform Resource Identifiers (URIs) (Sauermann & Cyganiak, 2008). Web addresses like "http://www.google.com" are a special kind of URI, namely a Uniform Resource Locator (URL) which not only identifies a resource, but also locates it (Berners-Lee et al., 2005). A major advantage of URIs on the World Wide Web (WWW) is their global uniqueness. Therefore, URIs facilitate the unambiguous identification of resources. However, there are several limitations on the WWW that may disturb the unambiguous identification of a resource via its URI. The resource which is identified by the URI may over time disappear or its meaning may change. Moreover, it is possible that the URL of one resource is redirected to the URL of another resource. In order to avoid changes, URIs should be designed carefully so that they can be held stable and lasting (cf. Berners-Lee, 1998a).

4.2.2 Core RDF Syntax: Triples, Literal Triples, and RDF Links

The core structure of RDF are so called triples. Triples allow the definition of statements in a subject, predicate, object format as illustrated in figure 23 (cf. Klyne & Carroll, 2004). With the triple structure, it is possible to draw relationships (predicates) between two entities or between an entity and the state of a property (subject, object). Therefore, the predicate position of a triple is always reserved for a property "that denotes a relationship" (Klyne & Carroll, 2004). Properties are always identified via URIs. Combinations of multiple triples form a graph (cf. Grimm et al., 2007, p. 84).

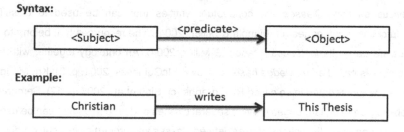

Figure 23: Syntax of RDF triples (cf. Klyne & Carroll, 2004)

We can differentiate between two different types of RDF triples, namely "Literal triples" and "RDF links" (Heath & Bizer, 2011). RDF links are triples with URIs in subject and object position (Heath & Bizer, 2011). Hence, the predicate of RDF links connects two resources with each other (Heath & Bizer, 2011). RDF links can, therefore, be used to describe relationships between two resources (cf. Heath & Bizer, 2011). RDF links have so called object properties in predicate position when using OWL (cf. Hitzler et al., 2009). Literal triples have data values in the object position which are known as literals (cf. Heath & Bizer, 2011). They may be restricted to a certain datatype and contain a language tag indicating the language in which the literal is represented (cf. Heath & Bizer, 2011). Literals with datatype indication are called typed literals, literals without datatype indication are called plain literals (cf. Heath & Bizer, 2011). Thus, Literal triples can be used to assign values to properties of a resource. In other words, Literal triples describe the states of properties of an entity (cf. Heath & Bizer, 2011). For example the triple `http://example.org/JonMyer foo:hasBirthday` "`1970-01-01`" is a Literal triple because the object position of the triple contains the literal "`1970-01-01`". Literal triples can be modeled using OWL datatype properties in predicate position. An example for an RDF link triple would be `http://example.org/JonMyer` `foo:hasMother` `http://example.org/JanetMyer`, since two resources with URIs are linked to each other.

4.2.3 Constructing an Ontology with RDF, RDFS, and OWL

Main elements of ontologies in Semantic Web architectures are classes and properties. *Properties* are in predicate position of a triple and, therefore, define relationships between resources or describe facts about resources as explained in the previous section. *Classes* are conceptual entities that can be used to classify resources into categories (cf. Manola & Miller, 2004). The resources that belong to a class are called its *instances* (Manola & Miller, 2004). An ontology together with its instances is called a *knowledge base* (cf. Noy & McGuinness, 2001, p. 3). Knowledge bases are represented in so called RDF graphs (cf. Sirin et al., 2007, p. 12). Semantic Web programming languages provide several classes and properties that can be used to model semantic distinctions of user-defined classes and properties in a standardized and machine-interpretable way. In the following, core modeling constructs of RDF, RDFS, and OWL are explained which are important for the understanding of this thesis.

Datatype properties: With OWL, a property can be declared as a datatype property meaning that the property can only have literals in the object position. The range of the property may be restricted to a certain datatype either by using XML Schema datatypes[13] or via self-defined datatypes with OWL 2 (cf. Hitzler et al., 2009).

Language tag assignment: Language tags can be assigned at the end of literals to indicate the language in which the literal is written (cf. Alvestrand, 2001; Beckett, 2004).

Domain of a property: The property `rdfs:domain` is a property of RDF-properties. It can be used to specify classes that hold individuals which can be used as a subject for the described property (cf. Brickley & Guha, 2004). In other words, `rdfs:domain` specifies the class of individuals which may be described by the property. E.g. the domain of the property `foo:hasEAN` is the class `foo:Material`.

Range of a property: The property `rdfs:range` is also a property of RDF-properties. It is used to specify the allowed types used for the values of a property, i.e. which datatype the values must have or to which class the values must belong (cf. Brickley & Guha, 2004). E.g. the property `foo:hasName` has a range of datatype `xsd:string`. It is important to note that the consequences of applying a property to an instance of another type is that an additional class membership is inferred (cf. De Bruijn et al., 2005, p. 5).

Class membership: RDF allows the definition of class memberships of entities (cf. Brickley & Guha, 2004). E.g. the triple `Christian rdf:type PhD-Student` expresses that the individual "`Christian`" belongs to the class of PhD Students.

Class and property hierarchies: RDFS allows the expression of hierarchic relationships between classes and properties (cf. Brickley & Guha, 2004). For example, we can define that the class `PhD-Students` is a sub-class of the class `Person` or that the property `lastName` is a sub-property of the property `name`.

Equivalence between classes / properties: With the OWL properties `owl:equivalentClass` and `owl:equivalentProperty` we can express that classes or properties are equivalent in terms of that equivalent properties share the same values and equivalent classes share the same individuals (cf. Bechhofer et al., 2004; Hitzler et al., 2012).

---

[13] XML Schema datatypes, http://www.w3.org/TR/2004/REC-xmlschema-2-20041028/

Identity between individuals: With the OWL property `owl:sameAs` we can express semantic equality between individuals, i.e. the resources connected with `owl:sameAs` represent the same real-world object (cf. Bechhofer et al., 2004).

Disjointness of classes: The property `owl:disjointWith` facilitates the expression of disjointness between two classes, i.e. that individuals cannot be member of both classes at the same time (cf. Bechhofer et al., 2004).

Transitivity of a property: OWL supports the definition of transitive properties by making the properties instances of the class `owl:TransitiveProperty`. Transitivity in this context means that the property relationship will also apply for the subject of one triple and the object of a second triple if the object of triple one is also the subject of triple two, although they are not directly connected to each other. E.g. if the property `foo:subProductOf` is defined to be a transitive property and the two triples X `foo:subProductOf` Y and Y `foo:subProductOf` Z exist, then we can derive that X `foo:subProductOf` Z (cf. Bechhofer et al., 2004).

Symmetry of a property: A property is symmetric if the subject and the object of the triple, in which the property is used, can be substituted without making an incorrect statement. Symmetric properties can be defined via OWL by making the property an instance of the class `owl:SymmetricProperty` (cf. Bechhofer et al., 2004). E.g. the property `foo:marriedTo` is symmetric because a marriage is always mutual.

Inverse properties: With OWL, we can define that one property is an inverse of another property (cf. McGuinness & van Harmelen, 2004). E.g. the property `foo:writtenBy` is an inverse of the property `foo:authorOf`.

Functional properties: Functional properties are properties "that can have only one (unique) value y for each instance x" (Bechhofer et al., 2004). A property is defined as functional by making it an instance of the class `owl:FunctionalProperty`. Functional properties are a way to express global cardinality restrictions (cf. Bechhofer et al., 2004). E.g. a car can only have one active license plate number.

Inverse functional properties: Inverse functional properties uniquely identify the subject in a triple. In other words, a value of an inverse functional property must only belong to the same individual. A property is defined as inverse functional by making it an instance of the class `owl:InverseFunctionalProperty`. Inverse functional properties are a way to express global cardinality restrictions (cf. Bechhofer et al., 2004). E.g. a certain social security number can only belong to one person.

Cardinality restrictions: OWL provides the properties `owl:maxCardinality`, `owl:minCardinality`, and `owl:Cardinality` to define cardinality restrictions on ranges of properties. The OWL cardinality properties hold values of datatype `xsd:nonNegativeInteger`. A restriction with `owl:maxCardinality` "describes a class of all individuals that have *at most* N semantically distinct values (individuals or data values) for the property concerned, where N is the value of the cardinality constraint" (Bechhofer et al., 2004). Analogous to the `owl:maxCardinality`, `owl:minCardinality` describes a class of individuals that must at least have N semantically distinct values, and `owl:Cardinality` describes a class that has exactly N semantically distinct values (cf. Bechhofer et al., 2004). Since the cardinality only applies to semantically distinct values and the same individuals may be represented by syntactically distinct values, it is possible that, although `owl:maxCardinality` has value "1", an instance has two values for a property that represent the same individual. If both values represent the same individual, then the restriction will still be followed.

The Semantic Web programming languages RDF, RDFS, OWL, and OWL 2 allow many more formal semantic expressions which are not explained in this thesis due to their lack of relevance for the focus of this work.

4.2.4 Language Profiles of OWL and OWL 2

The Web Ontology Language OWL has three common language profiles, namely OWL Lite, OWL Description Logic (DL), and OWL Full (Bechhofer et al., 2004). A language profile thereby provides a subset of language constructs of OWL and may constrain their usage (Bechhofer et al., 2004). In OWL Full, all elements of the language can be used with no restrictions as long as valid RDF documents are produced (Bechhofer et al., 2004). OWL DL and OWL Lite are subsets of OWL (Bechhofer et al., 2004). One of the major distinctions between OWL Full and OWL DL is the meta-modeling capability of OWL Full. In OWL Full, classes and properties can also be used as an individual. This is not allowed in OWL DL to provide a language profile for decidable reasoning, i.e. automated inferencing of implicit knowledge within finite time

63

(Bechhofer et al., 2004). OWL Lite is the simplest of all OWL profiles and provides a minimal subset of OWL with the most important ontological constructs to provide an easy way to engineer an ontology (cf. Hitzler, 2008, p. 151ff.). At present, most ontologies are coded in OWL DL.

OWL 2 introduces three new language profiles, namely OWL 2 EL, OWL 2 RL, and OWL 2 QL (W3C-OWL-Working-Group, 2012). The different language profiles of OWL 2 have been composed for specific cases. For example, OWL 2 EL is optimized for very large ontologies with many classes and properties (W3C-OWL-Working-Group, 2012). OWL 2 QL was designed to provide "sound and complete query answering" (Motik et al., 2009) at a reasonable time. And OWL 2 RL is optimized for reasoning (W3C-OWL-Working-Group, 2012). For a detailed overview about the different language profiles for OWL 2, please see (Motik et al., 2009).

Thus, when designing new ontologies, it is important to consider the required level of expressivity and the scenarios in which the ontology shall be used, in order to identify a proper language profile. In the following, the acronym OWL is used to refer to both, OWL and OWL 2.

4.3 SPARQL Query Language for RDF

Query languages have been used for several decades, e.g. the Structured Query Language (SQL) to update and retrieve data from relational databases (Oracle, 2013). The Semantic Web provides its own query language, called the SPARQL query language for RDF (SPARQL) (Harris & Seaborne, 2010). SPARQL can be used to store, update, retrieve, and delete data in knowledge bases and provides several mechanisms, such as aggregations, subqueries, or filters, that are very similar to features of SQL (cf. Harris & Seaborne, 2010). Other than with SQL, SPARQL can be combined with reasoners to also retrieve information that is not explicitly represented[14]. E.g. a SPARQL query asking for instances of the class Person could also retrieve instances of subclasses of the class Person, if subclass reasoning was enabled. A lot

---

[14] There has been work on deductive databases that combine logic programming and database management systems. However, to the best of the author's knowledge they are not widely used in business information systems.

of triplestores and Semantic Web tools, such as Virtuoso[15] or TopBraid Composer[16], provide so called SPARQL endpoints (Feigenbaum et al., 2013) with query interfaces to access the knowledge base or RDF files via SPARQL queries. Moreover, a lot of the available SPARQL query interfaces provide additional, proprietary SPARQL functions (also known as SPARQL extensions), that extend the SPARQL standard functionalities[17] as specified by the World Wide Web Consortium (W3C). At time of this thesis, SPARQL 1.1 provides a mostly stable and expressive syntax that is already implemented in many commercial and non-commercial Semantic Web tools.

4.4 Reasoning and Inferencing

Besides the plain retrieval of Semantic Web data via SPARQL queries, it is also possible to employ the expressiveness of ontologies and the represented knowledge via so called reasoners (cf. Hebeler et al., 2009, p. 285). Reasoners are programs that use the represented logic of ontologies and / or user-defined rules (1) to infer implicit knowledge and (2) to check the logical consistency at ontology and instance level (cf. Antoniou & van Harmelen, 2008, pp. 97-103; Fensel & van Harmelen, 2007). According to Hebeler et al. (Hebeler et al., 2009, p. 285), there are two different types of reasoners which can also be combined in a single engine, namely inference reasoners and rule-based reasoners. Inference reasoners infer implicit knowledge and check logical consistency based on the axioms represented via RDFS and OWL (cf. Hepp, 2008b, p. 15f.). Rule-based reasoners process user-defined rules that are represented additionally to the axioms of an ontology (cf. Hebeler et al., 2009, pp. 231-233). Similar to the axioms of RDFS and OWL, user-defined rules can also be used to infer new knowledge or check consistency, but provide more flexibility for the definition of axioms (cf. O'Connor et al., 2005, p. 975). Depending on the processing capabilities of the reasoner, rules can be represented in different languages, such as the Semantic Web Rule Language (SWRL)[18] or via the vocabulary of the SPARQL Inferencing

---

[15] http://virtuoso.openlinksw.com/dataspace/dav/wiki/Main/VOSIntro (Last accessed on April 10th 2012)
[16] http://www.topquadrant.com/products/TB_Composer.html (Last accessed on April 10th 2012)
[17] http://www.w3.org/TR/2010/WD-sparql11-query-20100126/ (Last accessed on April 10th 2012)
[18] http://www.w3.org/Submission/SWRL/ (Last accessed on April 11th 2012)

framework (SPIN)[19]. A popular open source reasoner that combines both, inference and rule-based reasoning, is Pellet[20].

The inferable knowledge via inference reasoning depends on the formal elements that are used within the ontology. In the following, we provide some examples of potential inferences that can be made when reasoning knowledge provided by an OWL DL ontology (cf. Hitzler, 2008, p. 176f.).

Class equivalency: Based on equivalency relationships, it can be inferred which classes belong to a specific domain concept. E.g. by specifying that class `Person` and class `HumanBeing` are equivalent, a reasoner can process this information to automatically infer the members of both classes.

Subclass relationships: Based on the definition of subclass relationships, a reasoner can derive all members of a superclass including members that are not explicit members of the superclass. E.g. a reasoner could infer that the individual `Christian` not only belongs to the class `PhD-Student`, but also belongs to the class `Person`, since the class `PhD-Student` is a subclass of the class `Person`. In the following, we will use the term "subclass reasoning" to refer to this kind of inferencing.

Disjunctive classes: With OWL, classes can be defined as disjunctive, i.e. that members of class A cannot also be members of class B at the same time, if class A and class B are disjunctive. Based on this knowledge representation, reasoners can identify individuals that are members of disjunctive classes and, thus, identify and report inconsistent class memberships.

Additional inferencing capabilities for knowledge represented in ontologies based on RDFS and OWL can be found in (Hitzler, 2008). As mentioned in the previous section, the more formal elements and axioms are used within an ontology, the more resources are needed for the reasoning based on the ontology (cf. Antoniou & van Harmelen, 2008, p. 158; Fensel & van Harmelen, 2007; Gómez-Pérez et al., 2004, p. 204). Hence, for efficient reasoning it is important to pay attention to the design of an ontology, especially regarding the chosen language profile.

---

[19] http://spinrdf.org/ (Last accessed on April 11th 2012)
[20] http://clarkparsia.com/pellet/features (Last accessed on April 11th 2012)

4.5 Ontologies and Relational Databases

Ontologies and relational databases (RDB) are related to each other in at least two aspects. First, a lot of data that is currently available on the Semantic Web has been published via mapping technologies between RDB and ontologies (cf. Bizer, Heath, et al., 2009). Secondly, some triplestores use the efficient and mature technologies of RDB management systems (RDBMS) to store RDF triples (Heymans et al., 2008, p. 92). In this section, we examine how data from relational databases can be linked to conceptual elements from ontologies and exposed as RDF data. Relational data can be lifted into the Semantic Web space, namely (1) virtually without a persistent representation of the data in RDF or (2) persistently with a persistent conversion of the data into RDF (Sahoo et al., 2009). In both cases, the elements of the relational schema have to be mapped to the target ontology. Table 6 shows how the different elements of an RDB schema can be mapped to the elements of an ontology based on findings from Astrova (Astrova, 2009).

Table 6: Simplified mapping between RDBs and ontologies (cf. Astrova, 2009)

RDB Element	Ontology Element
Table[21] / View	Class
Table with only two foreign key columns	Object property
Column containing datatype values	Datatype property
Column containing foreign keys	Object property
Primary keys	Individuals / URIs
Row	Instance

It must be stressed that there may also be much more individual mappings between elements of an RDB to elements of an ontology. E.g. one might want to populate tuples of a specific table to multiple different classes based on filters on certain column values. However, there are many ways to easily expose relational sources to the Semantic Web spaces, such as D2RQ or Virtuoso RDF-Views (please see (Sahoo et al., 2009)

---

[21] Tables that only contain two columns with foreign keys are mapped to object properties

67

for a survey about RDB2RDF mapping technologies). In summary, we can conclude that relational data can be used in Semantic Web architectures via mappings to ontology elements. This facilitates the use of Semantic Web technologies to process data of RDB.

5 Data Quality in the Semantic Web

The Semantic Web is an initiative of the World Wide Web Consortium (W3C) with the vision to evolve the traditional Web, which is essentially a graph of interlinked documents, into a "Web of Data" (Berners-Lee et al., 2001; cf. W3C, 2013). One of the major goals of the Semantic Web is the supply of machine-interpretable data at Web scale to gain a higher degree of automation and to facilitate more complete processing of information (cf. Berners-Lee et al., 2001). For example, if the prices of all consumer products were published in a machine-readable format and structure throughout the whole Web, then more complete price comparisons at global scale would be possible with minimal manual effort. While the traditional Web is mainly used to publish information in a form that empowers a Web browser to render the contents in a form suitable for human consumption, the Semantic Web shall additionally allow computer-based devices to extract and process the meaning of the contents (cf. Berners-Lee et al., 2001). To facilitate the publication and use of structured data at Web scale, Semantic Web formalisms such as RDF (Manola & Miller, 2004), RDFS (Brickley & Guha, 2004), and OWL (Bechhofer et al., 2004; Hitzler et al., 2012) have been developed to support the publication of data. Semantic Web applications can then extract and use the published data, e.g. to derive decisions to automate tasks or to answer complex queries (cf. Berners-Lee et al., 2001). However, Semantic Web-based applications have a high risk to fail if the processed data is of insufficient quality.

In this chapter, we give an overview of existing data sources on the evolving Semantic Web vision and discuss data quality problems and their impact.

5.1 Data Sources of the Semantic Web

As already explained, data on the Semantic Web is mostly published according to the RDF data model (cf. Heath & Bizer, 2011; Manola & Miller, 2004, see also section 4.2.2), which represents graphs of information in the form of simple statements known as triples with the basic structure of subject, predicate, object (cf. Manola & Miller, 2004). The Semantic Web already provides billions of such triples with data about several different domains such as geography, media, health care, life sciences, linguistics, and e-commerce (cf. Bizer, Heath, et al., 2009, p. 5f.; Heath & Bizer, 2011;

69

Mühleisen & Bizer, 2012). Figure 24 shows the well-known linking open data (LOD) cloud diagram[22] which represents a large part of available data on the Semantic Web (Cyganiak & Jentzsch, 2011a).

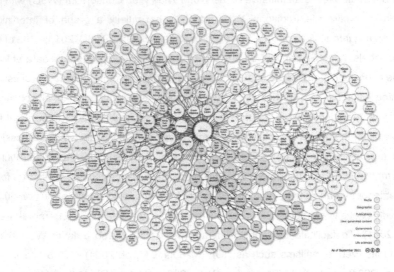

Figure 24: Linking Open Data (LOD) cloud diagram[22] (Cyganiak & Jentzsch, 2011a)

The amount of triples of the LOD cloud was estimated to be around 31 billion triples in September 2011 (Cyganiak & Jentzsch, 2011b). But the LOD cloud only represents part of the Semantic Web, since the latest available version of the diagram was created on September 19th 2011, and data sources have to meet certain criteria to be included in the diagram. For instance, a data source must contain at least 1000 triples and have at least 50 RDF links to other data sets in the diagram (cf. Cyganiak & Jentzsch, 2011a). Hence, a large amount of data that is not linked to data sets in the LOD cloud is not part of the diagram and its statistics. For example, a lot of product data published via the GoodRelations ontology[23], a popular vocabulary for publishing E-Commerce data (Hepp, 2008a), lack explicit links to the LOD cloud and is, therefore, not visible in the diagram despite its significance for the practical application of the Semantic Web.

In addition to the intended usage of data published in the LOD-cloud, like intelligent information processing (cf. Bizer, Lehmann, et al., 2009) or entity recognition in natural language processing (cf. Kobilarov, Scott, et al., 2009, p. 732; Reuters, 2013), the data

---

[22] Linking Open Data cloud diagram, by Richard Cyganiak and Anja Jentzsch. http://lod-cloud.net/ (Last accessed on April 2nd 2012)

[23] http://purl.org/goodrelations (Last accessed on April 12th 2012)

70

can also be a relevant source for data quality management. Several data quality management heuristics use reference data sets to identify data quality problems (cf. Apel et al., 2010, p. 74; English, 1999, p. 166; Loshin, 2001, p. 161). In (Fürber & Hepp, 2010a), we have shown that Semantic Web data can particularly be useful for the identification of illegal values or functional dependencies between attribute values in the geographic domain with minimal effort. To proof its practical usefulness for DQM, we performed a data quality analysis of real address data from BestBuy stores, a popular North American retailer for consumer electronics (cf. Fürber & Hepp, 2011a). The address data contained addresses of BestBuy stores which were published on the Web via the GoodRelations ontology and the vCard ontology[24], a vocabulary for publishing business card data. We compared the BestBuy data with data from Geonames[25], a Semantic Web data source for geographical information, and identified several data quality problems such as mistyped values and a few illegal city / country combinations. We only used the reference data as provided by Geonames for the data quality analysis which contained all valid city / country combinations and, therefore, saved the tremendous manual effort that would have to be invested for the manual creation and maintenance of this data. Despite these promising first results, it must be stressed that the Semantic Web data sets should be also frequently monitored for data quality errors, when used as a trusted reference. Otherwise, data quality problems in the reference data will be spread to other data sources without being noticed.

In near future, the Semantic Web will most likely further grow and expand its data diversity to additional domains. Therefore, we can expect that more useful data will be published that will open further possibilities for DQM. On the other hand, the number of individuals and organizations who publish data will grow, which may make it more difficult to evaluate the reliability of data from the Semantic Web as reference data for data quality management.

5.2 Semantic Web-specific Quality Problems

In section 3.3, data quality problems types have been shown that are typical for data in relational databases. While most of the illustrated problems may also occur in

---

[24] http://www.w3.org/2006/vcard/ns-2006.html (Last accessed on April 12th 2012)
[25] http://www.geonames.org (Last accessed on April 12th 2012)

Semantic Web data, there are some quality problems that are specific for Semantic Web data. In the following, we enumerate and describe several Semantic Web-specific quality problems based on findings by (Hogan et al., 2010; Lei & Nikolov, 2007; Lei et al., 2007). We thereby use the term "conceptual elements" to refer to classes and properties. Moreover, we sort the different types of errors into problems related to (1) document content, (2) data format, (3) data definitions and semantics, (4) classification, and (5) hyperlinks. The following representation of Semantic Web data quality problems does not claim to be complete. In fact, due to missing research in this area, additional quality problem types of Semantic Web data will most likely be discovered in future.

5.2.1 Document Content Problems

Missing structured data: In the Semantic Web, it is often expected that machine-processable data is returned when looking up links. But in many cases, the returned content type indicates unstructured data which is not as useful for Semantic Web agents (cf. Hogan et al., 2010).

Imprecise / misreported content types: Although Web documents on the Semantic Web are published in one of the various syntaxes for RDF, like RDF/XML, the content type as returned by the Hyper Text Transfer Protocol (HTTP) response header may be incompatible or more generic than the actual type of the content (cf. Hogan et al., 2010).

5.2.2 Data Format Problems

Document syntax errors: Semantic Web data is usually encoded according to W3C standards for the syntactical representation or formal semantics, such as RDF, RDFS, or OWL (cf. Hogan et al., 2010). These standards provide syntactic and structural requirements which may sometimes be violated. The W3C provides validation

72

applications which test documents for compliance to the syntax rules of such standards[26].

Misplaced conceptual elements: As stated in section 4.2.2, triples consist of subjects, predicates, and objects. Properties should only be used in the predicate position and classes should usually be the only objects of an `rdf:type` property. Therefore, the URIs of classes and properties may be considered as misplaced, if they do not obey these position rules (cf. Hogan et al., 2010). However, it must be stressed that in OWL Full knowledge bases, properties may also be in subject position of a triple. In OWL Full, it depends on the conceptual model whether the appearance of a class or property URI in another position of a triple is a data quality problem or an intended form of meta-modeling.

Violation of datatype syntax: In RDF documents, it is possible to define XML datatypes for literal values. Such datatypes indicate syntactic rules for literal values of such datatype properties without strictly enforcing them (cf. Hogan et al., 2010). E.g. the datatype `xsd:date`[27] requires date values in the syntax YYYY-MM-DD.

Missing language tags: In RDF documents, it is possible to define so called language tags for literal values indicating the language in which the literal is written (Heath & Bizer, 2011). Language tags are especially useful for multilingual support. However, if language tags are not assigned, then automated multiple language support is obviously not possible. Therefore, some applications may assume missing language tags as a data quality problem.

5.2.3 Problems of Data Definitions and Semantics

Undefined conceptual elements: In RDF documents, it is best practice to publish definitions of all conceptual elements, i.e. classes and properties with a formalism like RDFS (Brickley & Guha, 2004) or OWL (Bechhofer et al., 2004; Hitzler et al., 2012), within the data set, so that they are retrievable and reusable on the Web. However, a significant amount of conceptual elements are still undefined in Semantic Web data (cf. Hogan et al., 2010).

---

[26] See http://www.w3.org/RDF/Validator/ for the W3C RDF Validation service (Last accessed on April 12th 2012)

[27] See http://www.w3.org/TR/xmlschema-2/#date for a full description of the required syntax (Last accessed on July 20th 2014)

Ontology hijacking: Ontology hijacking is "the redefinition [...] of external classes/properties" by third parties (Hogan et al., 2010). In other words, conceptual elements of existing ontologies are reused in a way that conflicts with the initial definition, e.g. by adding additional axioms to the URI of the original element that are incompatible with the original meaning.

Ambiguous inverse functional property values: In OWL, the objects of inverse functional properties uniquely identify an individual (Bechhofer et al., 2004). The use of ambiguous values in the object position of inverse functional properties may cause that reasoners assume two or more individuals to be identical, although they are different individuals. Thus, ambiguous functional property values represent a severe data quality problem when reasoning shall be applied (cf. Hogan et al., 2010).

Misuse of `owl:DatatypeProperty` and `owl:ObjectProperty`: Datatype properties usually contain a resource in subject position and a literal value in object position (cf. Bechhofer et al., 2004). Object properties usually relate two resources (cf. Bechhofer et al., 2004). Cases where datatype properties connect resources to each other and object properties contain literal values in subject or object positions may be considered as misuse of these two property types (cf. Hogan et al., 2010). However, it must be stressed that datatype properties with datatype range `xsd:anyURI` may also contain literal values that look like resources (cf. Biron & Malhotra, 2004).

5.2.4 Problems of Data Classification

Imprecise classification: Imprecise classification occurs when instances are not classified to the most specific available class (cf. Lei et al., 2007, p. 139). E.g. `Peter Miller` belongs to the class `foo:Agent` and not to the class `foo:Person`.

Missing classification: Sometimes instances may not be classified at all, i.e. do not belong to a class more specific than `owl:Thing` or `rdfs:Resource` (cf. Lei & Nikolov, 2007; Lei et al., 2007). E.g. the individual `Peter Miller` does not belong to a class, although it should be member of the class `foo:Person`.

Incorrect classification: Instances are incorrectly classified when they belong to a wrong class, i.e. they actually cannot be a member of this class due to their real-world semantics (cf. Lei & Nikolov, 2007). E.g. the individual `Peter Miller` is member of the class `foo:PopulatedPlace`.

Spurious conceptual elements: Sometimes not all conceptual elements of an ontology are used, i.e. not all classes have instances or not all properties have values. Unused conceptual elements may, therefore, be considered as spurious (cf. Lei et al., 2007, p. 139).

Membership in disjoint classes: With the OWL property `owl:disjointWith` two classes can be connected that do not share the same individuals. Hence, an individual cannot be member of two or more disjoint classes or their subclasses at the same time (cf. Hogan et al., 2010; Lei & Nikolov, 2007).

Membership in deprecated conceptual elements: In OWL, classes and properties may be flagged as deprecated via the classes `owl:DeprecatedClass` and `owl:DeprecatedProperty` when they are shall not be used anymore (Bechhofer et al., 2004). In OWL 2, alternatively the annotation property `owl:deprecated` with value "`true`" annotates deprecated classes and properties (Bao et al., 2012). Hence, the usage of such deprecated conceptual elements may be considered as a quality problem, although it may not be as severe as other quality problems (cf. Hogan et al., 2010).

5.2.5 Problems of Hyperlinks

Dereferencability problems: In Semantic Web environments, it is recommended to use HTTP URIs to represent individuals, properties, and classes in order to be able to look up names and link data (cf. Berners-Lee, 2006). Sometimes the links may not be dereferencable, i.e. we receive an error when looking up the URI on the Web. In most of these cases the target data source of the link address is missing (cf. Hogan et al., 2010).

5.3 Distinct Characteristics of Data Quality in the Semantic Web

There are major differences between data quality in business information systems (BIS) and data quality in open environments such as the Semantic Web. The World Wide Web and the Semantic Web architecture facilitates that anyone that has an internet connection and Web space can publish anything about anything (cf. Berners-Lee, 1998b). In other words, anyone with access to a Web server can publish any data on the Semantic Web, even non-sense data. In opposite to the Web, traditional business information systems usually put control upon the creation and maintenance of data, e.g. via constraints or role and authorization systems to avoid the creation of heterogeneous and willfully conflicting data. These different policies are driven by different needs. While in BIS it may be necessary to establish a common way to create, update, and publish information in order to manage and control business processes, the Web relies on an open architecture to use the creativity and intelligence of the crowd and to serve as an open platform for information exchange (cf. Berners-Lee & Fischetti, 2000). In fact, the large-scale introduction of firm constraints and authorization systems in the Semantic Web would violate freedom of speech and other human rights. Moreover, while large BIS may have a couple of 100.000 users, the Web has most likely several billion users. Thereby, the amount of users also raises the level of heterogeneity. Consequently, the diversity of quality perceptions and data requirements is likely much bigger on the World Wide Web than in BIS. Furthermore, not existing information underlies different interpretations in the Web and in BIS. The Semantic Web assumes an open world, i.e. everything that we do not know is not defined, yet, and, therefore, is neither wrong nor right (cf. Hebeler et al., 2009, p. 103f.). Traditional BIS follow the opposite interpretation, i.e. they close the world and assume that everything that is not represented can be assumed as false (cf. Hebeler et al., 2009, p. 103f.). In other words, a missing instance in BIS would be assumed to not exist, while in the Semantic Web it would be assumed that additional instances may exist, but are currently not member of the class. During the interpretation of data, especially aggregated data, it is important to be aware that knowledge may be incomplete and, therefore, information may be missing. While data quality metrics typically assume a closed world, human interpretation of data quality assessment results can assume an open world, even for traditional BIS, since it is unlikely that all data requirements are known at all times. E.g. an accuracy score of 97 % should be interpreted with special regard to the assumed data requirements. Thus, the score may be higher or lower, when further knowledge about data requirements is added or different data requirements apply.

However, the Web's openness must be respected by data quality management systems for the Semantic Web, especially with regard to the large diversity of data requirements. But data quality management systems can be a good support to identify and monitor deficient data according to specific quality perspectives and thereby help to improve processing of heterogeneous data for specific tasks, even for the open Semantic Web.

PART III – Development and Evaluation of the Semantic Data Quality Management Framework

6 Specification of Initial Requirements

This chapter specifies the requirements for an ontology-based data quality management framework, called Semantic Data Quality Management Framework (SDQM), which shall be developed to support data quality management activities by the use of ontologies. We thereby apply the Design Science Research Methodology (DSRM, cf. Peffers et al., 2008) process as explained in section 2.4. We start with describing the required artifacts with a motivating scenario that illustrates the needs related to data quality management. Based on the motivating scenario, we derive initial requirements for the framework.

6.1 Motivating Scenario

We assume that a large organization aims to improve the quality of its data that is already used throughout the organization because the organization often suffers from costly process failures due to poor data quality. The data is managed by an information system that is based on a relational database and used for the support of business process execution. The quality requirements for data are not centrally documented and only known to domain experts who are dispersed across the organization. In the best case, the quality requirements are an implicit part of design documentations and manuals that have been created several years ago when the information system had been developed. To avoid the creation of poor data, the organization has implemented some quality requirement checks into the program code of their information system, but does barely review the implemented requirements as to whether they are still valid. This is because the required experts do not have time to support this action or do not understand the program code. Moreover, it is not known whether the data requirements are consistent with each other. In order to improve the situation, the organization seeks to establish a data quality management method which helps to gain a higher transparency about the organization's data requirements and the state of data quality of its data sources without the need for personal interaction with experts. Therefore, the organization seeks for a tool that supports

- collection of data requirements across the organization,
- documentation of data requirements in a standardized way,
- comparison of data requirements, as well as the identification and harmonization of inconsistent data requirements,
- central availability of data requirements including its documentation across the organization, and
- automated processing of data requirements to derive reports about data with requirements violations and reports that provide an overview about the quality state of a data source.

Based on the requirement violation reports the root causes of data quality problems shall be analyzed, in order to improve data quality at a sustainable level.

6.2 Initial Requirements for SDQM

In this section, we describe the initial requirements for the SDQM that can be derived from the motivating scenario and the theoretical findings about data quality management in chapter 3. According to (Grande, 2011, p. 37ff.), there are several different types of requirements. Grande distinguishes between functional and non-functional requirements. From Grande's viewpoint, functional requirements "describe the functionality and the behavior of the product" (Grande, 2011, p. 37). Non-functional requirements are quality requirements and requirements introduced by boundary conditions (cf. Grande, 2011, p. 37f.).

Although this categorization provides a first help to structure the definition of requirements, it is insufficient for the analysis of requirements in the context of artifact design. Therefore, we developed our own requirements typology as depicted in figure 25.

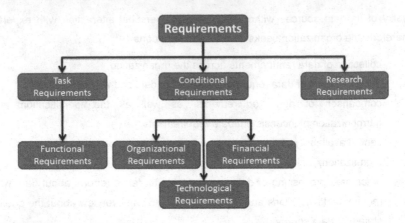

Figure 25: Typology of requirements for artifact design

On a high level, we distinguish between (1) task requirements, i.e. requirements of the tasks that shall be performed with the help of the framework, (2) conditional requirements, i.e. external requirements that are implied by the environment in which the framework shall be used, and (3) research requirements which need to be addressed in order to achieve the research goal as defined in section 2.1. Functional requirements describe the desired functions of the artifact and can be derived from the task requirements (cf. Grande, 2011, p. 37). Conditional requirements are non-functional requirements that can be further distinguished as organizational requirements, i.e. requirements derived from the organizational environment, technological requirements, i.e. requirements derived from the technological environment in which the artifact shall be integrated, and financial requirements, i.e. limitations on resources that are necessary for the development of the artifact. In the following, we describe the requirements of SDQM separated by these categories.

6.2.1 Task Requirements

The major goal of all data quality management activities is the continuous and sustainable improvement of data quality (cf. English, 1999, pp. 39, 69f.; Wang, 1998). To achieve this goal, a methodology for the continuous identification and removal of the causes of data quality problems is needed. In section 3.5, we have described the two most popular methodologies to improve data quality, namely Total Data Quality Management (TDQM) and Total Information Quality Management (TIQM). In section

3.5.3, the following common activities of TDQM and TIQM have been identified (cf. Batini & Scannapieco, 2006, p. 171f.):

- Identification and definition of quality-relevant metadata and requirements,
- Information quality measurement and assessment,
- Analysis of the root causes of identified data quality problems, and
- Resolution of the identified root causes

The organization in the motivating scenario requires the implementation of a data quality management methodology. We use the findings from the comparison of TDQM and TIQM added by the information from the motivating scenario to define a data quality management process that fits to the organization's needs. Hence, the data quality management process of the organization contains the following subtasks:

Identification / collection and formulation of data requirements: Data requirements shall be collected / identified from documents and expert knowledge distributed across the organization. Moreover, the requirements shall be formulated in a common language and structure, so that they are comparable and reusable.

Identification of requirement violations: Based on the formulated data requirements, requirement violation reports shall be generated.

Evaluation of the quality state of data sources: Based on the data requirements, transparency about the quality state of a data source shall be generated.

Identification and removal of root causes of requirement violations: Based on the requirement violation reports, root causes of the requirement violations shall be identified and removed.

Table 7: Tasks in the SDQM framework and their equivalencies in the TDQM method (based on Wang, 1998)

Total Data Quality Management Phase	Semantic Data Quality Management Framework
Define	Identification / collection and formulation of data requirements
Measure	Identification of requirement violations
	Evaluation of the quality state of data sources
Analyze	Identification of root causes of requirement violations
Improve	Removal of root causes of requirement violations

The enumerated tasks represent the task requirements of SDQM and can be aligned according to the TDQM cycle (cf. Wang, 1998) as shown in table 7.

6.2.2 Functional Requirements

Functional requirements are requirements that describe the desired functions of an artifact (cf. Grande, 2011, p. 37). The functional requirements of SDQM can be derived from the task requirements, since functions of the artifact shall support the execution of the identified tasks. The following functional requirements can be derived from the task "Identification / collection and formulation of data requirements":

- the artifact shall be used to collect requirements,
- the requirements shall be collected in a structured and comparable form, and
- some requirements may be in draft status and, therefore, not usable for measurement, yet.

The task "Identification of requirement violations" requires the following functions:

- use the approved data requirements to identify requirement violations in the tested data and
- generate a report with violated instances indicating the type of violation / data quality problem.

The following functional requirements can be derived from the task "Evaluation of the quality state of data sources":

- generate a report with key performance indicators (KPI) that show the ratio between correct instances and instances with requirement violations separated by quality dimensions,
- automated calculation of KPI's based on data requirements, and
- reference objects of KPI's must be visible in report.

The identification and removal of root causes of data quality problems is not part of the requirements, since these tasks require a thorough manual analysis and coordination, e.g. with the help of brainstorming, Ishikawa diagrams, or "Why analysis" (cf. English, 1999, pp. 294-297). Data cleansing via simple database updates is not an option for the organization in the motivating scenario since the data is highly integrated into transactions that must be audit compliant and, therefore, cannot be changed while used in transactions. Table 8 summarizes the functional requirements for SDQM and already indicates the expected deliverable that satisfies the requirement.

Table 8: Summary of functional requirements including expected deliverables

Task Requirement	Functional Requirement	Expected Deliverable
Identification / Collection and formulation of data requirements	Distributed acquisition of data requirements	Web-based platform for collaborative development of data requirements
	Data requirements shall be captured in structured and comparable shape	Data requirement forms
	Not all requirements may be immediately usable for measurement	Feature to flag approved data requirements
Identification of requirement violations	Use the approved data requirements to identify requirement violations in the tested data	Data quality monitoring algorithms
	Generate a report with violated instances indicating the type of violation / data quality problem	Data quality monitoring reports
Evaluation of the quality state of data sources	Use the approved data requirements to calculate KPIs for data quality separated by quality dimensions	Data quality assessment algorithms
	Generate a report with KPIs for each data quality dimension with reference to the assessed object	Data quality assessment reports

6.2.3 Conditional Requirements

Conditional requirements in the understanding of this thesis are requirements that are implied by the environment in which the framework shall be used (cf. Grande, 2011, p. 37). Furthermore, we can differentiate between (1) organizational requirements, i.e. conditions related to the organizational environment, (2) technological requirements, i.e. conditions implied by the system environment, and (3) financial requirements, i.e.

83

limitations of the available resources for the development project (cf. Grande, 2011, p. 38f.). In the following, we describe the conditional requirements that are relevant for the development of the SDQM. The following organizational requirements have to be considered during the development of the SDQM:

Ability to capture distributed knowledge: Knowledge about data requirements is (similar to other business knowledge) distributed across the organization and, therefore, difficult to capture (cf. Huang et al., 1999, pp. 44-47; Loshin, 2001, p. 9f.).

Ability to identify contradictory data requirements: Due to different perspectives and heterogeneity, data requirements may be contradictory. Hence, comparability of data requirements is important (cf. Loshin, 2001, p. 198f.).

Ability to create data requirements within a limited time: Expert knowledge is a very precious but limited resource, since it is the source for business success and time of domain experts is very limited (cf. Loshin, 2001, p. 15). Hence, expert knowledge should be captured as efficiently and used as effectively as possible.

Ability to create data requirements without programming knowledge: Business experts are the main contributors to the creation and maintenance of data requirements, since data requirements often have their origin in business decisions (cf. Loshin, 2001, p. 15). Therefore, the design of the framework must consider that the creators and maintainers of data requirements usually have limited programming knowledge.

Moreover, the following technological requirements must be considered by the SDQM:

Data retrieval from relational sources: The information system used in the motivating scenario is based on a relational database which limits the types of quality problems that can occur.

Different optimization of transactional and analytical systems: Transactional systems are information systems optimized for the support business process execution (cf. Hansen & Neumann, 2004, p. 90f.). In contrast, analytical systems, e.g. for decision support, are usually optimized for data analysis (cf. Hansen & Neumann, 2004, pp. 789-794). Performing data quality analytics on a transactional system may, therefore, lead to unacceptable performance overhead. The data from the organization in the motivating scenario is located in a transactional system.

Performance and scalability: The artifact needs to have a sufficient performance and must be scalable for wide-spread use.

System constraints: The experiments in this thesis are performed on a specific operating system. Therefore, the architecture is constrained to artifacts that can be run on the available operating system.

Furthermore, the development of the SDQM underlies financial requirements. Since this thesis project has a very limited financial budget and limited manual resources, the reused artifacts that shall be integrated into the framework have to be freely available for research purposes.

Additionally to the enumerated requirements, there may be several more conditional requirements. However, this section contains the most important conditional requirements with regard to the development of the SDQM framework.

6.2.4 Research Requirements

Besides requirements originating from the application setting, SDQM also addresses research requirements, i.e. requirements that have to be considered to achieve the research goal or which are caused by the research conditions in which the artifact is developed. Since this thesis investigates the use of ontologies for data quality management (see section 2.1), one or more ontologies shall be part of SDQM.

6.3 Summary of SDQM's Requirements

Table 9 summarizes the initial requirements of SDQM in a structured form and assigns an identifier to each requirement. The requirements register will be used as a guideline for the development and evaluation of the SDQM framework.

Table 9: Initial requirements for the development of the SDQM framework

ID	Requirement	Requirement Type
R1	Distributed acquisition of data requirements	Functional
R2	Data requirements shall be captured in a machine-readable form	Functional
R3	Data requirements have to be approved before their use for data quality management	Functional
R4	The approved data requirements can be automatically applied to the tested data and will indicate violations	Functional
R5	Generate a report with violated instances indicating the type of violation / data quality problem	Functional
R6	The approved data requirements can be used to calculate KPIs for the data quality separated by quality dimensions	Functional
R7	Generate a report with KPIs for each data quality dimension with reference to the assessed object	Functional
R8	Ability to capture distributed knowledge	Organizational
R9	Ability to identify contradictory data requirements	Organizational
R10	Ability to create data requirements without programming knowledge	Organizational
R11	Ability to create data requirements under time constraints	Organizational
R12	Data retrieval from relational sources	Technological
R13	Different optimization of transactional and analytical systems	Technological
R14	Performance and scalability	Technological
R15	System constraints	Technological
R16	Use ontologies	Research
R17	Used artifacts must be freely available	Financial

7 Architecture of the Semantic Data Quality Management Framework (SDQM)

In this chapter, we define the objectives and justify the design decisions of the Semantic Data Quality Management framework (SDQM). We describe each component of SDQM's architecture as illustrated in figure 26, namely (1) the data acquisition layer, (2) the data storage layer, (3) the data quality management vocabulary (DQM Vocabulary), (4) the data requirements editor, and (5) the reporting layer. The design of the architecture is based on the requirements identified in the previous chapter. The following sections are organized according to these major components of the SDQM.

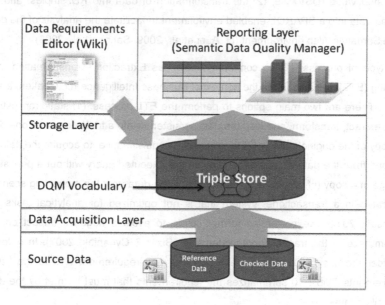

Figure 26: High-level architecture of the SDQM framework

In the first part of the following sections, we describe the purpose of the component of the high-level architecture and map the initial requirements to the accordant component. Additionally, we review the initial requirements since new requirements may arise with growing knowledge about the problem domain during the design process. In the second part of each section, we present the results of an analysis of existing artifacts regarding their reusability for the SDQM framework as part of the development process. At the end of each section, we briefly describe the final technical design of the component. The application procedure of SDQM's components is described in chapter 8. The use cases described in chapter 9 illustrate the actual use of SDQM in real-world settings.

7.1 Data Acquisition Layer

The data acquisition layer of SDQM shall be used to acquire (1) data for further data quality-related analyses and (2) reference data that may be needed for algorithms that compare the tested data with normative reference data. The acquisition process can be separated into (1) the extraction of data from a relational database or a delimiter-separated value (DSV) file, (2) the transformation of data into RDF triples, and (3) loading data into a SPARQL-enabled environment to facilitate the analysis of the data in the Semantic Web environment (cf. Auer et al., 2009; Sahoo et al., 2009).

This type of process is also commonly known as Extraction, Transformation, and Loading (ETL), in particular in the context of Business Intelligence (cf. Goeken, 2006, p. 29). There are two main options to perform the ETL process: (1) static replication, i.e. to extract, transform, and load the data persistently into a triplestore as a one-time full copy of the original data or (2) dynamic data acquisition, i.e. to acquire the data on demand from the data source depending on the executed query without a persistent storage of a copy (cf. Sahoo et al., 2009). Since the data from the motivating scenario is located in a transactional system that is not optimized for analytical tasks (cf. Microsoft, 2014), we prefer the former option to avoid a negative impact on the performance of the transactional systems (cf. Bizer & Cyganiak, 2007). In order to consider the use of DSV files, we added the new requirement R18 to the list of requirements. Table 10 summarizes the requirements that must be met by the data acquisition layer.

Table 10: Requirements for the data acquisition layer

ID	Requirement	Requirement Type
R12	Data retrieval from relational sources	Technological
R13	Different optimization of transactional and analytical systems	Technological
R18	Data retrieval from delimiter-separated files (DSV)	Technological

7.1.1 Reusable Artifacts for the Data Acquisition Layer

As of today, there are several tools that can be used to implement the SDQM data acquisition layer. In 2009, the W3C has published a survey about the state of the art of tools and techniques in the area of mapping relational databases to RDF (Sahoo et al., 2009). We analyzed a subset of these tools to identify an appropriate artifact for data acquisition in our scenario. Moreover, we added Google Refine with its RDF Extension (Google, 2011; Maali & Cyganiak, 2011) to the list which was not part of the W3C survey due to its novelty and the lack of direct connections to RDBMS. Our analysis focuses on the type of data acquisition, i.e. the possibility to load relational data to an RDF representation based on a mapping between both schemas, and the public availability of the tool for this research project. As explained in the previous section, there are two options to acquire data from relational sources, namely static data acquisition as one-time full copy and dynamic data acquisition that acquires data on demand. The results which are presented in table 11 are based on an analysis of the information provided by the respective project's Web site and the description in the W3C survey.

To minimize human effort, data acquisition tools should support scheduling the execution of data acquisition at certain points in time or triggered by certain events, and the visual modeling of ETL processes. To the best of our knowledge, none of the freely available tools currently support these mechanisms. Conventional data integration tools such as Talend Open Studio[28] or Pentaho Kettle[29] support scheduling and visual modeling, but do not support the conversion to RDF at the time of writing this thesis. However, for the purpose of this thesis a visual modeling tool with scheduling capabilities is not available, but also not necessary.

Table 11: Analysis of existing data acquisition tools with RDF conversion support

Tool	Data Acquisition Type	Free Availability
Virtuoso RDF Views (Erling, 2007)	Static and Dynamic	No[30]

---

[28] http://de.talend.com/products-data-integration/talend-open-studio.php (Last accessed on January 05th 2012)
[29] http://kettle.pentaho.com/ (Last accessed on January 05th 2012)
[30] Available in commercial release only (Last accessed on January 05th 2012)

D2RQ (Bizer, Cyganiak, et al., 2009; Bizer & Seaborne, 2004)	Static and Dynamic	Yes[31]
Triplify (Auer et al., 2009)	Static and Dynamic	Yes[32]
R2O (Rodriguez & Gómez-Pérez, 2006)	Static and Dynamic	Yes[33]
Dartgrid (Wu et al., 2006)	Dynamic	No[34]
RDBtoOnto (Cerbah, 2008)	Static	Yes[35]
Asio Semantic Bridge for Relational Databases (SBRD) and Automapper	Static and Dynamic	No[36]
Google Refine with RDF Extension (Google, 2011; Maali & Cyganiak, 2011)	Static[37]	Yes[38]

7.1.2 Data Acquisition for SDQM

In SDQM, data from relational databases and data from DSV files have to be converted into RDF before the data can be loaded into a triplestore. The conversion of the relational data in SDQM is done via D2RQ's RDF dump functionality (Cyganiak, 2012) since (1) it meets the requirements of SDQM, (2) it is publicly available, and (3) it is easy to use. Moreover, we use Google Refine with its RDF extension (Maali & Cyganiak, 2011) to convert data from DSV files into RDF. The loading procedure is done via the standard loading programs of the chosen triplestore in the data storage layer of SDQM.

---

[31] http://sourceforge.net/projects/d2rq-map/ (Last accessed on January 05th 2012)

[32] http://sourceforge.net/projects/triplify/ (Last accessed on January 05th 2012)

[33] Available as NeOn Toolkit plugin at http://neon-toolkit.org/wiki/ODEMapster (Last accessed on January 05th 2012)

[34] The project page http://ccnt.zju.edu.cn/projects/dartgrid was not available at the time of this analysis (Last accessed on January 05th 2012).

[35] http://www.tao-project.eu/researchanddevelopment/demosanddownloads/RDBToOnto.html (Last accessed on January 05th 2012)

[36] For availability see http://www.bbn.com/technology/knowledge/asio_sbrd (Last accessed on January 05th 2012)

[37] As of January 05th 2012 Google Refine allows the static conversion from TSV, CSV, DSV, Excel (.xls and .xlsx), JSON, XML, RDF as XML, and Google Data documents

[38] http://code.google.com/p/google-refine/ and http://lab.linkeddata.deri.ie/2010/grefine-rdf-extension/ (Last accessed on January 05th 2012)

7.2 Data Storage Layer

The data storage layer of SDQM serves the purpose of storage and supply of data and must, therefore, possess the following features:

- Storage of the acquired data,
- storage of data requirements,
- storage of ontologies,
- efficient data analysis capabilities, and
- free availability for research purposes.

In order to cover these functionalities, the storage layer consists of two artifacts: (1) a triplestore to store the data and (2) a server that exposes an endpoint with access to the triplestore for the execution of analytical queries and data updates by other artifacts. During the development of SDQM, we have discovered two more technological requirements that must be considered for the data storage layer:

- The storage artifact must provide a SPARQL 1.1[39]-compliant endpoint for data quality analyses (R19).
- The SPARQL endpoint must be extendable by custom SPARQL functions (R20).

Table 12 summarizes the requirements that must be addressed by SDQM's data storage layer.

Table 12: Requirements for the data storage layer

ID	Requirement	Requirement Type
R14	Performance and scalability	Technological
R15	System constraints	Technological
R16	Use ontologies	Research
R17	Used artifacts must be freely available	Financial
R19	SPARQL 1.1-compliant endpoint	Technological
R20	Support for User-Defined Functions (UDFs) in SPARQL	Technological

7.2.1 Reusable Artifacts for Data Storage in SDQM

---

[39] See http://www.w3.org/TR/sparql11-query/ for the SPARQL 1.1 syntax

At present, there are several triplestores that may meet the above requirements. As a basis for the further selection, we used the triplestores tested in the Berlin SPARQL Benchmark (Bizer & Schultz, 2011).

Table 13: Analysis of existing triplestores regarding their use for SDQM

Triplestore	Runs on used Operating System	Availability	SPARQL 1.1 compliant
4Store	No[40]	Yes[41]	Partially[42]
BigData	Yes	Yes[43]	Yes
BigOwlim	Yes	Yes[44]	Yes
Jena TDB	Yes	Yes[45]	Yes
Virtuoso	Yes	Yes[46]	Partially[47]

Since Virtuoso and 4store did not fulfill some of the requirements as illustrated in table 13, we had to choose between BigData, BigOwlim, and Jena TDB. Because of the strong support by the community, the openness of the framework, and its sufficient performance, we chose Jena TDB to be part of SDQM. Moreover, we chose Fuseki Server[48] to publish the SPARQL endpoint of our Jena TDB.

7.2.2 The Data Storage Layer of SDQM

The data storage layer of SDQM consists of the triplestore Jena TDB in Version 0.8.11 integrated into a Fuseki Server (Revision 8860). The Fuseki Server endpoint was slightly adjusted so that our custom SPARQL extensions can be interpreted by Fuseki's SPARQL query engine. In particular, we added the functions dqf:pattern,

---

[40] Our attempts for building a Windows 7 compatible version failed.
[41] http://4store.org/trac/wiki/Download (Last accessed on January 05th 2012)
[42] Supported: Aggregates and GROUP BY, not supported: property paths and sub queries ((Salvadores, 2012))
[43] http://sourceforge.net/projects/bigdata/
[44] OWLIM Lite freely available after registration at http://www.ontotext.com/owlim/owlim-lite-registration Last accessed on January 05th 2012)
[45] http://incubator.apache.org/jena/download/index.html (Last accessed on January 05th 2012)
[46] Open source edition available at http://sourceforge.net/projects/virtuoso/files/virtuoso/ (Last accessed on January 05th 2012)
[47] Although the syntax of virtuoso's SPARQL endpoint is very expressive, we discovered several differences to the SPARQL 1.1 syntax that would have caused a different (non-SPARQL1.1 compliant) query design
[48] http://openjena.org/wiki/Fuseki (Last accessed on January 05th 2012)

`dqf:dice`, and `dqf:requiredTimestamp` to the query engine. The prefix "`dqf:`" refers to the base URI http://semwebquality.org/function#.

The extension `dqf:pattern` can be used to analyze the syntactical differences between string patterns of the values of a certain property. It analyzes each character of a string and creates a new string based on standard character for each character type. E.g. capital letters are represented as "A", small letters as "a", numbers as "N", whitespaces as "_", and all other characters as "S". Commas and dots are not replaced by the function. As a result the function creates a new string "AaA_Aaaaaa" based on the existing string "PhD Thesis". This is especially useful in combination with frequency distribution statistics to get an impression of the different syntactical rules that apply for the values of a certain property.

The extension `dqf:dice` calculates the distance between two strings based on the dice coefficient. The dice coefficient is computed via the following formula (cf. Dice, 1945, p. 298):

$$d(a,b) = \frac{2 * H}{A + B}$$

The similarity between two strings, string a and string b, is thereby represented as d(a,b) (cf. Frakes & Baeza-Yates, 1992, p. 404f.). In our implementation of the dice coefficient, we extract all bigrams, i.e. the two adjacent characters, of each string, store each of the bigrams as a value within an array for each string, and compare both arrays with each other. Then we use the constructed arrays and the above formula to calculate the similarity between both strings. H is the number of matching bigrams between string a and string b, A is the number of bigrams of string a, and B is the number of bigrams of string b. As a result, `dqf:dice` produces a similarity score based on the number of identical bigrams of the two strings. The similarity d(a,b) between string a and string b lies between zero and one. A value of one means that both strings have all bigrams in common. Zero means that the two compared strings do not have any bigrams in common (cf. Dice, 1945, p. 298f.; Frakes & Baeza-Yates, 1992, p. 404f.). The extension `dqf:dice` can, therefore, be used to identify duplicates based on similar values. Due to heterogeneity, duplicates often cannot be identified via exact matches of property values.

Finally, we added the extension `dqf:requiredTimestamp` to Fuseki's query engine to support the computation of timeliness. The extension subtracts a value in `xsd:duration` format[49] from the current date and time. The `xsd:duration` value thereby indicates the maximum duration that may lapse between two updates. As a result `dqf:requiredTimestamp` creates an `xsd:dateTime` formatted[50] value that represents the latest timestamp an instance should have based of the required update duration information.

In summary, the data storage layer of SDQM facilitates communication with the triplestore via SPARQL 1.1 queries that are sent to the server's endpoint. Moreover, it is also suited to correctly interpret our custom SPARQL extensions.

7.3 Data Quality Management Vocabulary

One core requirement for the proposed approach is a common conceptual data model for capturing instance data, normative reference data, quality rules and quality metrics. Such shared data schemas are known as global or mediated schemas in the context of databases (cf. Alexiev et al., 2005, p. 154f.; Levy, 2000, pp. 7-10) or ontologies (cf. Alexiev et al., 2005, p. 154f.; Gruber, 1993, p. 199f.) in the context of intelligent systems, agents, knowledge representation, or the Semantic Web. The data quality management vocabulary presented in the following is an ontology that shall provide the unified data structure to store quality-relevant knowledge, so that generic SPARQL queries can process the knowledge and identify quality problems in data instances. Table 14 shows the initial requirements for the DQM vocabulary.

Table 14: Requirements for the data quality management vocabulary

ID	Requirement	Requirement Type
R2	Data requirements shall be captured in a machine-readable form	Functional
R3	Data requirements have to be approved before their use for data quality management	Functional
R4	The approved data requirements can be automatically applied to the tested data and will indicate violations	Functional
R6	The approved data requirements can be used to calculate KPIs for the data quality separated by quality dimensions	Functional

---

[49] http://www.w3.org/TR/xmlschema-2/#duration
[50] http://www.w3.org/TR/xmlschema-2/#dateTime

Besides these requirements, we have specified the requirements for the development of the ontology with the help of the ontology engineering methodology by Uschold and Gruninger (Uschold & Gruninger, 1996). The detailed requirements for the DQM vocabulary were described by using motivating scenarios for the use of the vocabulary itself. Based on the scenarios a set of competency questions has been derived such as the following:

- Which instances of a data source suffer from data quality problems according to predefined data requirements?
- What is the data quality state of a selected data source according to predefined data requirements?
- For which time-frame is the data requirement valid?
- Which data requirements have a confidence level above XY?
- Which data quality problems affect instances of class B and/or values of property X?
- Which data requirements are task-dependent?

The competency questions cover information that is required to represent quality-relevant knowledge for data quality monitoring and assessment and shall be answerable through queries against the DQM vocabulary assuming that the retrieved information is represented via the vocabulary. The competency questions, therefore, facilitate the identification of the required classes and properties of the ontology. A detailed description of the DQM vocabulary including its development can be found in (Fürber & Hepp, 2011b).

7.3.1 Reuse of Existing Ontologies

By the time of this thesis project, we did not find any suitable ontologies that fulfill the above requirements. However, there are multiple ontologies to represent provenance information of data in Semantic Web architectures, such as the Semantic Web Publishing Vocabulary (SWP[51]) or the Open Provenance Vocabulary (OPV[52]). Table 15 shows the existing vocabularies in the quality, provenance, and trust space of Linked Open Vocabularies (Vandenbussche, 2012), a Web site that maintains a list of

---

[51] http://www.w3.org/2004/03/trix/swp-2/
[52] http://purl.org/net/provenance/ns

open vocabularies of the Semantic Web. Although some provenance vocabularies may be expressive enough to represent some quality information relevant for the assessment of quality dimensions such as timeliness (Hartig & Zhao, 2009), they lack expressiveness for the representation of the different types of data requirements, such as legal values of a property or functional dependencies. Hence, we developed a new ontology called the DQM vocabulary from scratch.

Table 15: Ontologies in the data quality space of Linked Open Vocabularies[53]

Prefix	Namespace	Title
cert	http://www.w3.org/ns/auth/cert#	The Cert Ontology
dqm	http://purl.org/dqm-vocabulary/v1.1/dqm#	The Data Quality Management Vocabulary
irw	http://www.ontologydesignpatterns.org/ont/web/irw.owl#	The Identity of Resources on the Web ontology
opmv	http://purl.org/net/opmv/ns#	Open Provenance Model Vocabulary
pav	http://swan.mindinformatics.org/ontologies/1.2/pav/	Provenance, Authoring and Versioning Ontology Specification
prov	http://purl.org/net/provenance/ns#	Provenance Vocabulary Core Ontology
prvt	http://purl.org/net/provenance/types#	Provenance Vocabulary types
voag	http://voag.linkedmodel.org/schema/voag#	Vocabulary Of Attribution and Governance
wot	http://xmlns.com/wot/0.1/	Web Of Trust

7.3.2 Technical Design of the DQM Vocabulary

The DQM vocabulary currently consists of 68 classes, 46 object properties, and 54 data type properties and is coded in OWL DL (see section 4.2.4 for further explanations) to facilitate its adoption even in knowledge bases that depend on decidable reasoning. The DQM vocabulary serves the following basic purposes:

1. Representation of data requirements in a machine-readable way.
2. Annotation of quality-relevant meta-information to data elements.

---

[53] Picture retrieved from Mondeca Labs at
http://labs.mondeca.com/dataset/lov/details/vocabularySpace_Quality.html (Last accessed on January 05th 2012)

The DQM vocabulary uses the namespace http://purl.org/dqm-vocabulary/v1.1/dqm# which is abbreviated by the prefix "dqm:" in the following. A full visualization of the DQM vocabulary is shown in figure 27. Its central classes are highlighted in blue. The class `dqm:DataRequirement` is the superclass of all data requirements and, therefore, contains general properties that all data requirements have in common, such as the requirement's name, description, its importance, and source, the creator's confidence in accuracy of the requirement, the requirement's validity period, and information on whether the requirement shall be used for assessment or information filtering. The class `dqm:DataRequirement` is in the center of the DQM vocabulary due to its importance for data quality management. Since data requirements may be task-dependent, the object property `dqm:appliesFor` can be used to connect a specific requirement with an instance of the class `dqm:Task` (cf. Pipino et al., 2002, p. 211). This facilitates filtering of task-dependent data requirements based on specific tasks. Moreover, it helps to identify the tasks that may be affected in case the data requirement is violated.

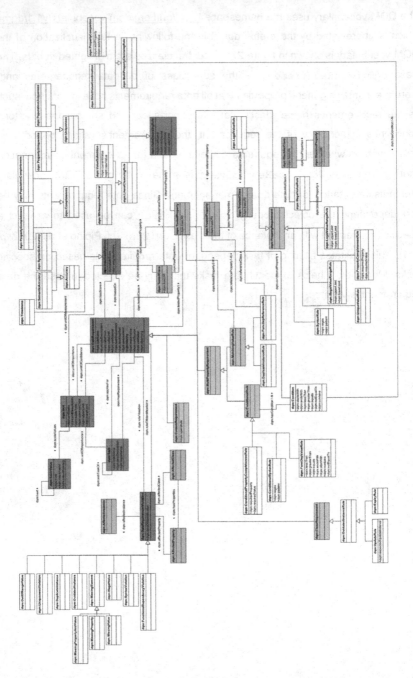

Figure 27: Visualization of the DQM vocabulary (cf. Fürber & Hepp, 2011b)

The instances of the class `dqm:DataRequirement` and its subclasses may be used to identify requirement violations and calculate data quality scores. Therefore, these instances can be used to derive other instances for `dqm:DataRequirementViolation` and `dqm:DataQualityScore`. The class `dqm:DataRequirementViolation` has the purpose of annotating instances that violate data requirements with information about the time of identification, the affected classes and properties, and the data requirement that identified the violation. The class `dqm:DataQualityScore` can be used to store the results of data quality assessments. The class, therefore, provides properties to identify the time when the assessment was conducted, the requirement the measurement is based on, the classes and properties that have been analyzed, the actual score and its unit. The class `dqm:DataElement` and its subclasses, which are highlighted in yellow in figure 27, are used to provide the range for the classes `dqm:DataRequirement`, `dqm:DataRequirementViolation`, and `dqm:DataQualityScore`. Hence, every class and property that is used in an instance of the class `dqm:DataRequirement` has to be either a direct instance of one of `dqm:DataElement`'s subclasses or mapped to one of its instances via its properties. In the latter option, the knowledge base stays in the OWL DL language profile. In the former option, the knowledge base becomes OWL Full. A full description of the DQM vocabulary can be found at http://semwebquality.org/dqm-vocabulary/v1/dqm.

7.4 Data Requirements Editor

The data requirements editor shall be used to collect data requirements in a structured and comparable form so that other artifacts can make use of the specified requirements, e.g. to automatically derive reports about requirement violations and the quality state of data sources (see section 6.2.2). Therefore, the requirements editor must address the requirements specified in table 16.

Table 16: Requirements for the data requirements editor

ID	Requirement	Requirement Type
R1	Distributed acquisition of data requirements	Functional
R2	Data requirements shall be captured in a machine-readable form	Functional
R3	Data requirements have to be approved before their use for data quality management	Functional
R8	Ability to capture distributed knowledge	Organizational
R9	Ability to identify contradictory data requirements	Organizational
R10	Ability to create data requirements without programming knowledge	Organizational
R11	Ability to create data requirements under time constraints	Organizational

7.4.1 Reusable Artifacts for SDQM's Data Requirements Editor

The collection of structured information can, in general, be supported by forms. However, platforms are needed that facilitate the collection of distributed knowledge and the creation of consensual agreement in an easy and efficient way. Wiki software addresses these issues and is especially useful in distributed environments (cf. Krötzsch et al., 2006, p. 935). Moreover, first experiences have been collected in the use of wikis for metadata management (Hüner, Brauer, et al., 2011; Hüner, Otto, et al., 2011). Therefore, we chose wiki technology as the platform for SDQM's data requirements editor. In order to meet the functional requirements, the data requirements need to be captured and stored in a structured way, so that external tools can retrieve the data requirements for further processing. We found two wiki-software platforms that already offer such functionalities, namely Atlassian Confluence[54] with the semantic plugin Wikidsmart[55] and MediaWiki[56] with the extensions Semantic MediaWiki[57] and Semantic Forms[58]. Atlassian Confluence is a popular commercial wiki software widely used in enterprises. According to Atlassian (Atlassian, 2012) Confluence is used by more than 8000 customers in over 94 countries. Not much is known about the usage of the Confluence plugin Wikidsmart. On the other hand MediaWiki is freely available. Its Semantic MediaWiki extension is already widely

---

[54] http://www.atlassian.com/software/confluence/overview (Last accessed on January 06th 2012)
[55] http://www.zagile.com/products/wikidsmart.html (Last accessed on January 06th 2012)
[56] http://www.MediaWiki.org/wiki/MediaWiki (Last accessed on January 06th 2012)
[57] http://semantic-MediaWiki.org/ (Last accessed on January 06th 2012)
[58] http://www.MediaWiki.org/wiki/Extension:Semantic_Forms (Last accessed on January 06th 2012)

used[59] and its documentation makes it easily adaptable. We, therefore, decided to build the data requirements editor based upon MediaWiki with the extensions Semantic MediaWiki and Semantic Forms.

7.4.2 Data Requirements Wiki

The architecture of SDQM's data requirements wiki makes use of standard features of MediaWiki (Version 1.17.0)[56], Semantic MediaWiki (Version 1.7)[57], and Semantic Forms (Version 2.3.2)[58]. The Semantic MediaWiki extension offers features to represent and use properties and classes in the MediaWiki environment (cf. Krötzsch et al., 2006, p. 937). For example the sentence "*Cologne has approximately 1,000,000 inhabitants*" can be expressed in a machine-interpretable way by adding property tags to the elements of a sentence, e.g. "*[[city::Cologne]] has approximately [[population::1000000]] inhabitants*". The tags [[city::]] and [[population::]] represent properties that can by freely defined and retrieved via so called inline queries within the wiki (cf. Dauw et al., 2014). Moreover, the wiki page that contains this text could be categorized into the wiki category "Location" which can be seen as a class for all wiki pages that describe locations. Based on the annotation of properties and categories, it is now possible to query the data in a structured way. Figure 28 shows an inline query and its results. The inline query can be saved on regular wiki pages to integrate dynamically retrieved wiki content (cf. Dauw et al., 2014).

---

[59] See http://semantic-MediaWiki.org/wiki/Sites_using_Semantic_MediaWiki for a list of wikis using Semantic MediaWiki (Last accessed on February 12th 2012)

```
{{#ask: [[Category:Location]]
 | mainlabel=Wikipage
 | ?city
 | ?population
 | format=table
}}
```

⬍	City ⬍	Population ⬍
Berlin	Berlin	3,500,000
Bonn	Bonn	325,000
Cologne	Cologne	1,000,000
New York City	New York City	8,100,000

Figure 28: Example for an inline query and its result (cf. Dauw et al., 2014)

In order to alleviate the complexity and heterogeneity related to the manual annotation of properties and categories, it is possible to define wiki-based forms with help of the Semantic Forms extension for Semantic MediaWiki. Semantic Forms allows defining input elements for properties and categories of Semantic MediaWiki which can be organized within forms. Therefore, users do not need to bother annotating the right property and category to the information stored in the wiki. They rather have to fill in forms to express the information. The data requirements wiki offers several different forms to capture data requirements (F1-6) and to register tested and trusted data elements (F7-F11). The forms and its purpose are listed in

table 17. The forms offer several possibilities to enter data such as checkboxes, dropdown lists, or text areas. Each of the form elements is bound to an internal property that can be defined via the Semantic MediaWiki extension. The binding between the form and the properties is done via a MediaWiki template (cf. Koren, 2012, pp. 147-150; Koren, 2014). The internal categories and properties of the data requirements wiki are mapped to external classes and properties of the DQM vocabulary via a standard vocabulary import function[60]. Due to the mapping, all data captured via the forms is stored with the URIs of the classes and properties of the DQM vocabulary. Moreover, the captured data is automatically stored in SDQM's triplestore in real-time via a

---

[60] The vocabulary import function of Semantic MediaWiki is described in detail at http://semantic-MediaWiki.org/wiki/Help:Import_vocabulary (Last accessed on February 12th 2012)

Standard MediaWiki triplestore connector and is, therefore, immediately available for data quality analyses within SDQM's architecture. Figure 29 illustrates the technical design of the data requirements wiki.

Table 17: Forms provided by SDQM's data requirements wiki

No.	Form	Purpose
F1	Property requirements	Capture data requirements bound to single properties.
F2	Conditional requirements	Capture data requirements that are valid for a specific subset of instances of a class.
F3	Timeliness requirements	Capture data requirements related to the timeliness of instances of a class.
F4	Duplicate rules	Capture data requirements that can identify duplicate instances.
F5	Functional dependency reference rules	Capture data requirements that refer to a trusted data source to identify functional dependency violations.
F6	Custom requirements	Capture data requirements that are not expressible with the above forms.
F7	Tested Classes	Register classes with instances that shall be analyzed for data quality problems.
F8	Tested Properties	Register properties that shall be analyzed for data quality problems.
F9	Conditions	Define conditions that shall be used for conditional requirements to filter a relevant subset of a class.
F10	Trusted Classes	Register classes of another data source as a trusted reference for legal value rules and functional dependency reference rules.
F11	Trusted Properties	Register properties of another data source as a trusted reference for legal value rules and functional dependency reference rules.

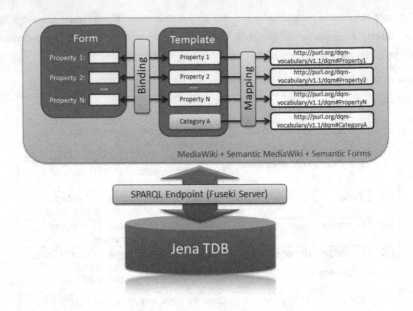

Figure 29: Architecture of SDQM's data requirements wiki

7.5 Reporting Layer

The reporting layer of SDQM shall provide data quality monitoring and data quality assessment reports that are automatically generated based on the data requirements that were previously created and approved within the data requirements wiki. Data quality monitoring reports shall contain information about instances of the data source that violate approved requirements. The data quality monitoring report shall also indicate which requirement was violated to support root cause analysis. The data quality assessment report shall provide an overview about the quality state of a data source separated by quality dimensions. Table 18 summarizes the requirements of the reporting layer.

Table 18: Requirements of the reporting layer

ID	Requirement	Requirement Type
R4	Use the approved data requirements to identify requirement violations in the tested data	Functional
R5	Generate a report with violated instances indicating the type of violation / data quality problem	Functional
R6	The approved data requirements can be used to calculate KPIs for the data quality separated by quality dimensions	Functional
R7	Generate a report with KPIs for each data quality dimension with reference to the assessed object	Functional

7.5.1 Reusable Artifacts for SDQM's Reporting Layer

The reporting layer of SDQM has to be able to process data specified in the DQM vocabulary. Since there is currently (by the time of this thesis project) no artifact available that can meet this specific requirement, we have to build our own reporting frontend, called Semantic Data Quality Manager (SDQMgr). To minimize the development effort we chose to use the Jena Semantic Web framework[61] for processing of Semantic Web data and Vaadin[62], a Java framework for building Web-based user interfaces. We chose the Jena framework since it is freely available and supports the most recent version of the SPARQL query language syntax as defined by the W3C. Vaadin was chosen since (1) it is written in the same programming language as the Jena framework, (2) it is also freely available and actively maintained, and (3) it provides appropriate graphical elements for the definition of modern user interfaces.

7.5.2 Semantic Data Quality Manager

The Semantic Data Quality Manager (SDQMgr) is one of the major artifacts of this thesis project. SDQMgr is a Web-based frontend application with a user interface for ad-hoc data quality monitoring and assessment based on approved data requirements

---

[61] http://incubator.apache.org/jena/ (Last accessed on February 12th 2012)
[62] https://vaadin.com/home (Last accessed on February 20th 2012)

expressed in the syntax of the DQM vocabulary. It is programmed in Java and uses the Jena Semantic Web Framework[63] for processing the data from SDQM's triplestore.

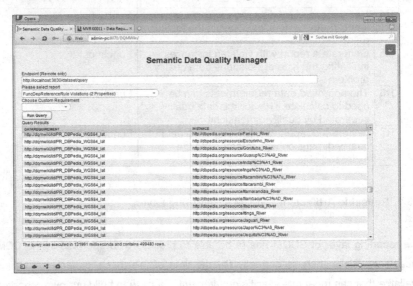

Figure 30: Web-based user interface of the Semantic Data Quality Manager

SDQMgr's graphical user interface is Web-based and, therefore, callable from any Web browser. Thus, users of the SDQMgr only require a Web browser as a prerequisite for using the application. Figure 30 shows a screenshot of the user interface of the SDQMgr. In the heart of SDQMgr are Java classes for data quality monitoring and data quality assessment which contain generic SPARQL queries for processing the data in SDQM's triplestore. The generic use of the queries is achieved by using only the terms provided by the DQM vocabulary. Users can choose from 32 predesigned reports for the identification of instances with requirement violations (data quality monitoring reports) and 32 reports for the evaluation of the quality state of data elements (data quality assessment reports). The reports can be chosen from a dropdown box below "Please select report" in SDQMgr's user interfaces (see Figure 30). The data quality monitoring reports are organized according to the type of quality problem and the data quality assessment reports according to data quality dimensions. Table 19 provides an overview about the SDQMgr's reports.

Table 19: Reports of SDQMgr

---

[63] http://incubator.apache.org/jena/ (Last accessed on February 12th 2012)

Data Quality Monitoring Reports	Data Quality Assessment Reports
Missing Values and Properties	Completeness
Conditional Missing Values and Properties (1 – 5 Conditions, 5 Reports)	Completeness (Conditional Rules, 5 Reports)
Syntax Violations	Syntactic Accuracy
Conditional Syntax Violations (1 – 5 Conditions, 5 Reports)	Syntactic Accuracy (Conditional Rules, 5 Reports)
Illegal Values (Legal Value Rules)	Syntactic Accuracy
Out Of Range Values	Semantic Accuracy
Illegal Values (Illegal Value Rules)	Semantic Accuracy
FuncDepReferenceRule Violations (2 - 5 Properties, 4 Reports)	Semantic Accuracy (4 Reports)
FuncDepValueRule Violations (1 – 5 Conditions, 5 Reports)	Semantic Accuracy (5 Reports)
Expired Instances	Timeliness
Exceeded Update Interval	Timeliness
Uniqueness Violations	Uniqueness in Depth
Duplicate Instances (1 – 5 Equal Values, 5 Reports)	Uniqueness in Scope (5 Reports)

The data quality assessment reports in the right column are thereby based on the heuristics of the data quality monitoring reports in the left column. The assessment reports compute a key performance indicator for each quality dimension which is based on the simple ratio between the number of correct instances $(I_R - I_V)$ and the number of all relevant instances I_R (cf. Fürber & Hepp, 2011a, p. 4f.; Pipino et al., 2002, p. 213).

$$DQ - Score_{Dimension} = \frac{(I_R - I_V)}{I_R}$$

The number of correct instances is thereby determined by subtracting the number of instances with requirement violations I_V from the number of all relevant instances I_R. The number of instances with requirement violations I_V is determined by the same heuristics as applied in the data quality monitoring reports. Figure 31 illustrates the relationship between the types of data requirement that are used to compute the quality scores for the accordant data quality dimension. For example, instances of the class `dqm:UpdateRule` are used to compute the timeliness of a specific data source. It is, therefore, not necessary to define own data requirements for data quality assessment. The data requirements that have been used to create data quality monitoring reports are automatically reused to compute the quality scores.

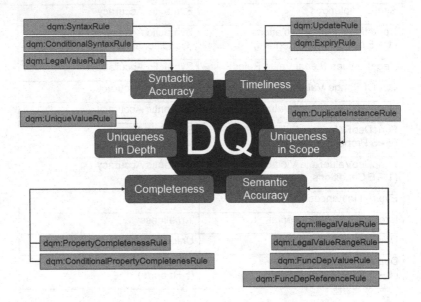

Figure 31: Configuration of data quality assessment reports in SDQMgr

The dimensional data quality scores presented in SDQMgr's data quality assessment reports allow the quick evaluation how complete, syntactic and semantically accurate, timely, and unique the tested data are based on the captured data requirements. The user only has to define his data requirements in the data requirements wiki once. Therefore, the manual effort is reduced. Figure 32 shows a data quality assessment report of the SDQMgr which contains the completeness scores of three different properties.

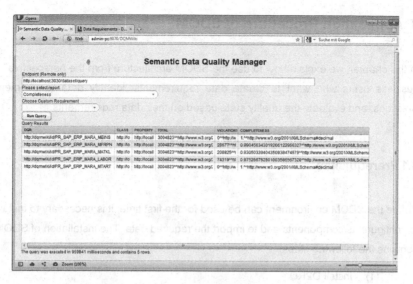

Figure 32: Data quality assessment report of SDQMgr

8 Application Procedure of SDQM

In this chapter, we explain how to use the SDQM architecture from the perspective of business users who want to create data requirements, identify data requirement violations, and evaluate the quality state based on their data requirements.

8.1 Prerequisites

Before the SDQM environment can be used for the first time, it is necessary to install, to configure its components and to import the required data. The installation of SDQM contains the following steps:

(1) Install D2RQ
(2) Extract the data to be tested from the relational database with D2RQ into a file in N-Triples format
(3) Install Google Refine with RDF Extension (optional)
(4) Convert DSV files into RDF files with Google Refine (optional)
(5) Setup, configure, and start the SDQM-optimized Fuseki server
(6) Import RDF and N-Triples files into Jena TDB of Fuseki via Fuseki's user interface or TDB's command line tool "tdbloader"
(7) Setup and configure MediaWiki with the extensions Semantic MediaWiki, Semantic Forms, Semantic Forms Inputs, and Category Tree including a database for MediaWiki (e.g. MySQL[64])
(8) Deploy the wiki via a PHP[65]-enabled Web server (e.g. WampServer[66])
(9) Import SDQM's forms, categories, properties, templates, and the DQM vocabulary mapping

Most of the above steps have to be performed only once before the first use of the SDQM framework. Steps (2), (4), and (6) may be performed each time new test or reference data is required. However, in practical settings these processes will usually be automated with the help of ETL tools that support visual modeling.

---

[64] http://mysql.com/ (Last accessed on February 22th 2012)
[65] Hypertext Preprocessor (Programming language for web applications)
[66] http://www.wampserver.com/en/ (Last accessed on February 22th 2012)

8.2 The Data Quality Management Process with SDQM

The general application procedure of SDQM is based on the main activities of the data quality management process as identified in section 3.5.3.

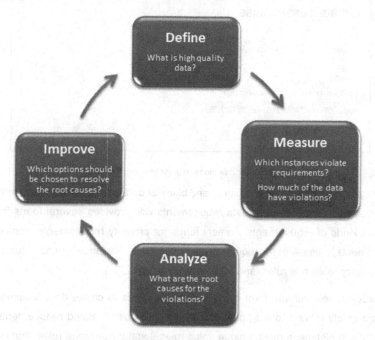

Figure 33: DQM process as supported by SDQM (based on Wang, 1998)

During the definition phase one has to define "What is high quality data?". This definition can be performed by using data requirements. SDQM's data requirements wiki provides standard forms for this purpose which can be used to express data requirements and, therefore, define data quality from a specific perspective. In order to create data requirements with SDQM's data requirements wiki, the user has to first register the classes and properties that shall be tested. Figure 34 shows the form of SDQM's data requirements wiki that can be used to register new classes that shall be analyzed for data quality problems. Besides this form, the data requirements wiki also contains similar forms to register tested properties, trusted classes, trusted properties, and blacklist classes and properties. The forms only require the specification of the URI of the class or property that shall be registered. The form then automatically classifies the registered class into one of the classes of the DQM vocabulary, i.e. the classes `dqm:TestedClass`, `dqm:TestedProperty`, `dqm:TrustedClass`, `dqm:TrustedProperty`, `dqm:BlacklistClass`, or `dqm:BlacklistProperty`.

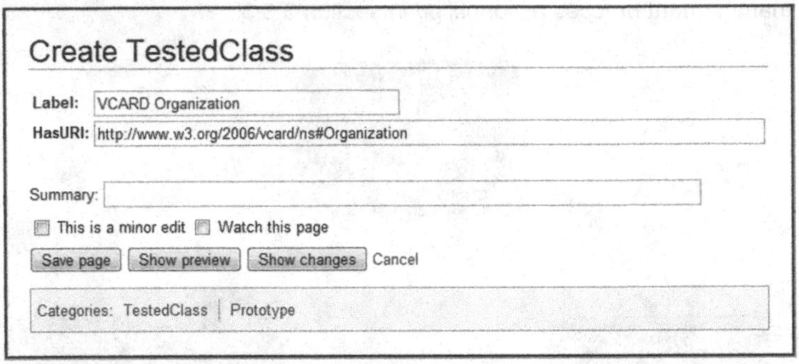

Create TestedClass

Label: VCARD Organization
HasURI: http://www.w3.org/2006/vcard/ns#Organization

Summary:
☐ This is a minor edit ☐ Watch this page
[Save page] [Show preview] [Show changes] Cancel

Categories: TestedClass | Prototype

Figure 34: SDQM's form to register new tested classes

After registration of the tested, trusted, and blacklist data elements, data requirements can be added. Therefore, the data requirements wiki provides several forms for the different kinds of requirements, namely forms for property requirements, conditional requirements, timeliness requirements, duplicate instance rules, functional dependency reference rules, and custom requirements.

The property requirement form contains form elements to create data requirements that are solely related to a single property. Such property-related requirements are property completeness rules, unique value rules, legal value range rules, legal value rules, and illegal value rules (cf. Loshin, 2001, pp. 171-179). Figure 35 shows the form used to capture property requirements with SDQM's data requirements wiki.

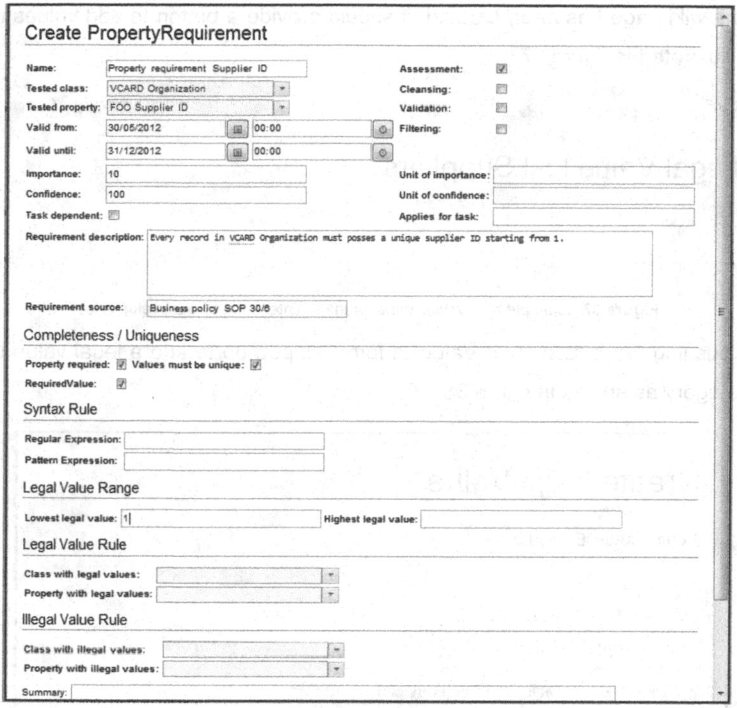

Figure 35: SDQM's property requirement form

The legal and illegal value rules thereby make use of a separate class and property that contains the legal / illegal values in a list. Such a list can also be generated within the data requirements wiki. Therefore, one has to first create a category for the list in the wiki. In case the list shall represent legal values, the new category has to be defined as subcategory of the category "LegalValue" and needs to be registered as trusted class via the trusted class form. In the other case, the new category has to be defined as subcategory of the category "IllegalValue" and has to be registered as blacklist class with the blacklist class form. After that, a new wiki page should be created for the maintenance of the list. In case of a legal value list, the legal values could be retrieved and maintained within a wiki page via the inline query shown in figure 36.

```
{{#ask: [[Category:<CategoryOfLegalValueList>]]
| mainlabel=Page name
| ?legalValue
}}
{{#formlink:form=LegalValue|link type=button|link text=Add Value|popup}}
```

Figure 36: Code for a wiki page to maintain lists in the data requirements wiki

113

After the wiki page has been created, it should provide a button to add values to the list as illustrated in figure 37

Figure 37: Example of new wiki page for the maintenance of legal value lists

When pushing the button "Add Value" a form will pop up to add a legal value to the new category as shown in figure 38.

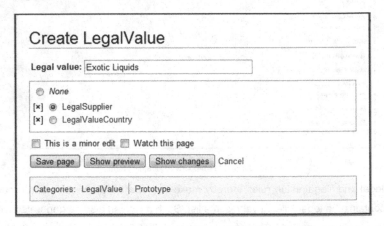

Figure 38: Example of SDQM's form to add legal values

After entering a new legal value and choosing the appropriate category, a list with the legal values of the category will be shown and dynamically updated each time a new value is added to the category. Figure 39 shows the dynamic list which contains the new value captured with the form from figure 38.

Figure 39: Example of legal value list in SDQM's data requirements wiki

After the legal value list has been completed, it can be selected in the property requirement form to define a legal value rule.

The conditional requirement form allows the definition of conditional mandatory value requirements, conditional syntax requirements, and functionally dependent values. The form design is thereby aligned to the structure of a conditional rule, i.e. if / then expressions (cf. Loshin, 2001, p. 170). The if-part allows the expression of conditions to filter a relevant subset of a class. The current form facilitates the selection of up to five different filter conditions that are connected with logical AND relationships. The conditions have to be defined by a separate form of SDQM before it can be selected in the conditional requirement form. Figure 40 displays the condition form of SDQM's data requirements wiki.

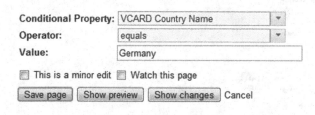

Figure 40: SDQM's form to define conditions

The then-part of the requirement represents certain characteristics that are expected for all values of a certain property that are part of instances that meet the previously defined conditions (cf. Loshin, 2001, p. 170). Such consequences are for example a specific syntax requirement, a conditional completeness requirement, or a functionally dependent value for a specific subset of a class / table. Figure 41 shows the conditional requirement form of SDQM's data requirements wiki.

Figure 41: SDQM's conditional requirement form

Functionally dependent value requirements can also be captured with the functional dependency reference rule form of SDQM. The form allows the definition of a reference data source that holds the legal value combinations. Hence, a lot of manual work can be saved in cases where there is a reference data source that already contains the valid property value combinations. A popular example is zip code data which can often be purchased from the countries' mail companies. The functional dependency reference rule form currently allows the definition of dependencies between up to five property values. Figure 42 shows the functional dependency reference rule form as it can be called in SDQM's data requirements wiki.

Functional Dependency Reference Rule: MVR 00001

Name:	Locality Country Combinations		Assessment:	☑
Valid from:	30/05/2012	00:00	Cleansing:	☐
Valid until:	31/12/9999	00:00	Validation:	☐
			Filtering:	☐
Importance:	10		Unit of importance:	
Confidence:	90		Unit of confidence:	
Task dependent:	☐		Applies for task:	

Requirement description: `Locality country combinations in VCARD Organization must be correct.`

Requirement source:

Tested class:	VCARD Organization
Tested property 1:	VCARD Locality
Tested property 2:	VCARD Country Name
Tested property 3:	
Tested property 4:	
Tested property 5:	
Reference class:	TrustedClass Locality Country Comb
Reference property 1:	TrustedProperty Locality
Reference property 2:	TrustedProperty Country
Reference property 3:	
Reference property 4:	
Reference property 5:	

Figure 42: SDQM's functional dependency reference rule form

Timeliness requirements can be captured with the outdated instance rule form of SDQM's data requirements wiki. The timeliness requirement can thereby be defined in two different ways: (1) We can define an update interval (cf. Oliveira, Rodrigues, Henriques, et al., 2005, p. 3) or (2) we can define a property that represents the date of expiry (cf. Oliveira, Rodrigues, Henriques, et al., 2005, p. 3). The update interval has to be specified in xsd:duration syntax[67] and represents the duration in which the instances of a specific class / table have to be periodically updated. The update rule requires the existence of a property that indicates the timestamp of the last update of an instance in order to work. The expiry rule requires the existence of a property that indicates the date of expiry of an instance. In cases, where none of these properties are available, it is not possible to assess timeliness with SDQM. Figure 43 shows the form of SDQM's Data requirements wiki that can be used to capture timeliness requirements.

---

[67] We refer to http://www.w3.org/TR/xmlschema-2/#duration for the syntax of xsd:duration values

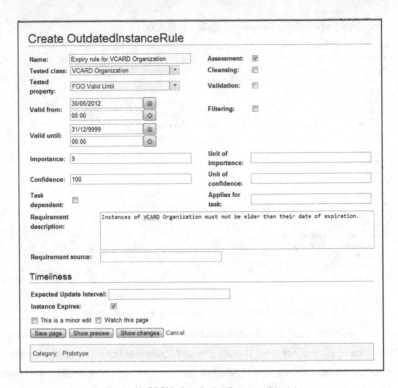

Figure 43: SDQM's form for timeliness requirements

Moreover, SDQM provides a form to capture duplicate rules. Duplicate rules are data requirements that can be used to identify potential duplicates of a class. The respective form of SDQM's data requirements wiki allows to define up to five properties of a class that are used to check whether there are instances with identical values for these properties. The SDQMgr's data quality monitoring reports then show all instances with identical values for these properties, since they are suspicious to be duplicates. Figure 44 shows SDQM's form to capture duplicate instance rules.

Figure 44: SDQM's duplicate instance rule form

Since there may be some requirements that cannot be expressed by using the above forms, SDQM also provides a form to define custom requirements in SPARQL syntax.

After a data requirement has been captured by the data requirements wiki, it is recommended to approve the requirement by independent experts or an expert group. This has the purpose of resolving contradicting data requirements and to facilitate a common definition of the desired state of data. Only if the data requirements are consistent to each other, it is technically possible to reach 100% data quality (cf. Loshin, 2001, p. 198f.).

After approval the data requirements can be flagged, e.g. with the assessment checkbox which is available in all data requirement forms of SDQM. The approved data requirements are then used by the SDQMgr to produce the reports for data quality monitoring and assessment during the measurement phase. The data quality monitoring reports thereby contain information about instances that violate the defined requirements. The data quality assessment reports indicate how many instances contain violations compared to the whole data set by providing scores for each quality dimension as explained in the previous section. Figure 45 shows a data quality monitoring report that was generated based on the requirement specified in figure 44.

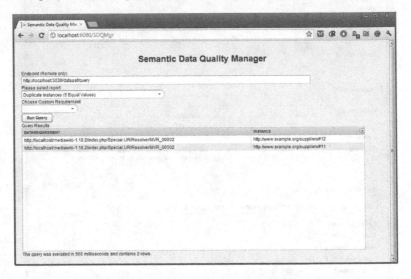

Figure 45: Data quality monitoring report of SDQMgr

Based on the generated data quality monitoring and assessment reports, a thorough analysis is required to identify the root causes of the requirement violations. The identification of the root causes is very important, because as long as the root cause is not removed, the problem may return (cf. English, 1999, pp. 80f., 286-289). The causes for requirement violations may be manifold (cf. Loshin, 2001, p. 381f.). For example programs that create data may contain errors, business process manuals may provide outdated or incorrect information, or people who capture data do not have time for quality checks. Any of these issues may lead to the production of incorrect data. Moreover, also the data requirement used for the measurement should be checked, since the requirement itself may be incomplete, outdated, or even wrong (cf. Loshin, 2001, p. 198f.). After the root causes of the requirement violations have been identified, they need to be removed to avoid the return of the data quality problem. Therefore, options for the removal of the root causes have to be identified, compared, and implemented during the improvement phase (cf. English, 1999, pp. 289-302; Wang, 1998, p. 65). Besides the removal of the root cause, it is usually also necessary to cleanse the data, i.e. to update the data that violate requirements (cf. English, 1999, pp. 77-80).

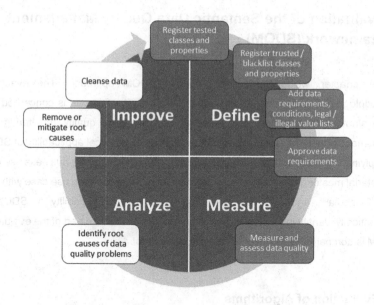

Figure 46: SDQM application procedure (based on Wang, 1998)

Figure 46 illustrates the application procedure of the SDQM framework based on the TDQM cycle by (Wang, 1998). The blue-colored process steps are fully supported by SDQM. At present, the white-colored process steps have to be performed outside of the SDQM framework. However, the identification and removal of the root causes of data requirement violations are at present predominantly manual process steps and can be supported by creativity techniques such as mind mapping, process analysis, or root cause analysis (cf. English, 1999, pp. 295-302; Loshin, 2001, pp. 381-397; Wang, 1998, p. 64f.).

9 Evaluation of the Semantic Data Quality Management Framework (SDQM)

In this chapter, we evaluate the proposed SDQM approach. The evaluation methodology of SDQM is separated into three parts. The first part is concerned with the evaluation of precision and recall of SDQM's data quality monitoring and assessment algorithms. The second part evaluates the practical applicability of SDQM by applying the framework to three different use cases, namely one business use case on material master data of a large organization, one Semantic Web use case with data from DBpedia[68], and one use case that examines the capability of SDQM to automatically identify inconsistent data requirements. In the third part of the evaluation, SDQM is compared to a conventional data quality tool.

9.1 Evaluation of Algorithms

9.1.1 Algorithm Evaluation Methodology

In this section, we will apply the notions of recall and precision from the field of Information Retrieval to data quality management and use them as indicators for the performance of our approach (cf. Batini & Scannapieco, 2006, pp. 125-127; Buckland & Gey, 1994; Raghavan et al., 1989). This is based on the idea that essentially our algorithms attempt to retrieve all requirement violations. Precision can be defined as the degree to which an information retrieval result contains relevant information (cf. Buckland & Gey, 1994, p. 12f.). It is measured via the ratio between true positives (TP) and the sum of true positives (TP) and false positives (FP) (Batini & Scannapieco, 2006, p. 126). True positives are thereby instances that are correctly identified to be relevant (Batini & Scannapieco, 2006, p. 125f.). False positives are relevant instances that were incorrectly identified to be relevant (Batini & Scannapieco, 2006, p. 125f.). In our case, true positives are correctly identified data requirement violations and false positives are requirement violations that have not been identified.

---

[68] http://dbpedia.org

122

Hence, precision in our case measures how many of the identified data requirement violations have been identified correctly, i.e. really violate a data requirement (Batini & Scannapieco, 2006, p. 126).

$$Precision = \frac{TP}{TP + FP}$$

Recall is a measure that represents the ratio between the retrieved relevant instances and all relevant instances (cf. Buckland & Gey, 1994, p. 12). In our case, the equivalent is the number of correctly identified requirement violations (TP) and all requirement violations including false negatives (FN), i.e. requirement violations that have not been identified by the algorithms. Recall, therefore, measures how many data requirement violations have been identified by the algorithm compared to the whole population of data requirements violations (cf. Batini & Scannapieco, 2006, pp. 125-127).

$$Recall = \frac{TP}{TP + FN}$$

Since our algorithms attempt to identify all data quality problems related to a certain data requirement, the scores for precision and recall should be equal to one in the ideal case.

9.1.2 Application Procedure

In order to identify the required variables correctly, we created a small test data set with product and location data that contains all instance-related single-source data quality problem types as listed in table 5 of section 3.6.1. Additionally, we created 49 self-defined data requirements for the data, such as "Every instance of class Location must have a ZIP code." The full set of rules that were used to evaluate SDQM's algorithms can be found in appendix B. The full test data set including the reference data that was used in the evaluation can be found in appendix C. All requirement violations in the test data set were known, so that we were able to exactly identify all false positives and false negatives. In sum, we tested all 64 algorithms of SDQM for data quality monitoring and data quality assessment.

9.1.3 Results

As expected all tested algorithms returned perfect results for precision and recall. These perfect results are necessary before we apply the algorithms to real data, in order to make sure that they are able to identify all types of data quality problems. It must be stressed that the queries related to "Functional Dependency Reference Rules" return instances that miss one or more dependent values or properties as requirement violations, i.e. true positives, although the correct value may be located in a different attribute. E.g. the record with LOCID equal to 3 with city value "Nantes" and state value "France" returned as true positive since the correct dependent value "France" was not located in the property country, but located in the wrong property state. A full list of the algorithm evaluation results of SDQM can be found in appendices D and E. In summary, the evaluation results show that SDQM's algorithms are able to identify data requirement violations and assess the state of data quality correctly.

9.2 Use Case 1: Evaluation of Material Master Data

The first use case deals with a real business scenario that is concerned with the quality of master data of an information system. According to ISO 8000-102:2009 master data is defined as "data held by an organization that describes the entities that are both independent and fundamental for that organization and that it needs to reference in order to perform its transactions" (ISO, 2009). Hence, correct and complete master data is essential for the execution of business processes and, therefore, the organizational success. This first use case shall illustrate how the SDQM framework can be applied for master data quality management in real-world settings. We thereby evaluate SDQM especially regarding the following criteria:

- Ability of SDQM to represent the organization's data requirements
- ability to process the organization's data requirements to create data quality reports, and
- performance of SDQM's data quality reports

9.2.1 Scenario

A large public organization uses an ERP system to support its logistic processes. The system contains material master data as a source for process-relevant information that is used for process execution. The system uses the material master data to automate tasks such as the placement of purchase orders, storage management, or to inform people, e.g. about appropriate handling of materials. In order to avoid process failures, it is necessary to assure that the master data provided by the ERP system is of sufficient quality. Therefore, the organization seeks for a system that identifies data quality problems, i.e. instances with data that violate the organization's requirements, and that allows the quick evaluation of the overall quality state of data items.

9.2.2 Setup and Application Procedure of SDQM

The SDQM framework is used in the context of the above scenario to (1) represent data requirements, (2) identify requirement violations, and (3) evaluate the quality state of data items of the data source. Therefore, SDQM was set up with the data of the organization on a local server as explained in section 8.1. The server used is an AMD Athlon II X4 630 Processor 2.80 GHz with 8 GB RAM on a Windows 7 64bit operating system. The Fuseki server thereby received 4,600 megabyte of the RAM and the SDQMgr 1,536 megabyte of RAM. The capturing of data requirements and the execution of data quality measurement reports was performed as described in section 8.2. The organization provided 19 data requirements for their general material master data. The source data was stored in single table of a relational database. We converted the data into an N-Triples file via D2RQ[69] and imported the N-Triples file into the triplestore via the user interface of the Fuseki server[70]. In the relational database, the source table had 3.3 million records. Together with the data requirements the triplestore contained 53,077,730 triples. Before executing SDQM's reports, the hardware setup was optimized by comparing the execution time of a simple SPARQL query that counts all triples of the Jena TDB published by the Fuseki server. In the mentioned configuration, the COUNT query performed best and executed within 41,713 milliseconds. Table 20 shows the rules that have been collected from experts

---

[69] http://d2rq.org/ (Last accessed on 30.08.2014)
[70] http://jena.apache.org/documentation/serving_data/ (Last accessed on 30.08.2014)

of the organization and were applied on their material data to identify data quality problems.

Table 20: Data requirements that were collected and applied for use case 1[71]

Report	Rule
Missing values and properties (5 property requirements)	The following fields must have a value for all materials: - Lab/Office - Material group - Base unit of measure - Manufacturer part number - Material type
Conditional missing values and properties (1 requirement)	If the material type is set for non-valuated materials, then the field "Installation type" must always have a value.
Syntax violations (1 property requirement)	The field "Internal material number" must always have 9 digits.
Illegal values (Legal value rules) (6 property requirements)	The following fields can only obtain specific values: - Installation type - External material group - Material condition management - Serial number profile - Lab/Office - Material type
Out of range values (1 property requirement)	The field "Standard price" must not be lower than 0.02 € and not higher than 999,999,999.00 €.
Duplicate instances (3 equal values) (1 duplicate instance requirement)	If the material text, the manufacturer part number and the standard price have the same value for two or more instances, then the instances are potential duplicates.
Functional dependent value rule (4 requirements)	Furniture materials must have a specific installation type value. Certain material types are always in ownership of a specific office. Materials with a specific external material group are always in ownership of a specific office. Materials with a certain installation type must always have a price greater than 4,999.00 €.

---

[71] The rules are described on an abstract level in order to assure the anonymity of the organization.

9.2.3 Results and Findings

As shown in table 20, the data requirements delivered by the organization covered syntax rules, legal value rules, duplicate instance rules, property completeness rules, legal value range rules, and functional dependency rules. The standard forms of SDQM's data requirements wiki were expressive enough to cover all of the organization's data requirements. All data requirements were represented in the data requirements wiki and could be processed by the SDQMgr to generate reports about requirements violations and reports that reflect the overall quality state of the organization's data items. Figure 47 shows the data quality monitoring report with instances that violate a legal value range requirement of a certain property.

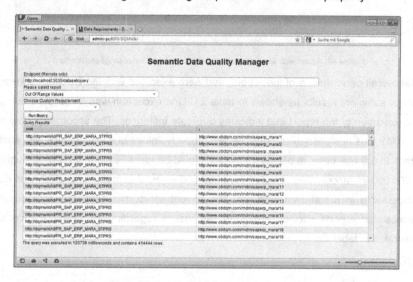

Figure 47: Report with legal value range violations

Figure 48 shows the accordant data quality assessment report which contains a score about the overall semantic accuracy of the property. The score has been computed based on the legal value range requirement which contains an upper and lower legal value for the property.

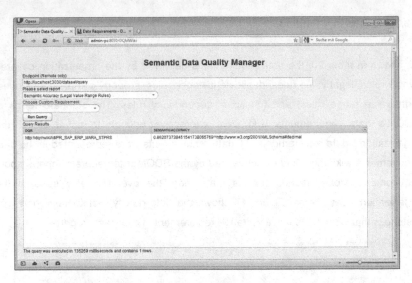

Figure 48: Report with semantic accuracy score based on value range requirement

The overall performance of the reports that were executed with the SDQMgr showed mostly sufficient results as shown in table 21. One exception was discovered during the execution of the report that indicates duplicate instances. The accordant query of SDQMgr was designed to compare certain property values of each instance with each other. In our use case, duplicate instances should be identified in a class with roughly 3,000,000 instances. This resulted in $(3,000,000 - 1)^2 / 2$ comparisons which was not processable in a sufficient time with the current setup. However, the data quality assessment reports showed also sufficient results regarding their performance as illustrated in table 22.

Table 21: Evaluation results of SDQMgr's data quality monitoring reports (use case 1)

Report	Result	Execution Time (in min:sec.ms)
Missing Values and Properties (5 requirements)	311,821 rows	10:02.901
Conditional Missing Values and Properties (1 requirement)	56 rows	01:43.038
Syntax violations (1 requirement)	7 rows	03:54.431
Illegal Values (Legal Value Rules) (6 requirements)	23,724 rows	18:35.353
Out of Range Values (1 requirement)	414,444 rows	02:00.738
Duplicate Instances (3 Equal Values) (1 duplicate instance requirement)	Did not finish	Did not finish
Functional Dependent Value Rule (4 requirements)	71 rows	02:02.784

Table 22: Evaluation results of SDQMgr's data quality assessment reports (use case 1)

Report	Result	Execution Time (in min:sec.ms)
Completeness (5 requirements)	Property 1: 100 % Property 2: 99,05 % Property 3: 93,05 % Property 4: 97,53 % Property 5: 100 %	15:59.841
Conditional Completeness (1 requirement)	Property 6: 99,93 %	01:50.137
Syntactic Accuracy (Syntax Rules) (1 requirement)	Property 7: 99,99 %	02:08.727
Syntactic Accuracy (Legal Value Rules) (6 requirements)	Property 8: 99,95 % Property 9: 100 % Property 6: 99,99 % Property 4: 99,97 % Property 10: 99,28 % Property 5: 100 %	27:18.928
Semantic Accuracy (Legal Value Range Rules) (1 requirement)	Property 11: 86,20 %	03:04.716
Semantic Accuracy FDV (1 Condition) (4 requirements)	FDV 1: 100 % FDV 2: 100 % FDV 3: 99,96 % FDV 4: 99,77 %	02:54.406

In summary, the evaluation results show that SDQM is basically capable to be used for quality management of master data in real-world business settings. However, there is room for improvement in several areas. In particular, future work on SDQM should regard the following options to increase performance:

- Jena's in-memory technology could be used to load the whole Jena TDB of SDQM into the computer's main memory before execution of SDQMgr's reports.
- The execution of queries and generation of data quality reports could be decoupled from each other. E.g. the queries could be executed at night and the reports would only access a cached query result.
- The CPU and main memory capacity could be extended to provide more resources for SDQM's applications.
- An authorization system could be added that requires user's login before the execution of data quality reports to avoid inappropriate use.

Moreover, SDQM's mechanisms for representing and processing duplicate instance requirements should be optimized to be applicable to larger data sets, e.g. by adapting duplicate detection algorithms as proposed in (Monge & Elkan, 1997) or (Herschel et al., 2011). For example the performance of SDQM's duplicate checking algorithm can be improved by adjusting the algorithm to search for duplicates only in a sorted neighborhood (Bitton & DeWitt, 1983) or by building clusters based on the transitivity of the "isDuplicateOf" relationship and thereby avoiding unnecessary comparisons (Monge & Elkan, 1997).

Despite the successful application of SDQM in this use case, it must be stressed that this is only a first step to prove SDQM's practical applicability. A longer practical application of SDQM in a realistic business setting would be needed to evaluate the strengths and weaknesses of SDQM with higher precision. For example the amount of data requirements will most likely increase over time and easily exceed the number of data requirements as applied in this use case. Furthermore, more complex functional dependencies may exist that may not be represented with the standard forms of SDQM.

9.3 Use Case 2: Evaluation of Data from DBpedia

The second use case attempts to investigate the applicability of SDQM for tasks related to data quality in Semantic Web scenarios. As for the evaluation, we chose DBpedia (Bizer, Lehmann, et al., 2009), a publicly available Semantic Web data source that contains structured information from Wikipedia. As DBpedia data stems from the open environment of Wikipedia where anyone can edit content, it raises new challenges for a data quality management tool especially regarding the heterogeneity of data and data requirements.

9.3.1 Scenario

Wikipedia is a public encyclopedia that can be edited by anyone who has access to the internet (cf. Voss, 2005, p. 1). As of June 2012 the English Wikipedia contains over 3.9 million articles about persons, locations, movies, species, and many other things[72]. The DBpedia project extracts the structured part of Wikipedia's articles regularly and publishes the data in the Semantic Web (cf. Kobilarov, Bizer, et al., 2009, p. 35f.) where it can be used by anyone for multiple different purposes. Due to the amount of data, it is not feasible to identify data quality problems manually. Thus, means are required to efficiently identify data quality problems and to evaluate the quality state of DBpedia's data items for the following purposes:

- Administrators of DBpedia and Wikipedia may want to efficiently identify vandalism caused by the openness of Wikipedia.
- Data consumers may want to evaluate the quality state of certain parts of DBpedia before relying on it.

In the following, we evaluate whether SDQM may help in these tasks.

---

[72] http://en.wikipedia.org/wiki/Main_Page (Last accessed on June 10th 2012)

9.3.2 Specialties of Semantic Web Scenarios

Data quality tasks in open environments such as the Semantic Web underlie different conditions than data quality management tasks of information systems in closed settings. Since data can be edited and used by anyone, the degree of heterogeneity is much larger in open settings than in closed settings (cf. Batini & Scannapieco, 2006, p. 15; Bizer, 2007, p. 44). Heterogeneity thereby does not only reflect on data, but also on data requirements due to different subjective preferences and different use cases, in which the data is used (Bizer & Cyganiak, 2009, p. 2). Hence, the definition of the characteristics of high quality data may be much more contrary in open settings, since it is more difficult to achieve agreement in a large and diverse environment such as the Web. In consequence, the goal of data quality management tasks is usually not primarily the correction of data according to specific requirements of single users. A consensual agreement would have to be first established about a data requirement before requirement violations can be corrected in the data source. Due to heterogeneous world views and ways of expression, it is not realistic to satisfy everyone's requirements.

9.3.3 Setup and Application Procedure

First of all, we downloaded the DBpedia ontology, the ontology infobox types, the property data including the specific properties, and the titles data which are all available at http://dbpedia.org/Downloads37. The downloaded data sets were extracted from the English Wikipedia in July 22nd 2011 and contain 35,823,373 million triples in summary. The data was loaded into SDQM's triplestore. We thereby used the same hardware configuration as in use case one. We also again used the application procedure as describe in figure 46 to create the requirement metadata for the data quality management tasks. Since (to the best of our knowledge) there is currently no community that establishes agreement among data requirements in Web environments such as DBpedia, we created our own subjective data requirements. It must be stressed that, therefore, the ability of SDQM to represent data requirements cannot be fully evaluated. However, this second use case rather focuses on collecting first evidence for the applicability of SDQM in Semantic Web environments. Table 23 lists the assumed data requirements for this use case.

Table 23: Assumed data requirements of use case 2

No.	Requirement Description
1	The property http://dbpedia.org/ontology/gender can only obtain the values http://dbpedia.org/resource/Female and http://dbpedia.org/resource/Male.
2	The property http://dbpedia.org/ontology/populationTotal can only obtain values between 0 and 7,000,000,000.
3	The property http://dbpedia.org/ontology/populationTotal can only obtain numeric values.
4	The property http://dbpedia.org/ontology/populationTotal should exist in all instances of the class http://dbpedia.org/ontology/PopulatedPlace.
5	The property http://www.w3.org/2003/01/geo/wgs84_pos#long must exist in all instances of class http://dbpedia.org/ontology/Place.
6	The property http://www.w3.org/2003/01/geo/wgs84_pos#long must have a specific syntax (Regular expression: "^(\-?\d+(\.\d+)?)").
7	The property http://www.w3.org/2003/01/geo/wgs84_pos#lat must exist in all instances of class http://dbpedia.org/ontology/Place.
8	The property http://www.w3.org/2003/01/geo/wgs84_pos#lat must have a specific syntax (Regular expression: "^(\-?\d+(\.\d+)?)").
9	Country – Capital combinations in DBpedia must match the country capital combinations of Geonames.

We focused on data requirements relevant for data usage of data from the DBpedia classes dbo:Place[73], dbo:PopulatedPlace[74], dbo:Country[75], and dbo:Person[76]. It must be stressed that the data requirements as listed above are the

---

[73] http://dbpedia.org/ontology/Place
[74] http://dbpedia.org/ontology/PopulatedPlace
[75] http://dbpedia.org/ontology/Country
[76] http://dbpedia.org/ontology/Person

subjective requirements of the author and do not necessarily represent a commonly accepted understanding of high-quality data in DBpedia.

9.3.4 Results and Findings

Our analyses identified several requirement violations. E.g. requirement no. 1 revealed that there are eight other values for the property http://dbpedia.org/ontology/gender in instances of the class http://dbpedia.org/ontology/Person besides "Male" and "Female" in the English Wikipedia as of July 2011, namely "Man", "Nerd", "Cylon (Battlestar Galactica)", "Elves (Shannara)", "Puppet", "Sex", and "Pantomime horse". Figure 49 shows the results as identified by the SDQMgr.

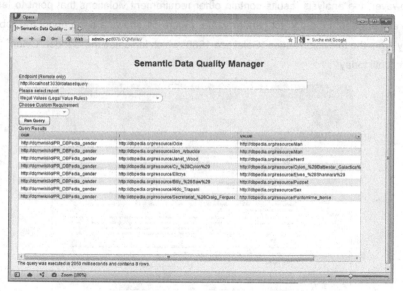

Figure 49: Result of legal value requirement analysis in DBpedia

An additional random check confirmed the usage of these values in the English version of Wikipedia. Figure 50 reveals that the Wikipedia page of the television character "Janet Wood" has been subject to assignment of the value "Nerd" as gender. In the meanwhile the value for gender has been changed by the Wikipedia community to "Female". This reflects agreement to the author's understanding of legal values for the properties representing the gender of a person.

```
{{Infobox character
| name      = Janet Wood
|image      = [[Image:Janet Wood 1982.png|220px]]
| caption   = Joyce DeWitt as Janet Wood
| first     = "A Man About the House"
| last      = "Friends and Lovers"
| nickname  =
| alias     =
| species   =
| gender    = [[Nerd|Female]]
| occupation = Florist, Aerobics instructor
| title     =
| family    = Roland Wood (father)<br>Ruth Wood (mother)<br>Jenny Wood (sister)<br>unnamed brother
| children  =
| relatives =
| portrayer = [[Joyce DeWitt]]
| creator   =
}}
```

Figure 50: Infobox source code of Wikipedia page "Janet Wood" as of June 27, 2011

However, the analysis results contain other requirement violations that point to less agreement about the correct gender value. Figure 51 shows a page about the robot "Cy" from the television series "Galactica 1980" which indicates the Gender "Cylon" for "Cy" until today[77].

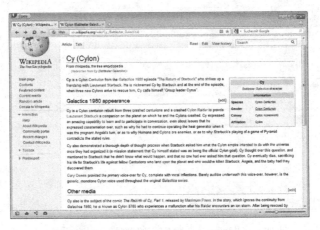

Figure 51: Wikipedia page "Cy (Cyclon)" as of June 10, 2012

To the best of our knowledge, there is no commonly accepted truth about the real gender of Cy. Therefore, the gender "Cylon" may be seen as valid. However, from our subjective perspective it is not harmful to regard "Cylon" as invalid value for representation of a gender. But most likely we are not able to change the value for "Cy" permanently to "Male" in Wikipedia without convincing the community. This example

---

[77] Today in this context equals June 10th 2012.

emphasizes the special problems related to data quality management in open environments such as the Web.

Moreover, we were able to detect obviously incorrect values for the property http://dbpedia.org/ontology/populationTotal. We found 47 instances of the class http://dbpedia.org/ontology/Place which contain a population value greater than 7,000,000,000. Figure 52 shows SDQMgr's report on out of range violations according to our data requirement No.2 of table 23.

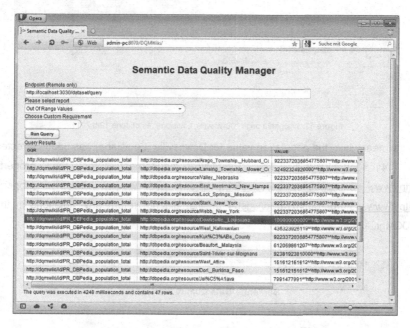

Figure 52: Out of range values for property "population" in DBpedia

The highlighted row in the result table shows that "Downsville Louisiana" has a population value of "100,000,000,000". The accordant Wikipedia page from June 19th 2011 confirms this result as illustrated in figure 53.

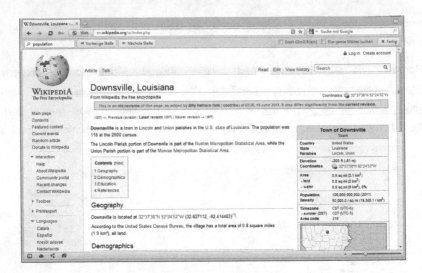

Figure 53: Wikipedia page "Downsville, Louisiana" as of June 19th 2011

In the meanwhile, the population value for Downsville (Louisiana) has been corrected to 141 inhabitants[78]. The syntactic requirements for the property http://www.w3.org/2003/01/geo/wgs84_pos#long and the property http://www.w3.org/2003/01/geo/wgs84_pos#lat did not return any violations in the SDQMgr.

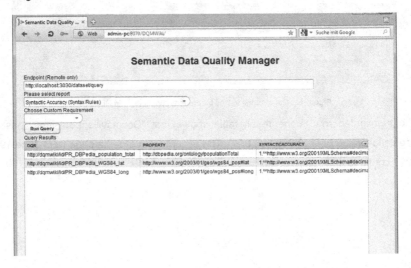

Figure 54: Data quality assessment report displaying syntactic accuracy results

---

[78] http://en.wikipedia.org/wiki/Downsville,_Louisiana (Last accessed on June 10th 2011)

Moreover, we generated data quality assessment reports to each of the requirements which are shown in table 24.

Table 24: SDQMgr's data quality assessment results on DBpedia

Report	Result	Execution Time (min:sec.ms)
Completeness (Requirement no. 4, 5, 7)	Population total: 61,21 % Latitude: 65,79 % Longitude: 65,79 %	01:27.221
Syntactic Accuracy (syntax rules) (Requirement no. 3, 6, 8)	Population total: 100 % Latitude: 100 % Longitude: 100 %	01:02.057
Syntactic Accuracy (legal value rules) (Requirement no. 1)	Gender: 99,99 %	00:47.565
Semantic Accuracy (out of range rules) (Requirement no. 2)	Population: 99,98 %	00:14.773
Semantic Accuracy (functional dependency reference rule) (Requirement no. 9)	Country Capital Combinations (Variant 1: Class Country): 0,07 % Country Capital Combinations (Variant 2: Class CurrentCountry): 46,22 %	00:06.100 00:01.701

It must be stressed that the interpretation of the above results must be performed very carefully. For example the analysis results show that DBpedia and, therefore, most likely also Wikipedia provides data on population, latitude, and longitude for almost two thirds of the documented places or populated places respectively. This does not mean that it makes sense to provide such data for all of Wikipedia's places and populated places, since these high level classes may combine different concepts. For example, the data quality monitoring report with missing latitude and longitude values contains a lot of rivers which do not have specific latitude and longitude values. Moreover, we identified almost perfect results regarding our syntactic requirements except for the gender values that were mentioned earlier. The semantic accuracy of the population values that were tested with help of a legal value range (requirement no. 2) is also on a very high level. The 0.02 % requirement violations are all caused by population values beyond 7,000,000,000 which have partly already been removed in Wikipedia as shown earlier. Finally, we tested country related data of DBpedia against Geonames[79], a publicly available data source for geographic data. We thereby downloaded the country info data of Geonames[80] as of June10th 2012 which contains information about 252 countries, such as population, capital, currency, format of postal codes, etc. The Geonames data was converted to be matched against data from DBpedia's `dbo:Country` class as trusted reference to check valid combinations of country names and its capital cities. The first run showed insufficient results as only 0.07 % of DBpedia's country data matched with the data in Geonames. One of the major reasons for this poor result was the fact that DBpedia represents current and historic countries while Geonames only represents current countries. Thus, we adjusted our data requirement by creating a new class `CurrentCountries` that contains all instances of DBpedia without a property value for `dbpedia-owl:dissolutionDate` or `dbpedia-owl:dissolutionYear`. In consequence, the semantic accuracy score raised up to 46.22 %. The remaining requirement violations are in majority caused by different naming, e.g. "Bogota" versus "Bogotá" or "China" versus "People's Republic of China". But besides these heterogeneities, there are also real errors. For example, DBpedia contains a triple that says that "La Paz" is the capital of "Bolivia". In fact, "Sucre" is the constitutional capital of Bolivia, while "La Paz" is only the seat of government. However, in cases where the seat of government is also regarded as capital, the combination "La Paz" and "Bolivia" would have to be added to the trusted reference.

In summary, SDQM indicates that it can be used in Semantic Web environments, such as DBpedia, (1) to spot potential data quality problems according to one's requirements

---

[79] http://www.geonames.org (Last accessed on June 2nd 2011)
[80] Available at http://download.geonames.org/export/dump/countryInfo.txt (Last accessed on June 10th 2011)

and (2) serve data consumers to quickly analyze a Semantic Web data source regarding their own quality perception. Moreover, the performance of SDQM showed promising results. But we also discovered several problems which have to be considered when using SDQM in Semantic Web settings:

- Agreement about data requirements is much harder to achieve in Web environments than in closed settings due to a greater heterogeneity of world views.

- Heterogeneity and different world views may lead to inconsistent data requirements. E.g. one may define "Cylon" as valid value for gender, while another person defines "Cylon" as invalid value for gender.

- Correction of an open data source, such as Wikipedia, usually requires agreement from the community to persist.

- Heterogeneity makes the definition of data requirements more complicated, since it raises the amount of acceptable states of values.

- The classes of the DBpedia ontology only barely distinguish between real entities and fictitious entities. This again complicates the definition of data requirements. For example the robot "Cy" from the television series "Battlestar Galactica" is considered as a person in DBpedia and, therefore, should have a gender.

- The classes of the DBpedia ontology do not distinguish between historic and currently existing entities. For example the German Democratic Republic is member of the class "Populated Place" in DBpedia.

As part of future work, SDQM could be deployed to the Web to generate commonly accepted data requirements by the Semantic Web community. Therefore, it can efficiently support data quality management on Web-scale and the improvement of Semantic Web data.

9.4 Use Case 3: Consistency Checks Among Data Requirements

In this use case, we intend to demonstrate how SDQM facilitates the automated identification of inconsistent data requirements.

9.4.1 Scenario

A large organization that performs data quality management has many data requirements which are used to improve data quality. The organization uses SDQM. The organization's data requirements have been previously represented via the data requirements wiki of SDQM. The organization seeks for an efficient automatic way to identify conflicting data requirements.

9.4.2 Application Procedure

In SDQM, all data requirements are represented in a common structure that is provided by the DQM vocabulary. The data requirements are themselves represented as data in RDF format. Therefore, we can use standard SPARQL queries to manage the quality of data requirements. In general, there are two different types of inconsistencies between data requirements, namely (1) duplicate, but consistent requirements, and (2) contradicting requirements (cf. Oliveira, Rodrigues, & Henriques, 2005, p. 8). Duplicate requirements typically refer to the same schema elements, i.e. classes and properties, which are tested for requirement violations. Contradicting requirements are two or more requirements about the same schema elements that oppose each other and, therefore, cannot be applied at the same time. In the following, we will provide some example queries that are based on fictitious data requirements. The data requirements are based on the test data with information about suppliers. The examples are separated according to the different types of data requirements, since they require different application procedures.

SDQM's property requirements can in general not become inconsistent due to the enforced naming convention of wiki pages in the data requirements wiki. By convention the property requirement title in the wiki is concatenated from the class and property name. Hence, if the tested class and property is only registered under one name in the data requirements wiki, it will not be possible to create duplicate property requirements. However, the naming convention may be modified to create duplicate requirements for the same property if the use case required capturing heterogeneous and potentially inconsistent requirements. In such cases, the same property may be associated to multiple different requirements. Due to the annotation of each requirement with the "testedClass" and "testedProperty" properties and their representation in RDF, it is possible to identify duplicate requirements and duplicate inconsistent requirements with standard SPARQL queries. To prove this, we created three property requirements for the property http://www.example.org/suppliers#supplierID. The first property requirement "PR Organization FOO Supplier ID" defines that unique values are required for this property in all instances of the class http://www.w3.org/2006/vcard/ns#Organization. The second property requirement "PR Organization EXAMPLE Supplier ID" refers to the same class and property, but does not define that unique values are required. Thus, the property requirement "PR Organization EXAMPLE Supplier ID" is not consistent with the original requirement "PR Organization FOO Supplier ID". The third property requirement "PR Organization Supplier ID" consistently defines that unique values are required for this property in all instances of the class http://www.w3.org/2006/vcard/ns#Organization. All of the three requirements make statements about the same tested class and property, but use different representations of the property http://www.example.org/suppliers#supplierID, since the same property has been registered with three different names in the data requirements wiki. Figure 55 shows a generic SPARQL query that identifies duplicate property requirements and its result based on our test data.

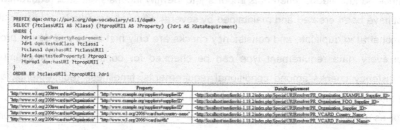

Figure 55: SPARQL query and result displaying duplicate property requirements

In general, it is possible to identify only such duplicate requirements that are inconsistent with each other. Figure 56 shows a SPARQL query and its result that can be used to identify inconsistent unique value rules, in case the requirements have been represented in the DQM vocabulary.

```
PREFIX dqm:<http://purl.org/dqm-vocabulary/v1.1/dqm#>
SELECT (?dr1 AS ?UniqueValueRequirement) (?dr2 AS ?InconsistentRequirement)
WHERE{
?dr1 a dqm:UniqueValueRule .
?dr1 dqm:testedClass ?class1 .
?class1 dqm:hasURI ?class1URI .
?dr1 dqm:testedProperty1 ?prop1 .
?prop1 dqm:hasURI ?prop1URI .
OPTIONAL{
    ?dr2 a dqm:PropertyRequirement .
    ?dr2 dqm:testedClass ?class2 .
    ?class2 dqm:hasURI ?class2URI .
    ?dr2 dqm:testedProperty1 ?prop2 .
    ?prop2 dqm:hasURI ?prop2URI .
    FILTER(str(?prop1URI) = str(?prop2URI) && str(?class1URI) = str(?class2URI) && ?dr1 != ?dr2)
    MINUS{
        ?dr2 a dqm:UniqueValueRule
    }
}
FILTER(bound(?prop2URI))
}
```

UniqueValueRequirement	InconsistentRequirement
<http://localhost/mediawiki-1.18.2/index.php/Special:URIResolver:PR_Organization_FOO_Supplier_ID>	<http://localhost/mediawiki-1.18.2/index.php/Special:URIResolver:PR_Organization_EXAMPLE_Supplier_ID>
<http://localhost/mediawiki-1.18.2/index.php/Special:URIResolver:PR_Organization_Supplier_ID>	<http://localhost/mediawiki-1.18.2/index.php/Special:URIResolver:PR_Organization_EXAMPLE_Supplier_ID>

Figure 56: SPARQL query for identification of inconsistent property requirements

9.4.3 Summary

The above queries are domain independent and can be reused to identify inconsistencies among unique value requirements in a data quality management system that represents its data requirements with the DQM vocabulary. Therefore, data quality management with SDQM is especially useful in large environments with distributed knowledge where it is important to identify inconsistent data requirements that have been created and maintained by several different individuals. However, the demonstrated duplicate and consistency checks are only first steps and do not prove that every data requirement type can be checked for consistency. For example, consistency checks among conditional requirements, timeliness requirements, and functional dependency reference rules have not been evaluated, yet. Moreover, as soon as reasoning is enabled, the identification of duplicates and conflicts may become more complex. Further research is needed in this area, to provide reliable information about the scope of consistency checks that is currently possible with SDQM. But the current results based on this evaluation are a promising first approach that may probably be extendable to other data requirement types.

9.5 Comparison with Talend OS for Data Quality

In this section, we compare SDQM with Talend Open Studio for Data Quality (Talend OS for Data Quality), a conventional data quality software tool from the software company Talend[81]. Talend OS for Data Quality can be used for analyzing the quality of data. It is open-source software that is freely available for download. The comparison is focused on the following issues:

- Representation of data requirements
- consistency checks among data requirements
- data quality monitoring and assessment reporting, and
- performance of data quality analyses

It must be stressed that Talend OS for Data Quality offers many more features, e.g. in the area of data profiling, that are beyond the scope of SDQM and, therefore, not subject of this comparison.

9.5.1 Representation and Management of Data Requirements

In Talend OS for Data Quality, data requirements can be represented with so called "SQL business rules". In order to represent a data requirement with Talend OS for Data Quality, the following three high-level steps are required (cf. Talend, 2012, p. 140ff.):

(1) Create SQL business rule
(2) Create new analysis
(3) Run analysis

As the name implies, SQL business rules are based on the relational query language SQL. The data requirement is thereby represented in SQL code which is later automatically embedded into the WHERE clause of an SQL query. Figure 57 shows an SQL business rule for the identification of missing values in the attribute "city".

---

[81] http://www.talend.com (Last accessed on June 2nd 2012)

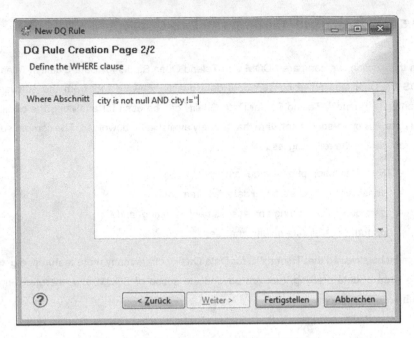

Figure 57: SQL business rule in Talend OS for Data Quality

After the data requirements have been represented as SQL business rules, they have to be attached to a so called analysis. Therefore, a new business analysis object has to be created in Talend OS for Data Quality. The tool provides a wizard for the creation of the analysis object in which the relevant table and the relevant SQL business rules can be chosen from a list. The latter is shown in figure 58. Based on these inputs the analysis can be run to identify requirement violations.

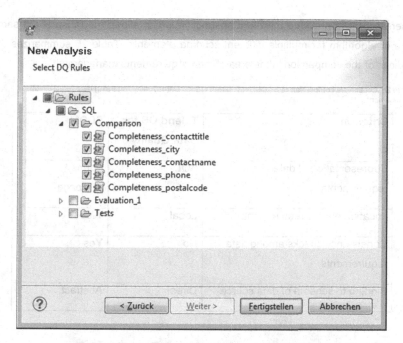

Figure 58: Selecting SQL business rules in Talend OS for Data Quality

In the area of data requirements management, there are three major differences between Talend OS for Data Quality and SDQM. The first difference lies in the way of representing data requirements. Talend OS for Data Quality uses plain SQL coding, while SDQM uses forms to capture data requirements which are automatically converted into RDF data. Other than the users of Talend OS for Data Quality, SDQM's users do not have to know any query language to create data requirements, since they just have to fill in wiki-based forms. The second difference is the location in which the data requirements are created and maintained. In Talend OS for Data Quality data requirements are typically created and maintained on the client of the software installation. Since SDQM uses the data requirements wiki to manage data requirements, they can be created and maintained at Web scale by anyone who has sufficient access rights. Lastly, due to the representation of the data requirements in RDF, it is possible to check consistency among data requirements with SDQM by using standard SPARQL queries. To the best of our knowledge, this is not possible with the data requirements represented in Talend OS for Data Quality, since the requirements are represented in plain SQL. Finally, in Talend OS for Data Quality the data requirements are hard-wired to the actual schema elements of the data source, whereas SDQM provides a level of abstraction which allows the reuse of the same type of algorithm for multiple different schema elements. Table 25 summarizes the findings of the comparison in the area of data requirements management.

Table 25: Qualitative comparison of SDQM and Talend OS for Data Quality regarding data requirements management

Criterion	Talend OS for Data Quality	SDQM
Representation of data requirements	SQL	Forms / Wikipage
Location of data requirements	Local	Web
Consistency checks among data requirements	No	Yes
Binding to schema of data source	Direct	Abstract

9.5.2 Data Quality Monitoring and Assessment Reporting

In this section, we compare the data quality reporting capabilities of Talend OS for Data Quality and SDQM. SDQM provides separate reports for data quality monitoring, i.e. the identification of instances with requirements violations, and for data quality assessment, i.e. the computation of dimensional quality scores. In Talend OS for Data Quality, these reports are combined. After data requirements have been represented and integrated into an analysis object, the execution process of Talend OS for Data Quality first computes a score which indicates the percentage to which the requirement has been met. Figure 59 shows such a report in which the completeness scores for five different attributes are shown. Based on this assessment report, it is possible to drill down to the tuples that violate data requirements via the context menu in the red box as shown in figure 59.

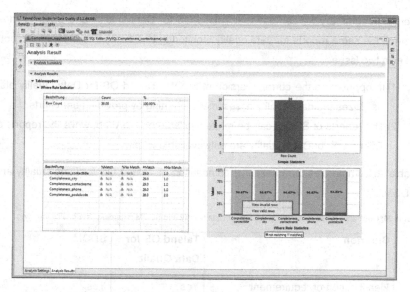

Figure 59: Data quality assessment report in Talend OS for Data Quality

When hitting the menu option "View invalid rows", an SQL query is automatically executed which retrieves the tuples violating the requirements. Figure 60 shows the result of such a query which can be viewed as the data quality monitoring reports of Talend OS for Data Quality.

Figure 60: Data quality monitoring report of Talend OS for Data Quality

149

Hence, in summary we can say that Talend OS for Data Quality and SDQM almost provide the same reports for data quality monitoring and assessment. However, both differ in two issues:

(1) In opposite to the current version of SDQM, Talend OS for Data Quality also visualizes the data quality assessment reporting by providing bar charts.
(2) The reports of SDQM can be made available on the Web, while the reports of Talend OS for Data Quality are only available locally.

Table 26 summarizes the qualitative comparison of Talend OS for Data Quality and SDQM.

Table 26: Qualitative comparison of Talend OS for Data Quality and SDQM regarding data quality reporting

Criterion	Talend OS for Data Quality	SDQM
Identification of requirement violations	Yes	Yes
Automated computation of data quality scores	Yes	Yes
Graphical visualization of data quality scores	Yes	No
Availability of reports	Local	Web-scale

Moreover, we compared the performance of a DQM architecture with Talend OS for Data Quality and our SDQM architecture. The Talend OS for Data Quality architecture uses a 64bit MySQL database and 4,600 megabytes buffer size. Moreover, we assigned 1,536 megabytes of main memory to Talend OS for Data Quality. This shall represent a similar configuration as used in use case one for the SDQM architecture. For the evaluation of the performance we used the same data corpus for both architectures with one exception: the Talend architecture processed the data in relational format, while SDQM processed it in the triple structure. We executed the same data requirements and created data quality assessment reports in both cases. The results of the performance analysis are listed in table 27.

The performance analysis shows that SDQM still has a significant performance drawback compared to conventional DQM architectures. But it must be stressed that SDQM is an early prototype, while the conventional DQM architecture with Talend OS for Data Quality and MySQL has already matured through practical experience over several years. However, we expect that with the optimization of SDQMgr's queries and with increasing maturity of triplestores the performance gap between both architectures will decrease.

Table 27: Results of performance analysis between Talend OS for Data Quality and SDQM

Report	Talend OS for Data Quality	SDQM (in mm:ss.ms)
Completeness (5 requirements)	00:23.790	15:59.841
Conditional Completeness (1 requirement)	00:07.800	01:50.137
Syntactic Accuracy (Syntax Rules) (1 requirement)	00:09.937	02:08.727
Syntactic Accuracy (Legal Value Rules) (6 requirements)	00:29.937	27:18.928
Semantic Accuracy (Legal Value Range Rules) (1 requirement)	00:07.504	03:04.716
Semantic Accuracy FDV (1 Condition) (4 requirements)	00:32.402	02:14.406

9.5.3 Summary

In summary, we can say that both architectures, the SDQM architecture and the conventional DQM architecture, have strengths and weaknesses and none of the architectures is superior in general. The strengths of SDQM lie in data requirements management. While Talend OS for Data Quality requires SQL knowledge to create data requirements, SDQM only requires users to fill in wiki-based forms which is much less time consuming and more convenient for business experts who often do not have programming skills. Also, in contrast to DQM tools based on the state-of-the-art, SDQM can identify inconsistencies among data requirements automatically. Moreover, SDQM provides a Web-based user interface for the management of data requirements which facilitates collaboration and the generation of agreement. A shared understanding of data requirements promises a more sustainable and effective improvement of data quality. A local data quality tool, such as Talend OS for Data Quality, hides data requirements in SQL code of client software which hinders the generation of a common understanding about data requirements. SDQM's data requirements are audit-proof due to its version-based storage in Semantic MediaWiki and they can be combined with other information due to the wiki architecture. A major weakness of SDQM compared to the conventional DQM architecture is currently the comparatively slow speed of execution. The current performance of SDQM is acceptable, but far away from the performance of a conventional DQM architecture. As mentioned earlier, the growing use of SDQM and the increasing maturity of triplestore technology will decrease this gap over time. Moreover, the use of Jena's in-memory features may close this gap in the future.

PART IV – Related Work

10 Related Work

This chapter summarizes research approaches in the area of ontology-based data quality management and compares the SDQM framework with such related work. Ontology-based data quality management frameworks in here are artifacts that make use of ontologies to support data quality management activities. In the following, we provide a high-level classification of the field, which is then used to organize the presentation of related work in this chapter.

10.1 High-Level Classification Schema

On a high level, we can distinguish work in the area of data quality management frameworks between (1) conventional rule-based approaches and (2) ontology-based approaches. The latter can be further distinguished into approaches that are (1) Web-oriented, i.e. aim to manage the quality of Web information, and approaches that are (2) oriented towards the management of data quality in databases of information systems (IS) that are used in closed environments. Figure 61 illustrates this high-level classification schema.

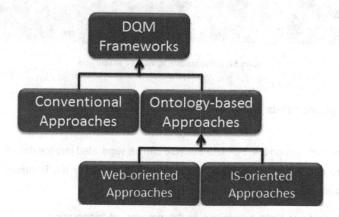

Figure 61: High-level classification of DQM frameworks

10.2 Categorization Schema

In order to provide a systematic account of existing data quality management approaches that make use of ontologies, we defined three different categories that further classify related approaches according to their application area. The categorization is based on our findings about the data lifecycle from section 3.4 and on a literature analysis of the related work. In order to classify the approaches, we try to answer the following questions:

1. For which step(s) of the data lifecycle was the approach designed?
2. Which representations of data are in the focus of the approach's data quality functionalities?
3. Which data quality tasks are supported by the approach?

Based on these questions, we defined the three categories (1) supported data lifecycle step, (2) supported data representation, and (3) supported data quality task to categorize the analyzed approaches. As illustrated in figure 62, these abstract categories are organized into several subcategories that classify common approaches. In the following, we will define each of the subcategories as applied in our analysis.

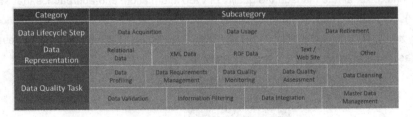

Category	Subcategory				
Data Lifecycle Step	Data Acquisition		Data Usage		Data Retirement
Data Representation	Relational Data	XML Data	RDF Data	Text / Web Site	Other
Data Quality Task	Data Profiling	Data Requirements Management	Data Quality Monitoring	Data Quality Assessment	Data Cleansing
	Data Validation	Information Filtering		Data Integration	Master Data Management

Figure 62: Categorization schema for related work

10.2.1 Supported Data Lifecycle Step

As explained in section 3.4, the data lifecycle can be separated into the data acquisition phase, the data usage phase, and the data retirement phase (cf. Redman, 1996, p. 217). Therefore, we define each of the steps as follows:

Data Acquisition: Data acquisition is the process of "generating new or retrieving existing data and storing it onto some kind of medium" (see section 3.4.1, cf. Olson, 2003, p. 44f.; Redman, 1996, pp. 219-222).

Data Usage: Data usage is the process of using data "as an information source for humans and machines in operational or decision-making processes" (see section 3.4.2, cf. Redman, 1998, p. 80f.).

Data Retirement: Data retirement is the process of deleting, deactivating or archiving data (see section 3.4.3, cf. Loshin, 2009, p. 223).

Research approaches in the area of data management usually attempt to support a specific problem of one or more data lifecycle phases. Therefore, we classify the related work according to these phases.

10.2.2 Supported Data Representation

Data quality tasks can be applied to various representations of data because data can be represented in many different formats, e.g. in proprietary formats of legacy databases, in relational database systems, in XML documents or within Web sites (cf. Bodendorf, 2006, p. 3). Therefore, different solutions may be required due to the nature of the format of the data. Our analysis, therefore, classifies the related work based on the following representations of data:

- Relational data, i.e. data that is stored in relational databases (cf. Codd, 1970),
- XML data, i.e. data that is stored in XML documents (cf. Bray et al., 2008),
- RDF data, i.e. data that is stored in RDF documents or databases that can store RDF structured data (cf. Beckett, 2004; Berners-Lee, 1998b; Sahoo et al., 2009), and
- Text / Web Site, i.e. data that is not structured, but stored on a Web site or within a text document.

Moreover, we added the category "Other" for approaches that focus on the quality of other data formats not covered by the enumerated categories, e.g. proprietary data streaming formats sent by sensors, etc.

10.2.3 Supported Data Quality Task

As outlined in section 3.5, data quality management consists of several different tasks. In order to easily find appropriate techniques, we try to classify the ontology-based approaches according to the data quality management task that they support. Specifically, the following tasks are part of the classification framework:

Data Profiling: Data profiling is the process of creating statistics about data, such as the used patterns and value distribution, the number of distinct values, the number of null values, etc. (cf. Apel et al., 2010, p. 110f.; Friedman & Bitterer, 2011, p. 3; Olson, 2003, p. 20).

Data Requirements Management: Data requirements management is the process of collecting, maintaining, and publishing data requirements (cf. Loshin, 2001, p. 197f.). Moreover, the process of the identification and resolution of conflicting data requirements may be part of data requirements management (cf. Loshin, 2001, p. 198f.).

Data Quality Monitoring: Data quality monitoring is the continuous process of monitoring the quality of data according to specified data requirements (cf. Friedman & Bitterer, 2011, p. 3; Olson, 2003, p. 20f.).

Data Quality Assessment: Data quality assessment is "the process of assigning numerical or categorical values (quality scores) to quality criteria in a given data setting" (Gertz et al., 2004, p. 129) based on previously defined measures and data requirements (cf. Ge & Helfert, 2008, p. 382).

Data Cleansing: In terms of this analysis, data cleansing encompasses the removal of errors from data by update, merge, or removal of data (cf. Friedman & Bitterer, 2011, p. 3; Rahm & Do, 2000, p. 1).

Data Validation: In the understanding of this thesis, data validation is the process of verifying the correctness of data during its creation according to previously specified requirements before it is passed to further processes (cf. Loshin, 2001, p. 54f.).

Information Filtering: Information filtering is the process of selecting and filtering relevant information from the available information according to previously defined requirements (cf. Bizer, 2007, p. 3f.).

Data Integration: Data integration is the process of "combining data residing at different sources, and providing the user with a unified view of these data." (Lenzerini, 2002, p. 233).

Master Data Management: In the understanding of this thesis, we use the category "Master Data Management" to classify approaches that are focused on the central management of master data. Management activities include the integration, harmonization, evaluation, and distribution of master data across a heterogeneous system landscape (cf. Loshin, 2009, p. 8f.). According to (ISO, 2009), master data is "data held by an organization that describes the entities that are both independent and fundamental for that organization, and that it needs to reference in order to perform its transactions" (ISO, 2009). Master data is typically used in different applications across and beyond an organization to supply business processes with information about these objects (cf. Loshin, 2009, p. 3f.). Examples of master data objects are material, customer, location, or contract (cf. ISO, 2009; Loshin, 2009, pp. 5-8).

10.3 Conventional Rule-Based Approaches

Rule-based approaches for data quality monitoring and assessment are similar to ontology-based approaches, since they aim to represent logic that is necessary for the measurement of data quality. Other than ontology-based approaches, the conventional approaches usually find alternative ways to represent and store the required logic. Since they still have some similarities to the proposed approach in this thesis, we briefly describe some related rule-based data quality management approaches in the following.

Loshin (2002) developed a framework called *GuardianIQ* that uses user-defined business rules to assess and monitor data quality. The business rules of GuardianIQ are thereby implemented automatically via SQL or Java code.

Categories: Relational Data, Data Quality Monitoring, Data Quality Assessment, Data Usage, Data Requirements Management

Hipp et al. (2007) propose an approach to measure the data quality dimension "accuracy" based on association rules. The association rules are thereby automatically derived from data via a complex outlier detection algorithm that considers confidence values.

Categories: Relational Data, Data Quality Assessment, Data Usage

More conventional rule-based approaches can be found in the *Gartner Magic Quadrant for Data Quality Tools* (Friedman & Bitterer, 2011), a yearly market analysis report about commercial software tools that support the data quality management process.

10.4 Ontology-based Approaches

In the following, related ontology-based data quality management frameworks are described. Specifically, we outline how they are related to SDQM, the artifact that has been developed in this thesis. Ontology-based data quality management approaches can be further distinguished into (1) IS-oriented approaches and (2) Web-oriented approaches. As explained in section 10.1, IS-oriented approaches are approaches that aim to improve the quality of data in IS of closed environments, while Web-oriented approaches aim to improve the quality of information in open Web environments.

10.4.1 Information System-oriented Approaches

Brüggemann et al. (Brüggemann, 2006, 2008a, 2008b; Brüggemann & Aden, 2007; Brüggemann & Grüning, 2008, 2009; Grüning, 2009) propose two major uses of ontologies for data quality management, namely: (1) the representation of functional dependencies between data values (Brüggemann, 2008b, p. 523f.; Brüggemann & Aden, 2007, p. 208) and (2) the representation of quality-relevant metadata. For the first purpose, legal and illegal attribute value combinations are defined within an ontology and used to identify incorrect value combinations in the tested data set (cf. Brüggemann & Aden, 2007, p. 208). In (Brüggemann, 2008b), the approach was extended to track user's cleansing decisions to increase automation in data cleansing operations. In addition, they use ontologies for the following purposes:

- to label potential duplicate instances (cf. Brüggemann & Grüning, 2009, p. 197),
- to annotate the correctness of instances (cf. Brüggemann, 2008b, p. 523; Brüggemann & Grüning, 2009, p. 195),

- to create a history of data manipulations (cf. Grüning, 2009, p. 67f.), and
- to annotate the scale of measurement for proper processing of property values during duplicate detection (cf. Brüggemann & Grüning, 2009, p. 196f.; Grüning, 2009, p. 66).

Moreover, the Brüggemann and Grüning (2009, p. 197f.) propose an ontology for DQM which contains a configuration for data quality assessment metrics based on identified data quality problems. The approaches of Brüggemann, Aden, and Grüning have a strong focus on data cleansing during the data acquisition phase of data warehouses. However, the approaches seem to be applicable also during the data usage phase. Although the approaches of Brüggemann et al. are a promising first step in the area of utilization of Semantic Web technologies for DQM, they seem to lack support for data quality problem types such as syntax or legal value violations. Moreover, the proposed solution for the representation of functional dependencies seems to only support binary relationships.

Categories: Data Acquisition, Relational Data, Data Quality Monitoring, Data Quality Assessment, Data Cleansing

Chen et al. (2007) propose an ontology-based framework to detect inconsistencies in biological databases. The addressed inconsistencies are mainly heterogeneous terminology as it typically occurs in multi-source scenarios. The attributes of different databases are linked to the concepts of a domain ontology (cf. Chen et al., 2007, p. 279f.). The domain ontology is thereby used as a controlled vocabulary to harmonize heterogeneous terms in the data sources and to identify equivalent concepts (cf. Chen et al., 2007, pp. 280-282). The approach also defines a metric to measure consistency between two data sources based on the mappings to the domain ontology with the goal to support the selection of a reliable data source for further data mining (cf. Chen et al., 2007, pp. 284-288). Hence, the approach rather accepts data deficiencies and heterogeneity between data sources and, therefore, does not focus on improving the quality of data directly in the data source.

Categories: Data Acquisition, Data Usage, Relational Data, Data Integration, Information Filtering

Curé and Jeansoulin (2007) also propose to use domain ontologies to represent data dependencies and to check data from multiple sources for violations. The framework provides reports which contain the results of a comparison of the source data with the data dependencies represented in the ontology (cf. Curé & Jeansoulin, 2007, pp. 1128-1130). The approach considers the completeness and correctness of data, but does not provide many details about the covered data quality problem types (cf. Curé & Jeansoulin, 2007, pp. 1128-1130). Moreover, it is focused on data from relational sources.

Categories: Data Usage, Relational Data, Data Quality Monitoring, Data Cleansing

Curé (2009) proposes another approach that uses a mapping between queries that are based on ontological concepts and SQL queries to identify functional dependency violations in databases. The advantage of the proposed approach is that it does not require the conversion of relational data to RDF. But in contrast to SDQM, the approach requires the representation of each functional dependency as an SQL query and is, therefore, not generic (cf. Curé, 2009, p. 4). Moreover, it does not cover other data quality problem types besides functional dependency and does not provide data quality assessment metrics.

Categories: Data Usage, Relation Data, Data Quality Monitoring

Preece et al. (2006) present an approach that utilizes a so called information quality ontology (IQ ontology) as the foundation to identify acceptable results of proteomic analyses. The IQ ontology contains generic and domain-dependent concepts and is used to classify and organize domain specific quality characteristics which are important for scientists to find appropriate data. The data to be analyzed predominantly stems from XML sources and relational databases. In contrast to SDQM, it focuses on the selection of information, rather than the monitoring and assessment of data quality. Moreover, it does not focus on the broad identification of typical data quality problems for their correction.

Categories: Data Usage, Information Filtering, Relational Data, XML Data

X. Wang et al. (2005) use a task ontology to describe data cleansing tasks for information systems. Suitable cleansing methods are identified based on user-defined cleansing goals that are translated into queries over a knowledge base (cf. X. Wang et al., 2005, p. 4). The appropriate cleansing method is then applied based on the results of the queries. In contrast to SDQM, the proposed approach puts the data cleansing task into the center of interest. We argue that it is first necessary to provide mechanisms to identify data quality problems based on requirements, since the cleansing goal is determined by the data requirements that shall be fulfilled. To the best of our knowledge, the research work for this task-centric approach has not been continued.

Categories: Data Usage, Data Cleansing, Relational Data

Kedad and Métais (2002) propose a framework that uses knowledge represented via domain ontologies to identify corresponding data values. The identification process is thereby based on a so called "level of accuracy" which represents a user-defined metric that defines the scope of values that are considered as semantically similar. The proposed approach is applied for data cleansing in data integration scenarios of predominantly relational data. While SDQM focuses on the identification of defective data, the approach of Kedad and Métais attempts to deal with data heterogeneity, rather than real data defects.

Categories: Data Acquisition, Data Usage, Relational Data, Data Cleansing, Data Integration

Another ontology-based approach in the area of data quality improvement, called *Context Interchange (COIN),* has been developed at the Massachusetts Institute of Technology (MIT) (Madnick & Zhu, 2006). Supposing that many data quality problems are based on misinterpretations, they developed a knowledge-based mediation technology that attempts to overcome semantic heterogeneities of the underlying data sources. With COIN the data consumer is empowered to formulate queries expressed in his context independent of the underlying data sources (cf. Madnick & Zhu, 2006, p. 466). A mediator executes the user's query by transforming the query into source-orientated sub-queries to retrieve the requested information (cf. Madnick & Zhu, 2006, pp. 470-473). The context mediator is able to identify and reconcile semantic differences by accessing domain knowledge about the underlying sources, which is represented in a shared ontology and context definitions (cf. Madnick & Zhu, 2006, pp. 470-473). With this technique the ontology and the related context definitions facilitate interoperability between users and heterogeneous information systems by providing access to knowledge, which helps overcoming semantic differences. In contrast to SDQM, COIN does neither attempt to identify quality problems in the data, nor monitor or assess the level of data quality in a data source. It rather tries to solve problems of heterogeneity during data consumption, in order to avoid the misinterpretation of data.

Categories: Data Usage, Relational Data, XML Data, Data Cleansing

OntoDataClean is an approach from (Perez-Rey et al., 2006) that uses an ontology to store information about the required transformation for preprocessing data as part of a knowledge discovery process. The approach supports harmonization and cleansing of data from heterogeneous data sources for various problem types, such as missing values, duplicate instances, heterogeneous syntaxes, and inconsistent terminology (cf. Perez-Rey et al., 2006, p. 266f.). However, the application domain of OntoDataClean differs significantly from SDQM due to OntoDataClean's focus on data cleansing for the knowledge discovery process.

Categories: Data Acquisition, Data Usage, Data Cleansing, Relational Data

The *Semantic Conflict Resolution Ontology (SCROL)* as proposed by (Ram & Park, 2004) is a domain-independent ontology to detect and resolve semantic differences at instance and schema level when integrating data from heterogeneous data sources. On instance level, the ontology can be used to store information to resolve heterogeneities, such as different units, representations, or different levels of precision (cf. Ram & Park, 2004, p. 197f.). On schema level, the ontology is able to represent information required to resolve schematic discrepancies and other schema-related conflicts (cf. Ram & Park, 2004, p. 198f.). In contrast to SDQM, SCROL was designed to integrate and harmonize data from multiple sources rather than for data quality monitoring, data quality assessment, or management of data requirements. Moreover, it is primarily focused on the data acquisition phase.

Categories: Data Acquisition, Relational Data, Data Integration

The *Ontology-based XML Cleaning (OXC)* framework from (Milano et al., 2005) uses a domain ontology for the identification and resolution of data quality problems in XML documents. A domain ontology is created and mapped to the Document Type Definition (DTD) of the XML document to serve as a reference for the identification of quality problems in the accordant XML document (cf. Milano et al., 2005, pp. 567-570). In contrast to SDQM, OXC requires the creation of a separate domain ontology before its application to a specific domain. Moreover, the approach is only focused on quality problems related to the completeness dimension.

Categories: Data Usage, Data Cleansing, Data Quality Monitoring, XML-Data

Semantic Master Data Management (SMDM) is an approach from IBM China Research Lab (Wang et al., 2009). SMDM extends the conventional MDM solution of IBM by Semantic Web technologies. The approach uses a core MDM ontology as a global schema for business entities and relationships (cf. Wang et al., 2009, p. 1594). The concepts of the ontologies are mapped to relational data entities (cf. Wang et al., 2009, pp. 1594-1596). The data in the relational databases can be queried via a SPARQL-to-SQL translation technology that also allows reasoning during query execution (cf. Wang et al., 2009, p. 1595). Additionally, it is possible to integrate user-defined rules into query execution (cf. Wang et al., 2009, p. 1595). Although the approach does not provide data quality management features, it could be combined with SDQM to provide a holistic platform for master data management that entails quality management of master data.

Categories: Data Usage, Relational Data, Master Data Management

Bidlack (2009) describes an industry-driven approach to data quality management with lightweight ontologies. The ontologies are thereby part of a Python program that can only be managed by programmers (cf. Bidlack, 2009, p. 4). The ontologies represent synonym mappings and reference data with functional dependencies and legal value lists (cf. Bidlack, 2009, p. 6). The stored information is then used for data cleansing operations. The proposed approach is focused on data cleansing in Customer Relationship Management (CRM) and does not seem to use any Semantic Web technologies.

Categories: Data Usage, Data Cleansing, Relational Data

Geisler et al. (2011) propose an ontology-based approach for data quality management in data streaming applications. The approach's ontology is thereby used to store information about quality assessment and monitoring metrics which are also mapped to data quality dimensions (cf. Geisler et al., 2011, p. 7f.). The ontology facilitates the flexible representation of user-defined metrics (cf. Geisler et al., 2011, p. 7f.). However, the approach focuses on data streaming applications in traffic management and does not fully materialize data requirements as SDQM does. Instead, it rather provides capabilities to store SQL code snippets.

Categories: Data Acquisition, Data Quality Monitoring, Data Quality Assessment, Other (Streaming Messages)

F. Wang et al. (2005) introduce an approach for the validation of geographic data based on rules expressed via the Semantic Web Rule Language (SWRL). The information system directly identifies potential data quality problems and risks based on the data quality constraints that have been previously expressed via SWRL (cf. F.

Wang et al., 2005, p. 5f.). The approach was especially designed for mobile users who capture geographic information in fields and meadows (cf. F. Wang et al., 2005, p. 1f.). In comparison to SDQM, the approach uses SWRL instead of a plain ontology and RDF instances to store quality requirements (cf. F. Wang et al., 2005, p. 3). This reduces the ability to automatically identify inconsistencies among requirements. Additionally, the proposed approach does not provide requirement templates, which raises the complexity for users to express data requirements.

Categories: Data Acquisition, Data Validation

Becker et al. (2008) propose an approach for ontology-based data quality management that utilizes domain ontologies as an independent conceptual layer to integrate data from disparate data sources. Queries are then executed based on the ontology to identify data quality problems (cf. Becker et al., 2008, p. 8f.). Other than SDQM, the approach does not utilize a special ontology for the domain of data quality management and does not materialize data requirements in RDF.

Categories: Data Usage, Data Quality Monitoring, Data Quality Assessment, Relational Data

In addition to the presented related work, the author of this thesis proposed an alternative approach which utilizes the SPARQL INferencing framework (SPIN) to materialize and process data requirements in RDF (Fürber & Hepp, 2010b). SPIN is a vocabulary that is able to represent SPARQL queries in RDF (Knublauch, 2011). Based on the materialized data requirements, data quality monitoring reports can be derived that identify the instances with requirement violations. Moreover, the data requirements can be used for data validation during data entry (cf. Fürber & Hepp, 2010b, p. 10f.). The author extended the SPIN-based framework by a data quality assessment component to compute scores for the data quality dimensions accuracy, completeness, timeliness, and uniqueness based on materialized data requirements (Fürber & Hepp, 2011a). The SPIN-based approaches are closely related to the SDQM framework. Other than the SPIN-based approaches, SDQM is strictly optimized for data quality management, since it uses a vocabulary that is especially designed for supporting data quality management activities. Moreover, sharing data requirements is much easier with the DQM vocabulary than with the SPIN-Vocabulary, since SPIN provides the full syntax of SPARQL and the DQM vocabulary is only focused on data quality management related information.

Categories: Data Acquisition, Data Usage, Relational Data, RDF Data, Data Quality Monitoring, Data Quality Assessment

10.4.2 Web-oriented Approaches

Web-oriented data quality management approaches focus on the quality of Web information. In the following, we describe related approaches that utilize Semantic Web technology for quality management of Web information.

Lei et al. (2007) present a framework to evaluate the quality of semantic metadata. The framework is based on an analysis of typical problems that may occur during the annotation of data sources with semantic metadata. In order to evaluate the quality, gold standard annotations that serve as a reference for quality checks have to be created which often do not exist in real-world scenarios and, therefore, require considerable human effort to create. In (Lei & Nikolov, 2007), the authors have addressed this limitation by using available domain ontologies, knowledge bases, and lexical resources as a substitute for the manually created reference as used in the initial proposal. This automatic approach thereby recognizes inconsistent, duplicate, ambiguous, inaccurate, and spurious annotations (cf. Lei & Nikolov, 2007, p. 3f.). Since the approach is focused on the quality of annotations, such as semantic tags of blogs, it cannot directly be compared to SDQM. However, the proposed approach is valuable for the quality evaluation of semantic annotations of unstructured resources.

Categories: Data Usage, RDF Data, Data Quality Assessment

The *Web Information Quality Assessment framework (WIQA)* as proposed by (Bizer, 2007; Bizer & Cyganiak, 2009) allows to filter Web data that corresponds to user-defined information filtering policies. The filtering policies have to be defined via the WIQA policy language (WIQA-PL), which is based on the SPARQL query language grammar (Bizer, 2007, pp. 95-97). Each WIQA policy consists of three parts, namely a name, a description, and a pattern (Bizer, 2007, p. 96f.). The pattern is used to express a set of filtering conditions to filter desired data out of the underlying data sources (Bizer, 2007, p. 97). The framework thereby relies on the availability of provenance information in the data sources, such as timestamps, authors of information, or ratings, depending on the type of filtering policy that shall be applied (cf. Bizer, 2007, pp. 101-103). Except for the domain-specific functions of WIQA, such as the "Tidal Trust" function (cf. Bizer, 2007, pp. 110-112) and the "More Positive Ratings" function (cf. Bizer, 2007, p. 109f.), most WIQA policies should now be representable with standard SPARQL 1.1 queries (Harris & Seaborne, 2010). However, WIQA is also able to provide explanations why certain information has been filtered (cf. Bizer, 2007, pp. 119-121). Moreover, the framework provides a browser add-on which facilitates information filtering based on WIQA policies and explains why the information has been filtered (cf. Bizer, 2007, p. 143). Compared to SDQM, WIQA does not attempt to improve information quality. It rather provides a filtering mechanism that finds information corresponding to the quality requirements of information consumers. Moreover, WIQA was primarily designed for Web information consumers, while SDQM shall provide tools for monitoring and assessing the quality of information sources.

Categories: Data Usage, RDF Data, Information Filtering

Hartig (2009) proposed an extension of the SPARQL query language for RDF called *tSPARQL* to query information based on previously assigned trust values. As a prerequisite, trust values have to be generated (cf. Hartig, 2009, p. 14f.). Compared to SDQM, tSPARQL uses a completely different approach to evaluate the quality of information. tSPARQL relies on subjective user judgments of the trustworthiness of information, rather than focusing on hard facts that are based on detailed and explicitly represented data requirements. Thus, the assumptions that lead users to create certain scores of trustworthiness are not explicit in tSPARQL.

Categories: Data Usage, RDF Data, Data Quality Assessment, Information Filtering

Hartig and Zhao (2009) propose a framework to assess the timeliness of Semantic Web data based on provenance information. The timeliness assessment is similar to the timeliness assessment as implemented by SDQM. However, SDQM uses a different formula to assess timeliness and is based on the previous creation of data requirements related to timeliness. Moreover, in contrast to SDQM, the approach from Hartig and Zhao does not directly allow to express a required update interval as a requirement for the timeliness assessment.

Categories: Data Usage, Data Quality Assessment, RDF Data

Pernici and Scannapieco (2002) propose a framework to monitor and assess the quality of published and unpublished Web sites. Quality meta-information such as the author and date of the last update are thereby attached to a Web site with the help of an RDF document, called "data quality file" (cf. Pernici & Scannapieco, 2002, p. 62f.).

Moreover, dynamic data quality dimension scores like completability, i.e. "how fast (the completeness of an information source) will grow in time" (Pernici & Scannapieco, 2002, p. 53), are computed and stored in the data quality file (cf. Pernici & Scannapieco, 2002, p. 62f.). A module of the framework called "Data Quality Viewer" displays the data of the data quality file to Web consumers in a browser (cf. Pernici & Scannapieco, 2002, pp. 63-65). Hence, the framework shall help information consumers to evaluate the quality of Web information and to select appropriate information. SDQM differs significantly from the proposed approach, since SDQM is focused on evaluating the quality of structured data and not of Web sites.

Categories: Data Usage, Text / Web Site, Information Filtering

ProLOD is a tool designed for profiling Linked Open Data introduced by (Böhm et al., 2010). ProLOD clusters the data on schema level based on similarity measures and generates several different statistics about the profiled data on instance level (cf. Böhm et al., 2010, p. 176f.). The statistics are similar to conventional profiling tools and amongst others, they provide information about datatypes, pattern distributions, and value frequencies. ProLOD is, therefore, very valuable to gain a quick insight into the content of Semantic Web data sets. But to the best of our knowledge, it does not allow the storage and evaluation of data requirements which is possible with SDQM. ProLOD may be used together with SDQM, for example during the definition phase to identify data requirements based on the generated statistics.

Categories: Data Usage, RDF Data, Data Profiling

Mendes et al. (2012) developed a framework for data cleansing and data quality assessment operations during the integration of linked data called *Sieve*. Sieve is part of the Linked Data Integration Framework (LDIF) and can be configured to user-specific needs. The assessment metrics are thereby encoded in a proprietary XML-based language. The assessment results can be used during the data integration process to decide how to cleanse the data (cf. Mendes et al., 2012, pp. 3-5). Sieve and SDQM differ significantly in two aspects. Firstly, Sieve is focused on the use in data integration, while SDQM is optimized for data quality monitoring and assessment during the data usage phase. Secondly, Sieve stores quality-relevant metadata with help of a proprietary XML-based language rather than within an ontology.

Categories: Data Acquisition, Data Quality Assessment, Data Cleansing, Data Integration, RDF Data

10.5 Summary

Our analysis of related work in the area of ontology-based data quality management shows that, in summary, no common approach has yet evolved in the area of utilizing ontologies for data quality tasks. But considering the diversity of different use cases for which the approaches have been designed, we can say that ontology-based techniques have shown to be applicable to a broad range of problems in the data quality domain, ranging from data quality monitoring and cleansing to master data management, data integration, and information filtering. The role of ontologies in the analyzed approaches is also very diverse. Some approaches make use of domain ontologies that represent and utilize domain knowledge of a specific data domain, e.g. to integrate semantically similar data elements from different sources via the ontology (e.g. Chen et al., 2007) and to resolve heterogeneities (Madnick & Zhu, 2006; e.g. Ram & Park, 2004). Furthermore, domain ontologies are used as reference data to identify functional dependency violations (e.g. Brüggemann & Aden, 2007; Curé & Jeansoulin, 2007). Other techniques use ontologies to represent and utilize quality-relevant metadata such as annotations related to the correctness of instances (cf. Brüggemann, 2008b, p. 523; Brüggemann & Grüning, 2009, p. 195), assessment metrics (e.g. Brüggemann & Grüning, 2009, p. 197f.; Preece et al., 2006, p. 478), data cleansing tasks (cf. X. Wang et al., 2005, p. 4), or data requirements (e.g. Perez-Rey et al., 2006, p. 267). Additionally, some approaches utilize provenance metadata, , e.g. about the publisher of data and its credibility, represented via ontologies to evaluate the quality of a data source (e.g. Bizer, 2007; Hartig & Zhao, 2009). Moreover, we can say that most of the approaches concentrate on the data lifecycle phases of data acquisition and data usage. In fact, we did not find any solution that actively supports data retirement, although especially information filtering approaches, such as the approach from (Preece et al., 2006), could also be used to identify data for retirement and archiving. Figure 63 provides an overview of the differences between the analyzed approaches and SDQM.

By comparing the number of approaches we can also say that, so far, only little work has been done to manage the quality of the Semantic Web as only a few Web-oriented approaches could be found. More work has been done with a focus on closed IS. However, a lot of work has to be done in both areas to account for the central management of data requirements, since it is the requirements that are the foundation of all activities within the data quality management cycle (cf. English, 1999, pp. 119-121; Wang, 1998, p. 61). To the best of our knowledge, the SDQM framework is the only framework that allows the representation of a broad range of data requirement types fully represented in RDF. Moreover, we did not find any other tool besides SDQM that integrates wiki-based requirements management with data quality monitoring and assessment functionalities. However, SDQM could be extended to support more Semantic Web-specific features, e.g. to evaluate the quality of annotations, and to support heterogeneity resolution when integrating data from different sources. Moreover, the integration of data profiling features into SDQM should be further investigated.

Author	Supported Data Lifecycle Step			Supported Data Representation					Supported Data Quality Task									Role of Ontologies			
	Acquisition	Usage	Retirement	Relational	XML	RDF	Text / Unstructured Data	Other	Data Profiling	Data Requirements Management	Data Quality Monitoring	Data Quality Assessment	Data Cleansing	Data Validation	Information Filtering	Data Integration	Master Data Management	Representation of Quality-relevant Metadata	Representation of Domain Knowledge	Representation of Provenance Metadata	SWRL / Reasoning rules
Conventional Rule-based Approaches																					
Loshin, 2002		X	X								X	X	X					X	X		
Hipp, Müller, Hohendorff, & Naumann, 2007		X	X								X	X	X					X	X		
Information System-oriented Approaches																					
Brüggemann, 2006, 2008a, 2008b; Brüggemann & Aden, 2007; Brüggemann & Gruening, 2008; Brüggemann & Grüning, 2009; Grüning, 2009	X	X		X								X	X			X		X	X		
Chen, Chen, & Zhang, 2007	X	X	X	X												X	X	X	X	X	
Curé & Jeansoulin, 2007		X	X	X								X	X			X		X	X		X
Curé, 2009			X	X								X						X			
Preece et al., 2006			X		X													X	X		
Xin Wang, Hamilton, & Bither, 2005			X	X												X		X	X		
Kedad & Métais, 2002	X			X									X			X		X	X		
Madnick & Zhu, 2006			X	X	X								X						X		
Perez-Rey, Anguita, & Crespo, 2006	X		X	X									X						X		
Ram & Park, 2004	X		X	X									X				X	X	X		
Milano, Scannapieco, & Catarci, 2005			X	X	X							X		X				X	X		
Xiaoyuan Wang et al., 2009			X	X										X			X	X	X		X
Bidlack, 2009			X	X								X	X					X	X		
Web-oriented Approaches																					
Geisler, Weber, & Quix, 2011	X							X				X	X	X				X	X		
F. Wang, Mäs, Reinhardt, & Kandawasvika, 2005	X							X							X			X	X		X
Becker, Matzner, Mueller, & Winkelmann, 2008		X	X	X							X	X						X	X		
Fürber & Hepp, 2010 and Fürber & Hepp, 2011		X	X	X		X					X	X				X		X	X		
Lei, Uren, & Motta, 2007 and Lei & Nikolov, 2007		X	X			X							X					X	X		
Bizer, 2007 and Bizer & Cyganiak, 2009		X	X			X						X	X		X			X	X	X	
Hartig, 2009		X	X			X									X			X	X	X	
Hartig & Zhao, 2009		X	X			X												X	X	X	
Pernici & Scannapieco, 2002		X	X			X	X									X		X	X		
Böhm et al., 2010		X	X			X				X						X		X	X		
SDQM	X	X	X			X				X	X	X	X			X		X	X		

Figure 63: Own classification of related work

170

PART V - Conclusion

11 Synopsis and Future Work

The research goal of this thesis was the investigation of the usefulness of ontologies for data quality management. In this thesis project, we created an ontology, called the Data Quality Management vocabulary (DQM vocabulary), to collect and store data requirements in a structured and linkable format. Moreover, we configured a wiki, called data requirements wiki, which contains standard forms to capture data requirements and to store them based on the elements of our ontology, the DQM vocabulary. Because of the storage of data requirements in the DQM vocabulary schema, we were able to create a reporting tool, called the Semantic Data Quality manager, that automatically processes the captured data requirements and creates data quality monitoring and assessment reports without any additional manual intervention. In the following, we review our initial research questions, provide answers, and highlight the findings and results of this thesis. Moreover, we draw a final conclusion on the usefulness of ontologies and provide starting points for future work.

11.1 Research Summary

In section 2.1, we have subdivided the initial research goal into five research questions, which served as the roadmap for this thesis. In the following, we provide a short summary of the answers to the research questions:

RQ1: What kind of data quality problems exist?

We have argued that, in order to develop solutions to improve data quality, the nature of data quality problems has to be understood. Therefore, we have developed a typology of data quality problems for relational systems (see section 3.3) and for the Semantic Web (see section 5.2). The derived typologies are based on an analysis of literature related to data quality problems in relational databases and the Semantic Web.

RQ2: Which activities have to be performed during data quality management?

Since we have aimed to develop an artifact that facilitates data quality management, we had to identify typical activities that are performed during data quality management. Consequently, we analyzed the two most popular data quality management methodologies, namely Total Data Quality Management (TDQM, Wang, 1998) and Total Information Quality Management (TIQM, English, 1999), for commonalities as part of section 3.5. Based on the commonalities, we defined a new data quality management process in section 8.2 that is fitted to SDQM, the major artifact of this thesis.

RQ3: Which knowledge has to be represented to support data quality management?

In section 3.6, we argued that data requirements represent knowledge about the characteristics of high-quality data. Assuming that data quality problems are the result of requirement violations, we derived ten generic data requirement types from the typology of data quality problems. We thereby focused on quality problems of relational data. The generic data requirement types represent the core knowledge concepts that have to be represented to support data quality management.

RQ4: How can we represent knowledge relevant for data quality management to reduce manual work?

Based on the generic requirement types, we developed an ontology, called the DQM vocabulary, that supports the representation of knowledge for data quality management activities, such as data requirements definition, data quality monitoring, and data quality assessment (see section 0 and (Fürber & Hepp, 2011b)). The development procedure followed the ontology development methodology as provided in (Uschold & Gruninger, 1996). The DQM vocabulary consists of classes and properties that can be used to represent data requirements in a machine-readable format. Due to this design, we reduced manual input by automating the generation of data quality monitoring and assessment reports based on the representation of data requirements knowledge via the DQM vocabulary.

RQ5: How can we utilize knowledge for data quality management represented within ontological structures?

In chapter 7, we have developed the SDQM framework, a data quality management framework that is based on other programming frameworks and artifacts primarily from the Semantic Web community. SDQM processes quality-relevant knowledge represented in the DQM vocabulary to derive data quality monitoring and assessment reports. Knowledge processing within the SDQM framework is based on generic SPARQL queries which provide the basis for the derived reports. Since the SPARQL queries only use elements from the DQM vocabulary, they are of generic use for any domain, as long as the data requirements are formulated based on the DQM vocabulary. SDQM's data requirements wiki can be used to capture data requirements from business experts via standardized forms. Thus, users of SDQM do not need to possess programming skills to evaluate the quality of data. Furthermore, we have shown in section 9.4 that the represented knowledge can also be used to automatically identify inconsistent or duplicate data requirements. Finally, we provided an installation and application procedure for SDQM in chapter 8 of this thesis so that our research project is reproducible.

11.2 Contributions

The contributions of this thesis can be separated into (1) practical and (2) theoretical contributions. On the practical side, we developed a new artifact, called SDQM, which solves real-world problems in the area of data quality management and integrates state of the art technology of the Web.

SDQM consists of three major artifacts that have been developed in the course of this thesis, namely (1) an ontology for representing knowledge that is relevant for data quality management, (2) a wiki for capturing and maintaining data requirements, and (3) a reporting frontend to create data quality monitoring and assessment reports. *SDQM's data requirements wiki* can be used to capture quality-relevant knowledge from business experts via standardized forms. Thus, users of SDQM do not need to possess programming skills to evaluate the quality of data. The captured data requirements are automatically represented in RDF based on the DQM vocabulary. Therefore, SDQM's reporting frontend, called *the Semantic Data Quality Manager (SDQMgr)*, can automatically process the captured knowledge to derive data quality monitoring and assessment reports without any additional programming. As evaluated in section 0, this is a major distinction from conventional data quality tools such as Talend OS for Data Quality, since they usually represent data requirements as part of programming code. Due to its integration with standard wiki software, SDQM is especially suited for large organizations with distributed knowledge. The reduced complexity of maintaining data requirements logic may mitigate the effort for data quality management. To the best of our knowledge, SDQM is the first data quality management framework that uses standard wiki software to capture, manage, and utilize data requirements for automated data quality monitoring and assessment. Moreover, SDQM facilitates the automated identification of inconsistent and duplicate requirements with standard SPARQL queries, since the captured data requirements are represented in RDF format. At present, we do not know of any data quality management software that has a similar feature.

Moreover, this thesis provided several theoretical contributions for data quality research as listed below:

(1) A typology of data quality problems in relational systems and the Semantic Web (sections 3.3 and 5.2).

(2) A requirement-centric methodology for data quality management (section 8.2).

(3) Ten generic data requirement types (section 3.6.1).

(4) A survey of related work (chapter 10).

These theoretical contributions of this thesis may be useful for future research and applications in the area of data quality management.

11.3 Conclusion and Future Work

In this thesis, we have shown a way how ontologies can be employed for data requirements management, data quality monitoring, and data quality assessment for information systems and Semantic Web data. The evaluation results documented in chapter 9 indicate that the developed approach is also usable in real-world settings. Furthermore, we have collected first evidence that Web and Semantic Web technologies can facilitate the management of data quality in several ways, namely

- Semantic wikis facilitate the generation of data requirements by non-programmers, since they offer standardized forms for knowledge capturing.
- Representation of data requirements within ontological structures facilitates the automated derivation of requirement violations and data quality scores.

- Representation of data requirements within ontological structures facilitates the automated identification of duplicate and inconsistent data requirements.

However, we also discovered some limitations. Compared to conventional data quality architectures, such as Talend OS for Data Quality with a MySQL database, SDQM still has a significant performance gap. Moreover, SDQM does not yet provide features for data profiling and may not be able to represent complex functional dependencies in RDF. Additionally, we discovered that the use of SDQM for open environments, such as the Semantic Web, has some limitations. For example, Semantic Web scenarios contain a large diversity of world views which may sometimes collide. Therefore, it may not be possible or even suitable to solely seek for consistent data requirements (cf. Madnick & Zhu, 2006, p. 460f.). In consequence, the perceived characteristics of high quality data may be diverse and contradictory. Thus, data quality improvement directed to a single, harmonized quality perception is most likely not applicable for the Semantic Web. However, the results of this thesis provide multiple possibilities for future work in several areas which are explained in the following.

Semantic Web settings: Currently, SDQM is focused on closed environments based on relational information systems. Future work could address the extension of SDQM to cover specific data quality problems of the Semantic Web as specified in section 5.2. Moreover, SDQM could be deployed to the World Wide Web to collect data requirements from the Web community about public Semantic Web data sources, such as DBpedia or Geonames. Based on the captured knowledge, agreement and disagreement about data requirements could be identified and further investigated.

Technological optimization: Currently, SDQM was mainly used in single source scenarios. Future work could address the investigation of SDQM's ability to cover multi-source scenarios, e.g. in which properties with identical intensions are stored in disparate data sources. Moreover, SDQM's duplicate checking algorithms require further performance optimizations as explained in section 9.2. Additionally, SDQMgr's reports could be extended by charts to visualize data quality scores. Finally, SDQM could be extended by data profiling features to identify data requirements via data analysis.

Economic impact: SDQM may save manual effort due to the provision of standardized forms for capturing data requirements and standardized data quality reports. However, solid evidence is still missing that really proves a higher efficiency and lower costs compared to conventional data quality management tools. Future studies could also address the potential of SDQM to reduce costs of information exchange among different parties within a supply chain. For example, SDQM could be used to express and publish data requirements of customers within supply chains in an audit-proof way. Then the delivered data of the supplier could be verified according to these explicitly specified data requirements with SDQM. As a potential outcome, ambiguity and misunderstandings during information exchange may be reduced and the result of the verification against the customer's data requirements could be part of contracts and, therefore, used as an incentive to improve the quality of the information exchange within the supply chain. SDQM could be applied in a study related to such a scenario to investigate its potential to reduce costs for information exchange within the supply chain.

Appendix A – Comparison of TIQM and TDQM

Table 28: Comparison of TIQM and TDQM, part one

TIQM		TDQM	
Process Group	Process Step	Process Step	Process Group
Assess data definition and architecture quality (English, 1999, pp. 72-74)	Identification of quality requirements for data definition quality		
	Selection of important information groups for the assessment		
	Identification of stakeholder categories of the selected information groups		
	Quality assessment of data definitions		
		Identify characteristics of the IP (cf. Wang, 1998, p. 61)	Definition phase
	Quality assessment of information architecture / database design,		
	Assessment of customer satisfaction with data definitions		
		Identify information manufacturing process (cf. Wang, 1998, pp. 61-63)	Definition phase

Table 29: Comparison of TIQM and TDQM, part two

TIQM		TDQM	
Process Group	**Process Step**	**Process Step**	**Process Group**
Assess information quality (English, 1999, pp. 74-76)	Reconfirmation or identification of relevant information groups		
	Establish information quality objectives and measures	Identify IQ expectations and perceptions of IP suppliers, manufacturers, consumers, and managers (cf.Wang, 1998, p. 61f.)	Definition phase
	Identification of the "information value and cost chain" of the relevant information groups	Develop IQ metrics (cf. Wang, 1998, p. 64)	Measurement phase
	Identification of the objects for the assessment, i.e. files, databases, or processes		
	Identification of appropriate reference sources for data validation		
	Extraction of a random sample of the data to be assessed		
	Measurement of information quality based on the sampled data via automated or physical assessment	Implement IQ metrics (cf. Wang, 1998, p. 64)	Measurement phase
	Presentation and interpretation of assessment results		

Table 30: Comparison of TIQM and TDQM, part three

TIQM			TDQM	
Process Group	**Process Step**		**Process Step**	**Process Group**
Measure nonquality information costs (English, 1999, p. 76f.)	Identify business performance measures / business drivers that may be effected by information quality problems, such as profits, customer satisfaction, or costs			
	Analyze cost of information, e.g. cost for infrastructure, value delivery, and cost-adding developments			
	Determination of costs resulting from data quality problems including cost of caused process failures			
	Identification of customer segments for customer lifetime value calculation			
	Calculation of customer lifetime value as basis of lost opportunity costs			
	Calculation of missed and lost opportunity cost resulting from information quality problems (Nonquality)			

Table 31: Comparison of TIQM and TDQM, part four

TIQM		TDQM	
Process Group	**Process Step**	**Process Step**	**Process Group**
Reengineer and cleanse data (English, 1999, pp. 77-80)	Identification of data sources that require data cleansing or reengineering	Perform root cause analysis for identified data quality problems (Wang, 1998, p. 64)	Analysis phase
	Extraction and Analysis of the relevant source data for anomalies and patterns		
	Data standardization based on semantic meaning		
	Manual or automated correction or completion of data		
	Consolidation of duplicate data		
	Analysis of data defect types		
	Data transformation to target state (data warehouse-specific)		
	(Re-)Calculation of aggregates and derivations (data warehouse-specific)		
	Audit and control of Extract-Transform-Load (ETL-) processes (data warehouse-specific)		

Table 32: Comparison of TIQM and TDQM, part five

TIQM			TDQM	
Process Group	**Process Step**		**Process Step**	**Process Group**
Improve information process quality (English, 1999, p. 80f.)	Initiation of process improvement activity including problem definition, identification of relevant processes, and establishment of process improvement team			
	Creation of improvement plan including identification of the root causes		Perform root cause analysis for identified data quality problems (Wang, 1998, p. 64)	Analysis phase
	Implementation of changes for process and information quality improvement			
	Effectiveness assessment of implemented changes			
	Standardization and enterprise-wide implementation of effective changes		Improve alignment between IP characteristics and business needs (cf. Wang et al., 2001, p. 14)	Improvement phase
			Improve alignment of information flow and workflow (cf. Wang et al., 2001, p. 14)	

Appendix B –Rules for the Evaluation of SDQM

Table 33: Overview of rules used for the validation of the SDQM algorithms

ID	Rule Category	Rule
1	Missing values and properties	Mandatory properties: - City - Zip - Streetno - Street - Country - Location ID - Quantity - Price - PCATID - PNAME - WEIGHT
2	Conditional missing values and properties (1 condition)	1) If city starts with an N, then property country must have a value. 2) If country has value "USA", then the property "state" must have a value.
3	Conditional missing values and properties (2 conditions)	If country has value "USA" and city has value "San Diego", then the property "state" must have a value
4	Conditional missing values and properties (3 conditions)	If the property country has the value "Deutschland" and the value of the property city starts with "Neu" and property streetno contains "39", then the property state must have a value.
5	Conditional missing values and properties (4 conditions)	If the property country has value "USA" and the value of property street ends with "Plaza" and the property city starts with "San" and the property streetno contains the value "3", then the property state must have a value.
6	Conditional missing values and properties (5 conditions)	If the property city starts with "San" and the property country has the value "USA" and the property streetno contains the value "3" and the property street ends with "Plaza" and the property zip is less than 95000, then the property state must have a value.
7	Syntax violations	1) The property streetno can only contain numbers, letters and whitespaces (Regular expression: ^[0-9A-Za-z\s]*$). 2) The street property can only contain numbers,

ID	Rule Category	Rule
		letters, whitespaces, and dots (Regular expression: ^[A-Za-z-\s\.]*$).
8	Conditional syntax violations (1 condition)	If the property country has the value "USA", then the property state must contain 2 letters (Regular expression: ^[A-Z]{2}$). If the property country has the value "Deutschland", then the property zip must contain 5 digits (Regular expression: ^[0-9]{5}$).
9	Conditional syntax violations (2 conditions)	If the property city has the value "Köln" and the property street starts with "Flughafen", then the property zip must contain 5 digits (Regular expression: ^[0-9]{5}$).
10	Conditional syntax violations (3 conditions)	If the property country has the value "Deutschland" and the property street starts with "Flughafen" and the property zip is less than 95000, then the property zip must contain 5 digits (Regular expression: ^[0-9]{5}$).
11	Conditional syntax violations (4 conditions)	If the property city has the value "San Diego" and the property country has the value "USA" and the property street no contains a "3" and the property zip is less than 95000, then the property zip must contain 4 digits (Regular expression: ^[0-9]{4}$).
12	Conditional syntax violations (5 conditions)	If the property city starts with value "San" and the property country has the value "USA" and the property street no contains a "3" and the property street ends with "Plaza" and the property zip is less than 95000, then the property location ID must contain 2 digits (Regular expression: ^[0-9]{2}$).
13	Out Of range values	1) weight: Lower Limit = 0 2) location_id: Lower Limit = 1 3) quantity: Lower Limit = 0 4) price: Lower Limit = 0, Upper Limit = 10000000 5) pcatid: Lower Limit = 1
14	Illegal values (Legal value rules)	The property country must have one of these values: "USA", "Germany", "France", "United States of America", "Deutschland"

ID	Rule Category	Rule
15	Illegal values (Illegal value rules)	The property pcatid cannot have the value "0".
16	FuncDepReferenceRule violations (2 properties)	Value combinations of instances of class `foo:Location` must match value combinations between properties of instances of class `tref:Location` within the following properties: - City - Country
17	FuncDepReferenceRule violations (3 properties)	Value combinations of instances of class `foo:Location` must match value combinations between properties of instances of class `tref:Location` within the following properties: - City - Country - Zip
18	FuncDepReferenceRule violations (4 properties)	Value combinations of instances of class `foo:Location` must match value combinations between properties of instances of class `tref:Location` within the following properties: - City - Country - Zip - Street
19	FuncDepReferenceRule violations (5 properties)	Value combinations of instances of class `foo:Location` must match value combinations between properties of instances of class `tref:Location` within the following properties: - City - Country - Zip - Street - Streetno
20	FuncDepValueRule violations (1 condition)	If the property city has the value "Stavern", then the property country must have value "Norway".

ID	Rule Category	Rule
21	FuncDepValueRule violations (2 conditions)	If the property city has the value "Köln" and the property street starts with "Flughafen", then the property zip must have the value "51147".
22	FuncDepValueRule violations (3 conditions)	If the property country has the value "Deutschland" and the property street starts with "Flughafen" and the property zip must have the value "3".
23	FuncDepValueRule violations (4 conditions)	If the property city has the value "San Diego" and the property country has the value "USA" and the property street no contains a "3" and the property zip is less than 95000, then the property zip must have the value "92102".
24	FuncDepValueRule violations (5 conditions)	If the property city starts with value "San" and the property country has the value "USA" and the property street no contains a "3" and the property street ends with "Plaza" and the property zip is less than 95000, then the property location ID must have the value "81".
25	Expired instances	If date and time of property validThrough is before the current date and time, then the instance is outdated.
26	Exceeded Update Interval	If timestamp of instances is elder than 6 months, then the instance is outdated.
27	Uniqueness violations	The values of the property location_id must always be unique.
28	Duplicate instances (1 equal value)	If two or more instances have the same values in the following properties, then the instances are potential duplicates: - Zip
29	Duplicate instances (2 equal values)	If two or more instances have the same values in the following properties, then the instances are potential duplicates: - City - Zip
30	Duplicate instances (3 equal values)	If two or more instances have the same values in the following properties, then the instances are potential duplicates: - Street - Streetno

ID	Rule Category	Rule
		- Zip
31	Duplicate instances (4 equal values)	If two or more instances have the same values in the following properties, then the instances are potential duplicates: - Zip - Country - Street - Streetno
32	Duplicate instances (5 equal values)	If two or more instances have the same values in the following properties, then the instances are potential duplicates: - City - Country - Street - Streetno - Zip

Appendix C – Test Data for SDQM's Evaluation

Table 34: Location test data for evaluating SDQM's algorithms

Instance	LOCID	STREET	STREETNO	ZIP	CITY	STATE	COUNTRY
<http://www.example.org/stockdblocation/1>	1	8489 Strong St.			Las Vegas	NV	USA
<http://www.example.org/stockdblocation/2>	1	636 St Kilda Road		3004	Melbourne	Victoria	Australia
<http://www.example.org/stockdblocation/3>	3	67, rue des Cinquante Otages		44000	Nantes	France	
<http://www.example.org/stockdblocation/4>	4	Erling Skakkes gate	78	4110	Stavern		Belgien
<http://www.example.org/stockdblocation/5>	5	5677 Strong St.		97562	San Rafael	CA	USA
<http://www.example.org/stockdblocation/6>	6	Werner-Heisenberg-Weg	39	85577	Neubiberg		Deutschland
<http://www.example.org/stockdblocation/7>	7	Werner-Heisenberg-Weg	39	85577	Neubiberg		Deutschland
<http://www.example.org/stockdblocation/8>	8	Horton Plaza	324	92101	San Diego		USA
<http://www.example.org/stockdblocation/9>	9	Flughafenstr.	1	5114	Köln		Deutschland

Table 35: Product test data for evaluating SDQM's algorithms

Instance	pid	pcatid	pname	price	weight	validThrough
<http://www.example.org/stockdbproducts/10>	10	10	lenux winshield wiper, audi	25000000	0.333	
<http://www.example.org/stockdbproducts/11>	11	1	funny t-shirt, white	-1	0.3	
<http://www.example.org/stockdbproducts/12>	12	6	funny t-shirt, black	15	0.3	
<http://www.example.org/stockdbproducts/1>	1	1	sloppy socks, red	12.22	0.2	
<http://www.example.org/stockdbproducts/2>	2	4	Panisony LCD, 42"	1333.99	35	2010-11-13T17:19:39.683
<http://www.example.org/stockdbproducts/3>	3	3	Peach Book Air, slim edition	1400	1.5	2012-11-13T17:20:21.179
<http://www.example.org/stockdbproducts/4>	4	3	suni waio, netbook	449.00	1.4	
<http://www.example.org/stockdbproducts/5>	5	0				
<http://www.example.org/stockdbproducts/6>	6	7	Daily sun	1.00	0.2	2012-11-13T17:20:21.179
<http://www.example.org/stockdbproducts/7>	7	6	pan, big	20	2	
<http://www.example.org/stockdbproducts/8>	8	8	gaox, business, black	75.00	0.8	
<http://www.example.org/stockdbproducts/9>	9	4	Peach Book Air, slim edition	1200	1.8	2012-11-13T17:20:21.179

Table 36: Stock quantity test data for evaluating SDQM's algorithms

Instance	spid	slocid	quantity
<http://www.example.org/stockdbstock/1/12>	<http://www.example.org/stockdbproducts/12>	<http://www.example.org/stockdblocation/1>	1
<http://www.example.org/stockdbstock/1/2>	<http://www.example.org/stockdbproducts/2>	<http://www.example.org/stockdblocation/1>	15000
<http://www.example.org/stockdbstock/3/5>	<http://www.example.org/stockdbproducts/5>	<http://www.example.org/stockdblocation/3>	844
<http://www.example.org/stockdbstock/6/6>	<http://www.example.org/stockdbproducts/6>	<http://www.example.org/stockdblocation/6>	-2
<http://www.example.org/stockdbstock/7/11>	<http://www.example.org/stockdbproducts/11>	<http://www.example.org/stockdblocation/7>	134

Table 37: Test reference data for evaluating SDQM's "FuncDepReferenceRules" with two properties

URI	City	Country
<http://www.example.org/trustedreference/locations#Location_2>	Melbourne	Australia
<http://www.example.org/trustedreference/locations#Location_7>	San Diego	USA
<http://www.example.org/trustedreference/locations#Location_5>	San Rafael	USA
<http://www.example.org/trustedreference/locations#Location_3>	Nantes	France
<http://www.example.org/trustedreference/locations#Location_8>	Köln	Deutschland
<http://www.example.org/trustedreference/locations#Location_1>	Las Vegas	USA
<http://www.example.org/trustedreference/locations#Location_6>	Neubiberg	Deutschland
<http://www.example.org/trustedreference/locations#Location_4>	Stavern	Norway

Table 38: Test reference data for evaluating SDQM's "FuncDepReferenceRules" with three properties

URI	ZIP	City	Country
<http://www.example.org/trustedreference/locations3#Location_7>	92101	San Diego	USA
<http://www.example.org/trustedreference/locations3#Location_2>	97562	San Rafael	USA
<http://www.example.org/trustedreference/locations3#Location_5>	4110	Stavern	Norway
<http://www.example.org/trustedreference/locations3#Location_3>	32532	Las Vegas	USA
<http://www.example.org/trustedreference/locations3#Location_8>	51147	Köln	Deutschland
<http://www.example.org/trustedreference/locations3#Location_1>	3004	Melbourne	Australia
<http://www.example.org/trustedreference/locations3#Location_6>	85577	Neubiberg	Deutschland
<http://www.example.org/trustedreference/locations3#Location_4>	44000	Nantes	France

Table 39: Test reference data for evaluating SDQM's "FuncDepReferenceRules" with four properties

URI	ZIP	City	Country	Street
<http://www.example.org/trustedreference/locations4#Location_2>	97562	San Rafael	USA	5677 Strong St.
<http://www.example.org/trustedreference/locations4#Location_7>	92101	San Diego	USA	Horton Plaza
<http://www.example.org/trustedreference/locations4#Location_8>	51147	Köln	Deutschland	Flughafenstr.
<http://www.example.org/trustedreference/locations4#Location_6>	85577	Neubiberg	Deutschland	Werner-Heisenberg-Weg
<http://www.example.org/trustedreference/locations4#Location_1>	3004	Melbourne	Australia	Mainstreet

Table 40: Test reference data for evaluating SDQM's "FuncDepReferenceRules" with five properties

URI	ZIP	City	Country	Street	Streetno
<http://www.example.org/trustedreference/locations5#Location_8>	51147	Köln	Deutschland	Flughafenstr.	1
<http://www.example.org/trustedreference/locations5#Location_6>	85579	Neubiberg	Deutschland	Werner-Heisenberg-Weg	39
<http://www.example.org/trustedreference/locations5#Location_7>	92101	San Diego	USA	Horton Plaza	324

Appendix D – Evaluation Results of SDQM's Data Quality Monitoring Queries

The table below shows the evaluation results of SDQM's data quality monitoring queries. Information about the evaluation procedure and interpretation of the results can be found in section 9.1 (TP = True Positives, FP = False Positives, FN = False Negatives).

Table 41: Evaluation results of SDQM's data quality monitoring queries

No.	Algorithm	TP	FP	FN	Precision	Recall
M1	Missing values and properties	9	0	0	1	1
M2	Conditional missing values and properties (1 condition)	2	0	0	1	1
M3	Conditional missing values and properties (2 conditions)	1	0	0	1	1
M4	Conditional missing values and properties (3 conditions)	2	0	0	1	1
M5	Conditional missing values and properties (4 conditions)	1	0	0	1	1
M6	Conditional missing values and properties (5 conditions)	1	0	0	1	1
M7	Syntax violations	4	0	0	1	1
M8	Conditional syntax violations (1 condition)	1	0	0	1	1
M9	Conditional syntax violations (2 conditions)	1	0	0	1	1
M10	Conditional syntax violations (3 conditions)	1	0	0	1	1
M11	Conditional syntax violations (4 conditions)	1	0	0	1	1
M12	Conditional syntax violations (5 conditions)	1	0	0	1	1
M13	Out of range values	4	0	0	1	1
M14	Illegal values (legal value rules)	2	0	0	1	1
M15	Illegal values (illegal value rules)	1	0	0	1	1
M16	FuncDepReferenceRule violations (2 properties)	2	0	0	1	1
M17	FuncDepReferenceRule violations (3 properties)	4	0	0	1	1
M18	FuncDepReferenceRule violations (4 properties)	5	0	0	1	1
M19	FuncDepReferenceRule violations (5 properties)	7	0	0	1	1

No.	Algorithm	TP	FP	FN	Precision	Recall
M20	FuncDepValueRule violations (1 condition)	1	0	0	1	1
M21	FuncDepValueRule violations (2 conditions)	1	0	0	1	1
M22	FuncDepValueRule violations (3 conditions)	1	0	0	1	1
M23	FuncDepValueRule violations (4 conditions)	1	0	0	1	1
M24	FuncDepValueRule violations (5 conditions)	1	0	0	1	1
M25	Expired instances	1	0	0	1	1
M26	Exceeded update interval	1	0	0	1	1
M27	Uniqueness violations	2	0	0	1	1
M28	Duplicate instances (1 equal value)	2	0	0	1	1
M29	Duplicate instances (2 equal values)	2	0	0	1	1
M30	Duplicate instances (3 equal values)	2	0	0	1	1
M31	Duplicate instances (4 equal values)	2	0	0	1	1
M32	Duplicate instances (5 equal values)	2	0	0	1	1

Appendix E – Evaluation Results of SDQM's Data Quality Assessment Queries

The table below shows the evaluation results of SDQM's data quality assessment queries. Information about the evaluation procedure and interpretation of the results can be found in section 9.1 (TP = True Positives, FP = False Positives, FN = False Negatives).

Table 42: Evaluation results of SDQM's data quality assessment queries

No.	Algorithm	TP	FP	FN	Precision	Recall
A1	Completeness	9	0	0	1	1
A2	Conditional completeness (1 condition)	2	0	0	1	1
A3	Conditional completeness (2 conditions)	1	0	0	1	1
A4	Conditional completeness (3 conditions)	2	0	0	1	1
A5	Conditional completeness (4 conditions)	1	0	0	1	1
A6	Conditional completeness (5 conditions)	1	0	0	1	1
A7	Syntactic accuracy (syntax rules)	4	0	0	1	1
A8	Conditional syntactic accuracy (1 condition)	1	0	0	1	1
A9	Conditional syntactic accuracy (2 conditions)	1	0	0	1	1
A10	Conditional syntactic accuracy (3 conditions)	1	0	0	1	1
A11	Conditional syntactic accuracy (4 conditions)	1	0	0	1	1
A12	Conditional syntactic accuracy (5 conditions)	1	0	0	1	1
A13	Semantic accuracy (legal value range rules)	4	0	0	1	1
A14	Syntactic accuracy (legal value rules)	2	0	0	1	1
A15	Semantic accuracy (illegal value rules)	1	0	0	1	1
A16	Semantic accuracy (FDR 2 properties)	2	0	0	1	1
A17	Semantic accuracy (FDR 3 properties)	4	0	0	1	1
A18	Semantic accuracy (FDR 4 properties)	5	0	0	1	1
A19	Semantic accuracy (FDR 5 properties)	7	0	0	1	1
A20	Semantic accuracy (FDV 1 condition)	1	0	0	1	1
A21	Semantic accuracy (FDV 2 conditions)	1	0	0	1	1
A22	Semantic accuracy (FDV 3 conditions)	1	0	0	1	1
A23	Semantic accuracy (FDV 4 conditions)	1	0	0	1	1
A24	Semantic accuracy (FDV 5 conditions)	1	0	0	1	1

No.	Algorithm	TP	FP	FN	Precision	Recall
A25	Timeliness (expiry rule)	1	0	0	1	1
A26	Timeliness (update rule)	1	0	0	1	1
A27	Uniqueness in depth	2	0	0	1	1
A28	Uniqueness in scope (1 equal value)	2	0	0	1	1
A29	Uniqueness in scope (2 equal values)	2	0	0	1	1
A30	Uniqueness in scope (3 equal values)	2	0	0	1	1
A31	Uniqueness in scope (4 equal values)	2	0	0	1	1
A32	Uniqueness in scope (5 equal values)	2	0	0	1	1

References

Ackoff, R. L. (1989). From Data to Wisdom. *Journal of Applied Systems Analysis, 16,* 3-9.

Alexiev, V., Breu, M., de Bruin, J., Fensel, D., Lara, R., & Lausen, H. (2005). *Information Integration with Ontologies: Experiences from an Industrial Showcase.* Chichester, Wiley.

Alvestrand, H. (2001). Tags for the Identification of Languages, Retrieved October 22, 2011, from http://www.ietf.org/rfc/rfc3066.txt.

Antoniou, G., & van Harmelen, F. (2008). *A Semantic Web Primer* (2nd ed.), MIT Press.

Apel, D., Behme, W., Eberlein, R., & Merighi, C. (2010). *Datenqualität erfolgreich steuern.* München, Carl Hanser Verlag.

Astrova, I. (2009). Rules for Mapping SQL Relational Databases to OWL Ontologies. In M.-A. Sicilia & M. D. Lytras (Eds.), *Metadata and Semantics* (pp. 415-424), Springer US.

Atlassian (2012). Atlassian Confluence Overview, Retrieved January 6, 2012, from http://www.atlassian.com/software/confluence/overview.

Auer, S., Dietzold, S., Lehmann, J., Hellmann, S., & Aumueller, D. (2009). *Triplify - Light-weight Linked Data Publication from Relational Databases.* In: Proceedings of the 18th International World Wide Web Conference. from http://www2009.eprints.org/63/.

Ballou, D., & Tayi, G. K. (1989). Methodology for Allocating Resources for Data Quality Enhancement. *Communications of the ACM, 32*(3), 320-329.

Ballou, D., Wang, R., Pazer, H., & Tayi, G. K. (1998). Modeling Information Manufacturing Systems to Determine Information Product Quality. *Management Science, 44*(4), 462-484.

Bao, J., Kendall, E. F., McGuinness, D. L., & Patel-Schneider, P. F. (2012). OWL 2 Web Ontology Language Quick Reference Guide. *W3C Recommendation,* Retrieved July 20, 2014, from http://www.w3.org/TR/2012/REC-owl2-quick-reference-20121211/.

Barnes, S., & Vidgen, R. (2002). An Integrative Approach to the Assessment of E-Commerce Quality. *Journal of Electronic Commerce Research, 3*(3), 114-127.

Batini, C., & Scannapieco, M. (2006). *Data Quality: Concepts, Methodologies and Techniques.* Berlin, Springer.

Bechhofer, S., van Harmelen, F., Hendler, J., Horrocks, I., McGuinness, D. L., et al. (2004). OWL Web Ontology Language Reference. *W3C Recommendation,* Retrieved September 24, 2011, from http://www.w3.org/TR/2004/REC-owl-ref-20040210/.

Becker, J., Matzner, M., Mueller, O., & Winkelmann, A. (2008). *Towards a Semantic Data Quality Management - Using Ontologies to Assess Master Data Quality in Retailing.* In: Proceedings of the Americas Conference on Information Systems (AMCIS 2008).

Beckett, D. (2004). RDF/XML Syntax Specification (Revised). *W3C Recommendation,* Retrieved August 14, 2010, from http://www.w3.org/TR/2004/REC-rdf-syntax-grammar-20040210/.

Berners-Lee, T. (1998a). Cool URIs don't change, Retrieved September 25, 2011, from http://www.w3.org/Provider/Style/URI.

Berners-Lee, T. (1998b). Relational Databases on the Semantic Web, Retrieved January 5, 2012, from http://www.w3.org/DesignIssues/RDB-RDF.html.

Berners-Lee, T. (2006). Linked Data, Retrieved September 30, 2011, from http://www.w3.org/DesignIssues/LinkedData.html.

Berners-Lee, T., Fielding, R., & Masinter, L. (2005). Uniform Resource Identifiers (URI): Generic Syntax, Retrieved September 25, 2011, from http://www.ietf.org/rfc/rfc3986.txt.

Berners-Lee, T., & Fischetti, M. (2000). *Weaving the Web: The Original Design and Ultimate Destiny of the World Wide Web by Its Inventor*, Paw Prints.

Berners-Lee, T., Hendler, J., & Lassila, O. (2001). The Semantic Web. *Scientific American, 284*(5), 34-43.

Bidlack, C. R. (2009). *Enabling Data Quality with Lightweight Ontologies*. In: Proceedings of the 21st Innovative Applications of Artificial Intelligence Conference (IAAI 2009). from http://www.aaai.org/ocs/index.php/IAAI/IAAI09/paper/view/259/1010.

Biron, P. V., & Malhotra, A. (2004). XML Schema Part 2: Datatypes (Second Edition). *W3C Recommendation*, Retrieved August 15, 2010, from http://www.w3.org/TR/2004/REC-xmlschema-2-20041028/

Bitton, D., & DeWitt, D. J. (1983). Duplicate Record Elimination in Large Data Files. *ACM Transactions on Database Systems, 8*(2), 255-265.

Bizer, C. (2007). *Quality-driven Information Filtering in the Context of Web-Based Information Systems*. Dissertation, Freie Universität Berlin, Berlin.

Bizer, C., & Cyganiak, R. (2007). D2RQ - Lessons Learned. *W3C Workshop on RDF Access to Relational Databases*, Retrieved January 4, 2011, from http://www.w3.org/2007/03/RdfRDB/papers/d2rq-positionpaper/.

Bizer, C., & Cyganiak, R. (2009). Quality-driven Information Filtering using the WIQA Policy Framework. *Journal of Web Semantics, 7*(1), 1-10.

Bizer, C., Cyganiak, R., Garbers, J., Maresch, O., & Becker, C. (2009). D2RQ Version 0.7 - User Manual and Language Specification, Retrieved January 4, 2011, from http://www4.wiwiss.fu-berlin.de/bizer/d2rq/spec/20090810/.

Bizer, C., Heath, T., & Berners-Lee, T. (2009). Linked Data - The Story So Far. *International Journal on Semantic Web and Information Systems, 5*(3), 1-22.

Bizer, C., Lehmann, J., Kobilarov, G., Auer, S., Becker, C., et al. (2009). DBpedia - A Crystallization Point for the Web of Data. *Journal of Web Semantics, 7*(3), 154-165.

Bizer, C., & Schultz, A. (2011). Berlin SPARQL Benchmark (BSBM) Results (February 2011), Retrieved January 4, 2012, from http://www4.wiwiss.fu-berlin.de/bizer/BerlinSPARQLBenchmark/results/V6/index.html.

Bizer, C., & Seaborne, A. (2004). *D2RQ - Treating Non-RDF Databases as Virtual RDF Graphs*. In: Proceedings of the International Semantic Web Conference (ISWC 2004). from http://sites.wiwiss.fu-berlin.de/suhl/bizer/pub/Bizer-D2RQ-ISWC2004-Poster.pdf.

Bodendorf, F. (2006). *Daten- und Wissensmanagement* (second ed.). Berlin, Springer.

Boehm, B., & In, H. (1996). Identifying Quality-Requirement Conflicts. *IEEE Software Magazine, 13*(2), 25-35.

Böhm, C., Naumann, F., Ziawasch, A., Fenz, D., Grütze, T., et al. (2010). *Profiling Linked Open Data with ProLOD*. In: Proceedings of the 2nd International Workshop on New Trends in Information Integration (NTII 2010).

Bray, T., Paoli, J., Sperberg-McQueen, C. M., Maler, E., & Yergeau, F. (2008). Extensible Markup Language (XML) 1.0 (Fifth Edition). *W3C Recommendation*, Retrieved 23.08.2014, 2014, from http://www.w3.org/TR/2008/REC-xml-20081126/.

Brickley, D., & Guha, R. V. (2004). RDF Vocabulary Description Language 1.0: RDF Schema. *W3C Recommendation*, Retrieved September 24, 2011, from http://www.w3.org/TR/2004/REC-rdf-schema-20040210/.

Brüggemann, S. (2006). *Ontologiebasierte domänenspezifische Datenbereinigung in Data Warehouse Systemen.* In: Proceedings of the Grundlagen von Datenbanken.

Brüggemann, S. (2008a). *Proaktives Management von Konsistenzbedingungen im Analytischen Performance Management.* In: Proceedings of the Data Warehousing (DW 2008).

Brüggemann, S. (2008b). *Rule Mining for Automatic ontology-based Data Cleaning.* In: Proceedings of the 10th Asia-Pacific Web Conference (APWEB 2008).

Brüggemann, S., & Aden, T. (2007). *Ontology Based Data Validation and Cleaning: Restructuring Operations for Ontology Maintenance.* In: Proceedings of the 37. Jahrestagung der Gesellschaft für Informatik e.V.

Brüggemann, S., & Grüning, F. (2008). *Using Domain Knowledge Provided by Ontologies for Improving Data Quality Management.* In: Proceedings of the International Conferences on Knowledge Management and New Media Technology (I-Know 2008 and I-Media 2008).

Brüggemann, S., & Grüning, F. (2009). Using Ontologies Providing Domain Knowledge for Data Quality Management In T. Pellegrini, S. Auer, K. Tochtermann & S. Schaffert (Eds.), *Networked Knowledge - Networked Media* (pp. 187-203). Berlin / Heidelberg, Springer

Buckland, M. K., & Gey, F. C. (1994). The Relationship between Recall and Precision. *Journal of the American Society for Information Science, 45*(1), 12-19.

Cerbah, F. (2008). *Learning Highly Structured Semantic Repositories from Relational Databases: the RDBToOnto Tool.* In: Proceedings of the 5th European Semantic Web Conference (ESWC 2008).

Chen, P. P.-S. (1976). The Entity-Relationship Model - Toward a Unified View of Data. *ACM Transactions on Database Systems, 1*(1), 9-36.

Chen, Q., Chen, Y.-P. P., & Zhang, C. (2007). Detecting Inconsistency in Biological Molecular Databases using Ontologies. *Data Mining Knowledge Discovery, 15*(2), 275-296.

Chiang, F., & Miller, R. J. (2008). *Discovering Data Quality Rules.* In: Proceedings of the VLDB Endowment.

Codd, E. F. (1970). A Relational Model of Data for Large Shared Data Banks. *Communications of the ACM, 13*(6), 377-387.

Codd, E. F. (1980). *Data Models in Database Management.* In: Proceedings of the Workshop on Data abstraction, databases and conceptual modeling.

Codd, E. F. (1990). *The Relational Model for Database Management: Version 2.* Reading, Massachusetts, Addison-Wesley.

Curé, O. (2009). *Improving the Data Quality of Relational Databases using OBDA and OWL 2 QL.* In: Proceedings of the Workshop OWL: Experiences and Directions (OWLED 2009).

Curé, O., & Jeansoulin, R. (2007). *Data Quality Enhancement of Databases Using Ontologies and Inductive Reasoning.* In: Proceedings of the Workshop On the Move to Meaningful Internet Systems (OTM 2007). from http://dx.doi.org /10.1007/978-3-540-76848-7_73.

Cyganiak, R. (2012). Dump-rdf: Dumping the Database to an RDF file, Retrieved January 5, 2012, from http://d2rq.org/dump-rdf.

Cyganiak, R., & Jentzsch, A. (2011a, 19.09.2011). The Linking Open Data Cloud Diagram, Retrieved April 12, 2012, from http://lod-cloud.net/.

Cyganiak, R., & Jentzsch, A. (2011b, 19.09.2011). State of the LOD Cloud, Retrieved July 20, 2014, from http://lod-cloud.net/state/.

Dauw, J. D., Hoffmeyer, K., & Katkov, Y. (2014). Semantic MediaWiki Help - Inline Queries, Retrieved July 27, 2014, from http://semantic-mediawiki.org/wiki/Help:Inline_queries.

De Bruijn, J., Lara, R., Polleres, A., & Fensel, D. (2005). OWL DL vs. OWL flight: Conceptual Modeling and Reasoning for the Semantic Web. In: Proceedings of the 14th International Conference on World Wide Web.

Deming, W. E. (1986). Out of the Crisis (2. print.. ed.). Cambridge, Massachusetts, Massachusetts Inst. of Technology, Center for Advanced Engineering Study.

Dice, L. R. (1945). Measures of the Amount of Ecologic Association Between Species. Ecology, 26(3), 297-302.

Eckerson, W. W. (2002). Data Quality and the Bottom Line: Achieving Business Success through a Commitment to High Quality Data (Report): The Data Warehousing Institute.

Eliot, T. S. (1934). The Rock. London, Faber & Faber.

English, L. P. (1999). Improving Data Warehouse and Business Information Quality: Methods for Reducing Costs and Increasing Profits. New York, Wiley.

Eppler, M. J. (2006). Managing Information Quality: Increasing the Value of Information in Knowledge-intensive Products and Processes (Second ed.). Berlin, Springer.

Erling, O. (2007). Declaring RDF Views of SQL Data, Retrieved January 5, 2012, from http://www.w3.org/2007/03/RdfRDB/papers/erling.html.

Feigenbaum, L., Williams, G. T., Clark, K. G., & Torres, E. (2013, 21.03.2013). SPARQL 1.1 Protocol. W3C Recommendation, Retrieved July 19, 2014, from http://www.w3.org/TR/2013/REC-sparql11-protocol-20130321/.

Fensel, D. (2001). Ontologies: Dynamic Networks of Formally Represented Meaning. In: Proceedings of the 1st Semantic Web Working Symposium. from http://sw-portal.deri.at/papers/publications/network.pdf.

Fensel, D. (2002). Intelligent Information Integration in B2B Electronic Commerce. Boston, Kluwer Academic Publishers.

Fensel, D., & van Harmelen, F. (2007). Unifying Reasoning and Search to Web Scale. IEEE Internet Computing, 11(2), 95-96.

Fink, A., Schneidereit, G., & Voß, S. (2005). Grundlagen der Wirtschaftsinformatik. Heidelberg, Physica-Verlag.

Fisher, C. W., & Kingma, B. R. (2001). Criticality of Data Quality as Exemplified in two Disasters. Information and Management, 39(2), 109-116.

Floyd, R. W. (1967). Assigning Meanings to Programs. In: Proceedings of the Symposium on Applied Mathematics.

Frakes, W. B., & Baeza-Yates, R. (1992). Information Retrieval: Data Structures and Algorithms, Prentice-Hall.

Friedman, T., & Bitterer, A. (2011). Magic Quadrant for Data Quality Tools, Retrieved July 29, 2011, from http://www.gartner.com/technology/reprints.do?id=1-16TGI70&ct=110729&s.

Fürber, C., & Hepp, M. (2010a). Using Semantic Web Resources for Data Quality Management. In: Proceedings of the 17th International Conference on Knowledge Engineering and Knowledge Management (EKAW 2010).

Fürber, C., & Hepp, M. (2010b). Using SPARQL and SPIN for Data Quality Management on the Semantic Web. In: Proceedings of the 13th International Conference on Business Information Systems 2010 (BIS 2010).

Fürber, C., & Hepp, M. (2011a). SWIQA – A Semantic Web Information Quality Assessment Framework. In: Proceedings of the European Conference on Information Systems (ECIS 2011).

Fürber, C., & Hepp, M. (2011b). *Towards a Vocabulary for Data Quality Management in Semantic Web Architectures*. In: Proceedings of the 1st International Workshop on Linked Web Data Management (LWDM 2011).

Gasevic, D., Djuric, D., & Devedzic, V. (2006). *Model Driven Architecture and Ontology Development*. Berlin, Springer-Verlag.

Ge, M., & Helfert, M. (2007). *A Review of Information Quality Research - Develop a Research Agenda*. In: Proceedings of the 12th International Conference on Information Quality (ICIQ 2007).

Ge, M., & Helfert, M. (2008). *Data and Information Quality Assessment in Information Manufacturing Systems*. In: Proceedings of the 11th International Conference on Business Information Systems (BIS 2008).

Ge, M., & Helfert, M. (2013). Cost and Value Management for Data Quality. In S. Sadiq (Ed.), *Handbook of Data Quality* (pp. 75-92). Berlin / Heidelberg, Springer.

Geisler, S., Weber, S., & Quix, C. (2011). *Ontology-Based Data Quality Framework for Data Stream Applications*. In: Proceedings of the 16th International Conference on Information Quality (ICIQ 2011).

Gertz, M., Ozsu, M. T., Saake, G., & Sattler, K.-U. (2004). Report on the Dagstuhl Seminar "Data Quality on the Web". *SIGMOD Record, 33*(1), 127.

Goeken, M. (2006). *Entwicklung von Data-Warehouse-Systemen Anforderungsmanagement, Modellierung, Implementierung*. Wiesbaden, Deutscher Universitätsverlag.

Gómez-Pérez, A., Fernández-López, M., & Corcho, O. (2004). *Ontological Engineering*. London, New York, Springer.

Google (2011). Google Refine, Retrieved January 5, 2012, from http://code.google.com/p/google-refine/.

Grande, M. (2011). *100 Minuten für Anforderungsmanagement: Kompaktes Wissen nicht nur für Projektleiter und Entwickler*. Wiesbaden, Vieweg / Teubner.

Grimm, S., Hitzler, P., & Abecker, A. (2007). Knowledge Representation and Ontologies. In R. Studer, S. Grimm & A. Abecker (Eds.), *Semantic Web Services - Concepts, Technologies, and Applications* (pp. 51-105). Berlin / Heidelberg, Springer.

Grosser, T., & Bange, C. (2009). *Datenqualität in SAP-Systemen*: Business Application Research Center.

Gruber, T. R. (1993). A Translation Approach to Portable Ontology Specifications. *Knowledge Acquisition, 5*(2), 199-220.

Grüning, F. (2009). *Datenqualitätsmanagement in der Energiewirtschaft*. Dissertation, Oldenburger Verlag für Wirtschaft, Informatik und Recht, Oldenburg.

Hammer, M., & Champy, J. (2002). *Reengineering the Corporation: A Manifesto for Business Revolution*. New York, HarperBusiness.

Hansen, H. R., & Neumann, G. (2004). *Wirtschaftsinformatik 1 - Grundlagen und Anwendungen* (9th ed.). Stuttgart, Lucius & Lucius.

Harris, S., & Seaborne, A. (2010, 26.01.2010). SPARQL Query Language 1.1. *W3C Working Draft*, Retrieved April 10, 2012, from http://www.w3.org/TR/2010/WD-sparql11-query-20100126/.

Hartig, O. (2009). *Querying Trust in RDF Data with tSPARQL*. In: Proceedings of the 6th European Semantic Web Conference (ESWC 2009).

Hartig, O., & Zhao, J. (2009). *Using Web Data Provenance for Quality Assessment*. In: Proceedings of the 1st International Workshop on the role of Semantic Web in Provenance Management.

Heath, T., & Bizer, C. (2011). Linked Data - Evolving the Web into a Global Data Space. *Synthesis Lectures on the Semantic Web: Theory and Technology* 1st Edition. Retrieved September 25, 2011, from http://linkeddatabook.com/editions/1.0/.

Hebeler, J., Fisher, M., Blace, R., & Perez-Lopez, A. (2009). *Semantic Web Programming*, Wiley Publishing.

Hepp, M. (2008a). *GoodRelations: An Ontology for Describing Products and Services Offers on the Web*. In: Proceedings of the 16th international conference on Knowledge Engineering: Practice and Patterns.

Hepp, M. (2008b). Ontologies: State of the Art, Business Potential, and Grand Challenges. In M. Hepp, P. De Leenheer, A. de Moor & Y. Sure (Eds.), *Ontology Management: Semantic Web, Semantic Web Services, and Business Applications* (pp. 3-22).

Herschel, M., Felix, N., Sascha, S., & Maik, T. (2011). Scalable Iterative Graph Duplicate Detection. *IEEE Transactions on Knowledge and Data Engineering, 99.*

Hevner, A., March, S., Park, J., & Ram, S. (2004). Design Science in Information Systems Research. *MANAGEMENT INFORMATION SYSTEMS QUARTERLY.*

Heymans, S., Ma, L., Anicic, D., Ma, Z., Steinmetz, N., et al. (2008). Ontology Reasoning with Large Data Repositories. In M. Hepp, P. De Leenheer, A. de Moor & Y. Sure (Eds.), *Ontology Management: Semantic Web, Semantic Web Services, and Business Applications* (pp. 89-128), Springer.

Hipp, J., Müller, M., Hohendorff, J., & Naumann, F. (2007). *Rule-Based Measurement Of Data Quality in Nominal Data*. In: Proceedings of the 12th International Conference on Information Quality (ICIQ 2007).

Hitzler, P. (2008). *Semantic Web: Grundlagen* (First ed.). Berlin, Springer.

Hitzler, P., Krötzsch, M., Parsia, B., Patel-Schneider, P. F., & Rudolph, S. (2009). OWL 2 Web Ontology Language Primer. *W3C Recommendation*, Retrieved September 24, 2011, from http://www.w3.org/TR/2009/REC-owl2-primer-20091027/.

Hitzler, P., Krötzsch, M., Parsia, B., Patel-Schneider, P. F., & Rudolph, S. (2012). OWL 2 Web Ontology Language Primer (Second Edition). *W3C Recommendation*, Retrieved July 19, 2014, from http://www.w3.org/TR/2012/REC-owl2-primer-20121211/.

Hogan, A., Harth, A., Passant, A., Decker, S., & Polleres, A. (2010). *Weaving the Pedantic Web*. In: Proceedings of the Workshop on Linked Data on the Web (LDOW 2010).

Hoyningen-Huene, P. (1998). *Formale Logik - Eine philosophische Einführung*. Stuttgart, Reclam.

Huang, K.-T., Lee, Y. W., & Wang, R. Y. (1999). *Quality Information and Knowledge*. Upper Saddle River, N.J., Prentice Hall PTR.

Hüner, K., Brauer, B., Otto, B., & Österle, H. (2011). Fachliches Metadatenmanagement mit einem semantischen Wiki. *HMD – Praxis der Wirtschaftsinformatik, 277*(48), 98-108.

Hüner, K., Otto, B., & Österle, H. (2011). Collaborative Management of Business Metadata. *International Journal of Information Management, 31*(4), 366-373.

ISO (2005). ISO 9000:2005, *Quality management systems - Fundamentals and vocabulary*: International Organization for Standardization.

ISO (2009). ISO 8000-102:2009, *Data quality - Part 102: Master data: Exchange of characteristic data: Vocabulary*: International Organization for Standardization.

ISO/IEC (1993). ISO/IEC 2382-1:1993, *Information technology - Vocabulary - Part 1: Fundamental terms*: International Organization for Standardization.

Juran, J. M. (1988). *Juran's quality control handbook* (Fourth ed.). New York, McGraw-Hill.

Kahn, B. K., Strong, D. M., & Wang, R. Y. (2002). Information Quality Benchmarks: Product and Service Performance. *Communications of the ACM, 45*(4), 184-192.

Kano, N., Seraku, N., Takahashi, F., & Tsuji, S. (1984). Attractive Quality and Must-Be Quality. *Journal of the Japanese Society for Quality Control, 14*(2), 147-156.

Kashyap, V., & Sheth, A. P. (1996). Semantic and Schematic Similarities Between Database Objects: A Context-Based Approach. *Very Large Data Base Journal*(5), 276–304.

Kedad, Z., & Métais, E. (2002). Ontology-Based Data Cleaning. In: Proceedings of the 6th International Conference on Applications of Natural Language to Information Systems-Revised Papers.

Klein, D. E., & Murphy, G. L. (2002). Paper has been my Ruin: Conceptual Relations of Polysemous Senses. *Journal of Memory and Language, 47*(4), 548-570.

Klyne, G., & Carroll, J. J. (2004). Resource Description Framework (RDF): Concepts and Abstract Syntax. *W3C Recommendation*, Retrieved September 24, 2011, from http://www.w3.org/TR/2004/REC-rdf-concepts-20040210/.

Knublauch, H. (2011). SPIN - SPARQL Syntax. *W3C Member Submission*, Retrieved August 19, 2014, from http://www.w3.org/Submission/2011/SUBM-spin-sparql-20110222/.

Kobilarov, G., Bizer, C., Auer, S., & Lehmann, J. (2009). *DBpedia-A Linked Data Hub and Data Source for Web and Enterprise Applications*. In: Proceedings of the 18th International World Wide Web Conference.

Kobilarov, G., Scott, T., Raimond, Y., Oliver, S., Sizemore, C., et al. (2009). *Media meets Semantic Web – How the BBC uses DBpedia and Linked Data to make Connections*. In: Proceedings of the 6th European Semantic Web Conference (ESWC 2009).

Kokar, M. M., Matheus, C. J., Baclawski, K., Letkowski, J. A., Hinman, M., & Salerno, J. (2004). *Use Cases for Ontologies in Information Fusion*. In: Proceedings of the 7th International Conference on Information Fusion.

Koren, Y. (2012). *Working with MediaWiki*, WikiWorks Press.

Koren, Y. (2014). Semantic Forms and Templates, Retrieved July 27, 2014, from http://www.mediawiki.org/wiki/Extension:Semantic_Forms/Semantic_Forms_a nd_templates.

Krötzsch, M., Vrandečić, D., & Völkel, M. (2006). *Semantic MediaWiki*. In: Proceedings of the International Semantic Web Conference (ISWC 2006). from http://dx.doi.org/10.1007/11926078_68.

Lee, Y. W. (2006). *Journey to Data Quality*. Cambridge, Mass., MIT Press.

Lei, Y., & Nikolov, A. (2007). *Detecting Quality Problems in Semantic Metadata without the Presence of a Gold Standard*. In: Proceedings of the 5th International Workshop on Evaluation of Ontologies and Ontology-based Tools (EON 2007).

Lei, Y., Uren, V., & Motta, E. (2007). *A Framework for Evaluating Semantic Metadata*. In: Proceedings of the 4th International Conference on Knowledge Capture.

Lenzerini, M. (2002). *Data Integration: a Theoretical Perspective*. In: Proceedings of the 21st ACM SIGMOD-SIGACT-SIGART Symposium on Principles of Database Systems.

Leser, U., & Naumann, F. (2007). *Informationsintegration: Architekturen und Methoden zur Integration verteilter und heterogener Datenquellen* (1st ed.). Heidelberg, dpunkt-Verl.

Levy, A. Y. (2000). Logic-based Techniques in Data Integration *Logic-based Artificial Intelligence* (pp. 575-595), Springer.

Loshin, D. (2001). *Enterprise Knowledge Management: The Data Quality Approach*. San Diego, London, Morgan Kaufmann Academic Press.

Loshin, D. (2002). *Rule-based Data Quality*. In: Proceedings of the 11th International Conference on Information and Knowledge Management.

Loshin, D. (2009). *Master Data Management*. Amsterdam, Elsevier/Morgan Kaufmann.

Maali, F., & Cyganiak, R. (2011). RDF Extension for Google Refine, Retrieved January 5, 2012, from http://lab.linkeddata.deri.ie/2010/grefine-rdf-extension/.

Madnick, S., & Zhu, H. (2006). Improving Data Quality through Effective Use of Data Semantics. *Data & Knowledge Engineering, 59*(2), 460-475.

Madnick, S. E., Wang, R. Y., Lee, Y. W., & Zhu, H. (2009). Overview and Framework for Data and Information Quality Research. *Journal of Data and Information Quality, 1*(1), 1-22.

Manola, F., & Miller, E. (2004). RDF Primer. *W3C Recommendation*, Retrieved September 24, 2011, from http://www.w3.org/TR/2004/REC-rdf-primer-20040210/.

McComb, D. (2004). *Semantics in Business Systems: The Savvy Manager's Guide*. San Francisco, Elsevier Science.

McGuinness, D. L., & van Harmelen, F. (2004). OWL Web Ontology Language Overview. *W3C Recommendation*, Retrieved September 24, 2011, from http://www.w3.org/TR/2004/REC-owl-features-20040210/.

Mendes, P. N., Mühleisen, H., & Bizer, C. (2012). *Sieve: Linked Data Quality Assessment and Fusion*. In: Proceedings of the 1st International Workshop on Linked Web Data Management (LWDM 2012).

Microsoft (2014). Data Warehousing and Online Analytical Processing, Retrieved August 31, 2014, from http://technet.microsoft.com/en-us/library/aa933152%28v=sql.80%29.aspx.

Milano, D., Scannapieco, M., & Catarci, T. (2005). *Using Ontologies for XML Data Cleaning*. In: Proceedings of the On the Move to Meaningful Internet Systems (OTM 2005).

Monge, A., & Elkan, C. (1997). *An Efficient Domain-Independent Algorithm for Detecting Approximately Duplicate Database Records*. In: Proceedings of the Workshop on Research Issues on Data Mining and Knowledge Discovery.

Motik, B., Grau, B. C., Horrocks, I., Wu, Z., Fokoue, A., & Lutz, C. (2009). OWL 2 Web Ontology Language Profiles. *W3C Recommendation*, Retrieved September 24, 2011, from http://www.w3.org/TR/2009/REC-owl2-profiles-20091027/.

Mühleisen, H., & Bizer, C. (2012). *Web Data Commons - Extracting Structured Data from Two Large Web Corpora*. In: Proceedings of the 4th Linked Data on the Web Workshop (LDOW 2012).

Niemi, T., Toivonen, S., Niinimaki, M., & Nummenmaa, J. (2007). Ontologies with Semantic Web/Grid in Data Integration for OLAP. *International Journal on Semantic Web and Information Systems, 3*(4), 25–49.

Noy, N. F., & McGuinness, D. L. (2001). *Ontology Development 101: A Guide to Creating Your First Ontology* (Technical Report): Stanford Knowledge Systems Laboratory.

Nuseibeh, B. (1996). Conflicting Requirements: When the Customer is Not Always Right. *Requirements Engineering, 1*(1), 70-71.

O'Connor, M., Knublauch, H., Tu, S., Grosof, B., Dean, M., et al. (2005). *Supporting Rule System Interoperability on the Semantic Web with SWRL*. In: Proceedings of the 4th International Semantic Web Conference (ISWC 2005).

Oliveira, P., Rodrigues, F., & Henriques, P. R. (2005). *A Formal Definition of Data Quality Problems*. In: Proceedings of the International Conference on Information Quality (ICIQ 2005)

Oliveira, P., Rodrigues, F., Henriques, P. R., & Galhardas, H. (2005). *A Taxonomy of Data Quality Problems*. In: Proceedings of the 2nd International Workshop on Data and Information Quality.

Olson, J. (2003). *Data Quality: The Accuracy Dimension*. San Francisco, USA, Morgan Kaufmann.

Oracle (2013). History of SQL. *Oracle Database SQL Language Reference*, Retrieved July 19, 2014, from http://docs.oracle.com/cd/B28359_01/server.111/b28286/intro001.htm#i1712.

Otto, I. B., Kokemüller, D.-P. J., & Gizanis, D. (2011). Stammdatenmanagement: Datenqualität für Geschäftsprozesse. *HMD Praxis der Wirtschaftsinformatik, 48*(3), 5-16.

Peffers, K., Tuunanen, T., Rothenberger, M., & Chatterjee, S. (2008). A Design Science Research Methodology for Information Systems Research. *Journal of Management Information Systems, 24*(3), 45-77.

Perez-Rey, D., Anguita, A., & Crespo, J. (2006). *OntoDataClean: Ontology-Based Integration and Preprocessing of Distributed Data* In: Proceedings of the Biological and Medical Data Analysis.

Pernici, B., & Scannapieco, M. (2002). *Data Quality in Web Information Systems*. In: Proceedings of the 21st International Conference on Conceptual Modeling.

Pipino, L. L., Lee, Y. W., & Wang, R. Y. (2002). Data Quality Assessment. *Communications of the ACM, 45*(4), 211-218.

Pohl, K., Böckle, G., & van der Linden, F. (2005). *Software Product Line Engineering: Foundations, Principles, and Techniques*. Berlin, Springer.

Porter, M. E., & Millar, V. E. (1985). How Information gives you Competitive Advantage. *Harvard Business Review*, 149-160.

Preece, A., Jin, B., Pignotti, E., Missier, P., Embury, S., et al. (2006). *Managing Information Quality in E-science using Semantic Web Technology*. In: Proceedings of the 3rd European Conference on the Semantic Web (ESWC 2006).

Raghavan, V., Bollmann, P., & Jung, G. S. (1989). A Critical Investigation of Recall and Precision as Measures of Retrieval System Performance. *ACM Transactions on Information Systems, 7*(3), 205-229.

Rahm, E., & Do, H.-H. (2000). Data Cleaning: Problems and Current Approaches. *IEEE Data Engineering Bulletin, 23*(4), 3-13.

Ram, S., & Park, J. (2004). Semantic Conflict Resolution Ontology (SCROL): An Ontology for Detecting and Resolving Data and Schema-Level Semantic Conflicts. *IEEE Transactions on Knowledge and Data Engineering, 16*(2), 189-202.

Redman, T. C. (1996). *Data Quality for the Information Age*. Boston, Artech House.

Redman, T. C. (1998). The Impact of Poor Data Quality on the Typical Enterprise. *Communications of the ACM, 41*(2), 79-82.

Redman, T. C. (2001). *Data Quality: The Field Guide*. Boston, Digital Press.

Reuters, T. (2013). How does Calais work?, Retrieved July 20, 2014, from http://www.opencalais.com/about.

Riemer, N. (2010). *Introducing Semantics*. Cambridge, New York, Cambridge University Press.

Rodriguez, J. B., & Gómez-Pérez, A. (2006). *Upgrading Relational Legacy Data to the Semantic Web*. In: Proceedings of the 15th International Conference on World Wide Web.

Rowley, J. (2007). The Wisdom Hierarchy: Representations of the DIKW Hierarchy. *Journal of Information Science, 33*(2), 163-180.

Sahoo, S. S., Halb, W., Hellmann, S., Idehen, K., Thibodeau, T., et al. (2009). A Survey of Current Approaches for Mapping of Relational Databases to RDF Retrieved January 4, 2012, from http://www.w3.org/2005/Incubator/rdb2rdf/ RDB2RDF_SurveyReport_01082009.pdf.

Salvadores, M. (2012). E-Mail Communication with Developer of 4store Regarding SPARQL 1.1 Compliance of 4Store.

Sauermann, L., & Cyganiak, R. (2008). Cool URIs for the Semantic Web, Retrieved September 25, 2011, from http://www.w3.org/TR/cooluris/.

Simsion, G. C., & Witt, G. C. (2005). *Data Modeling Essentials* (3rd ed.). Amsterdam ; Boston, Morgan Kaufmann Publishers.

Sirin, E., Parsia, B., Grau, B. C., Kalyanpur, A., & Katz, Y. (2007). Pellet: A practical OWL-DL reasoner, Retrieved April 11, 2012, from http://www.mindswap.org/ papers/PelletJWS.pdf.

Skog, I., & Handel, P. (2009). In-Car Positioning and Navigation Technologies - A Survey. *IEEE Transactions on Intelligent Transportation Systems, 10*(1), 4-21.

Skoutas, D., & Simitsis, A. (2007). Ontology-Based Conceptual Design of ETL Processes for Both Structured and Semi-Structured Data. *International Journal on Semantic Web and Information Systems, 3*(4), 1-24.

Smith, B., & Welty, C. (2001). *Ontology: Towards a New Synthesis*. In: Proceedings of the Formal Ontology in Information Systems.

Souza, D., Belian, R., Salgado, A. C., & Tedesco, P. A. (2008). *Towards a Context Ontology to Enhance Data Integration Processes*. In: Proceedings of the 4th Workshop on Ontologies-based Techniques for DataBases in Information Systems and Knowledge Systems (ODBIS).

Sowa, J. F. (2014). Semantic Networks. *Encyclopedia of Artificial Intelligence*, Retrieved April 16, 2014, from http://www.jfsowa.com/pubs/semnet.htm.

Talend (2012). Talend Open Studio for Data Quality User Guide, Retrieved June 8, 2012, from http://www.talend.com/resources/documentation.php.

Uschold, M., & Gruninger, M. (1996). Ontologies: Principles, Methods, and Applications. *The Knowledge Engineering Review, 11*(2), 93-155.

Vandenbussche, P.-Y. (2012). Linked Open Vocabularies (LOV) - Quality, Provenance and Trust Space, Retrieved January 5, 2012, from http://lov.okfn.org/dataset/ lov/details/vocabularySpace_Quality.html.

Voss, J. (2005). *Measuring Wikipedia*. In: Proceedings of the 10th International Conference of the International Society for Scientometrics and Informetrics.

W3C-OWL-Working-Group (2012). OWL 2 Web Ontology Language Document Overview (Second Edition). *W3C Recommendation*, Retrieved July 19, 2014, from http://www.w3.org/TR/2012/REC-owl2-overview-20121211/.

W3C (2013). Semantic Web Project Website, Retrieved July 19, 2014, from http://www.w3.org/standards/semanticweb/.

Wache, H., Voegele, T., Visser, U., Stuckenschmidt, H., Schuster, G., et al. (2001). *Ontology-Based Integration of Information - A Survey of Existing Approaches*. In: Proceedings of the Workshop on Ontologies and Information Sharing. from http://www.iwayan.powernet.or.id/Research/Ontology/Papers_Research/SUR VEY.pdf.

Wand, Y., & Wang, R. Y. (1996). Anchoring Data Quality Dimensions in Ontological Foundations. *Communications of the ACM, 39*(11), 86-95.

Wang, F., Mäs, S., Reinhardt, W., & Kandawasvika, A. (2005). *Ontology-Based Quality Assurance for Mobile Data Acquisition*. In: Proceedings of the 19th International Conference on Informatics for Environmental Protection: Networking Environmental Information.

Wang, R. Y. (1998). A Product Perspective on Total Data Quality Management. *Communications of the ACM, 41*(2), 58-65.

Wang, R. Y., & Strong, D. M. (1996). Beyond Accuracy: What Data Quality means to Data Consumers. *Journal of Management Information Systems, 12*(4), 5-33.

Wang, X., Hamilton, H. J., & Bither, Y. (2005). *An Ontology-Based Approach to Data Cleaning* (Technical Report No. 0773105336 9780773105331). Regina: Department of Computer Science, University of Regina.

Wang, X., Sun, X., Cao, F., Ma, L., Kanellos, N., et al. (2009). SMDM: Enhancing Enterprise-Wide Master Data Management Using Semantic Web Technologies. *VLDB Endowment, 2*(2), 1594-1597.

Wang, Y. R., Ziad, M., & Lee, Y. W. (2001). *Data Quality*. Boston, Kluwer Academic Publishers.

West, M. (2003). Developing High Quality Data Models. 1-56. Retrieved from https://d2024367-a-62cb3a1a-s-sites.googlegroups.com/site/drmatthewwest/publications/princ03.pdf

West, M. (2011). *Developing High Quality Data Models*, Elsevier.

Wijnhoven, F., Boelens, R., Middel, R., & Louissen, K. (2007). *Total Data Quality Management: A Study of Bridging Rigor and Relevance*. In: Proceedings of the 15th European Conference on Information Systems (ECIS 2007).

Wu, Z., Chen, H., Wang, H., Wang, Y., Mao, Y., et al. (2006). *Dartgrid: A Semantic Web Toolkit for Integrating Heterogeneous Relational Databases*. In: Proceedings of the International Semantic Web Conference (ISWC 2006).

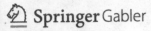

Printed in the United States
By Bookmasters